ENTREPRENEURIAL CONFESSIONS

ENTREPRENEURIAL CONFESSIONS

How Young Founders Found Their Way

ELLIOT LUM

SHATTERED GLASS MEDIA

ENTREPRENEURIAL CONFESSIONS

How Young Founders Found Their Way

ISBN 978-1-5445-0090-4 *Paperback*

978-1-5445-0091-1 *Ebook*

This book is dedicated to all the entrepreneurs I interviewed along my journey, especially Nina Alexander-Hurst, who pushed me to develop and grow emotionally, intellectually, and spiritually.

CONTENTS

PART III: CAREER MODELS

INTRODUCTION

In my tiny studio apartment in Washington, D.C., I was hunched over the stove watching tapioca balls boil in one pot, while black tea brewed in another. I wanted to get the texture of the tapioca balls just right for the bubble tea I was making. I had first heard about the bubble tea craze in Taiwan. It was 1999 and I thought I could be one of the first to introduce the concept to the States. I figured bubble tea wouldn't be hard to make since the product is just a combination of tea, powdered sugar, and tapioca balls. It would be easy money.

I invited my friends over for a bubble tea tasting, which they had never heard of before, so they were curious, or more likely, felt obligated to try the specialty because they were my friends. I ran a mini-focus group to collect their raw feedback and then asked them to fill out a survey based on their drink experience. The general consensus was that there was certainly promise in the bubble tea concept, but it wasn't the kind of drink they would crave like coffee. There was enough potential in the idea that I continued to pursue the idea of opening up my own bubble tea shop.

The owner of Cafe Asia, a popular Pan-Asian restaurant in Dupont Circle, offered me some advice. He said he worked hard for ten years before his restaurant became profitable. Given the emotional toll it took on him, he didn't recommend starting my own business in the food service industry. I still remember the weary look on his face that revealed the hardships he had experienced building his business. I looked at myself in the mirror. Could I realistically persist through the grind of making bubble tea my life? I didn't think so. I subsequently decided to continue down the path of corporate jobs until I had an idea that I truly believed in.

I have always admired entrepreneurs. Part of the appeal of entrepreneurship is creating something out of nothing. I've always thought that starting and running a business is one of the hardest things a person can do. Secretly, I've always wanted that challenge. I wanted to prove to the world that I was worthy of being an entrepreneur and then reap the financial rewards of investing my whole self into the effort.

I graduated from some of the best schools, including

Columbia University and MIT Sloan School of Management. I've worked at incredible companies like Colgate-Palmolive and Columbia Records. But I have never worked for myself. I've always been on somebody else's payroll. Every choice in my career was made to prepare myself and become as well rounded as possible so that I could one day be a great founder of a company.

At my first job at Corporate Executive Board, a strategy research firm, I learned how to write strategy reports, manage a team of researchers, and sell our research products. At MIT Sloan, I had the opportunity to round out my marketing and sales background with more quantitative, data-driven skills. More important, the MBA program's brand recognition gave me access to technical expertise, financial resources, and an entrepreneurial network that could catapult me to start my own business. At Sloan, I took classes in entrepreneurship, participated in the MIT $100K Entrepreneurship Competition, and even organized their first ever marketing conference. But I still didn't feel like my training was complete and decided I wasn't ready to start a business.

I secured an offer at Colgate-Palmolive, the global toothpaste company, and dug into Colgate's databases to see what was driving account sales on a monthly, weekly, and even daily basis. Questions raced through my head as I dove into the data. What promotions were we running at Walmart? Did we have a coupon that dropped in the Sunday newspaper? To what extent did the retail accounts execute our sales plan? What did our competitors do? Since I was accountable for sharing strategic and operational decisions with senior management, I immersed myself in the business of running a business.

At Colgate, I thought I was operating like an entrepreneur, but in reality, I wasn't. I was supported by a huge infrastructure that minimized all risks and maximized our profits for shareholder benefits. I understood how to play that game, but not the one I wanted to play for the long term.

Realizing this, I zeroed in on music as an industry that was undergoing significant disruption and change. My Colgate colleagues thought I was crazy for entering a business that was experiencing massive layoffs. They preferred a safer, more predictable path that valued education and experience. I wanted to be immersed in an environment with little to no structure, where I could see the direct impact of the deals that I identified, sourced, and executed. I didn't want to sit back and watch anymore. I wanted to go out into the world and meet the people who were making culture happen.

The music industry is made of entrepreneurs—artists who use their voices and creative vision to build a business around them. A hit song like Beyoncé's "Single Ladies" has the power to incite a movement, inspiring legions of fans to make and publish their own video renditions on YouTube. I wanted in.

At Columbia Records, my role was to connect with Fortune 500 companies, brands from Adidas to Marriott to Baskin-Robbins, and leverage their marketing muscle to drive awareness for our portfolio of artists. I built a vast network doing this work, which comforted me and made me feel like I was doing something to further my future business prospects while I was still figuring out what idea to pursue.

In my spare time, I absorbed as much as I could about entrepreneurship. I read books such as *Choose Yourself!* and *The $100 Startup*; listened to podcasts like Stanford's *Entrepreneurial Thought Leaders* and *Mixergy*; and subscribed to publications like *The Union Square Ventures Blog*, *Both Sides of the Table*, and *TechCrunch*. I was intoxicated with the concept of entrepreneurship, but I didn't act on any business ideas with serious conviction. I was just an outsider looking in, preferring the comfort of the sidelines to competing in the actual game. What I was really doing was preparing myself for a general management career instead of committing to starting a business.

During my time at Columbia Records, my wife took a

role working for a venture capital firm. She learned how he built businesses and applied those lessons to starting her own. For me, having a spouse who was an entrepreneur was exhilarating. She was doing what I had always wanted to do. In 2014, she quit her job to focus full time on building her technology business. Although she didn't code herself, she was a businesswoman who sensed a market opportunity and wanted to build a brand that capitalized on this shift in consumer taste.

I wanted to help her as much as I could as a sounding board who could share her initial frustrations or connect her with valuable contacts in my network. For example, early on I introduced her to a friend who gave her free office space for a year. I was excited to share her story with my friends, both personal and professional, because I was so proud of her.

Over time, though, the business started to consume all of her mindshare and we started to drift apart. I hated feeling the chasm between us. I loved my wife. I supported her fully so that she could realize her dream. But I was ill-equipped to talk about what was going on in our relationship. My preference was to bury the issue because I was scared of rocking the boat. In reality, these issues continued to fester and eventually led to our demise as a couple.

When we separated, I simply didn't understand why.

We never fought. I understood that she needed different things in her life, but I didn't understand why we couldn't be together. The best proxy for understanding her rationale, I figured, was to interview other entrepreneurs and get a sense of how I might be able to change based on their input.

The idea for this book was hatched during the Memorial Day holiday in 2015 on a marketing retreat in Cabo, Mexico, that my friends had organized. Our host was a young entrepreneur named Evan Burns, cofounder of Odyssey, a content media platform, and his investor was the owner of the huge compound we were staying at. Evan's room was right next to mine, and he and I spent one evening just talking. I didn't intend to spill out everything to him, yet I couldn't help but open up about the painful process of my recent separation.

He and I had one of the most enlightening conversations I've ever had. Even though Evan was still in his twenties and didn't have as much life experience as me, he had a wisdom that was beyond his years. For instance, he referred me to several books that might help contextualize my situation. Most important, he empathized with me, offering his own startup experience as a proxy for what my wife at the time might have been going through.

This was exactly the kind of conversation I hoped to have

with other founders as I set out to write *Entrepreneurial Confessions* in late 2015. Over the course of two years, I crisscrossed the country and interviewed more than 300 entrepreneurs to uncover what it takes to be an entrepreneur. The driving force behind this journey was a desire to hear their stories from the frontlines of entrepreneurship, gain insight into what my wife had gone through, and maybe even rekindle the entrepreneurial spark I once had myself when I was just a twentysomething hoping to open a bubble tea shop.

The criteria I used to select entrepreneurs for this book was that they had to be in their early twenties to mid-thirties and have started a company in the United States.

My first interview was Akash Malhotra, cofounder of Eventable, a company that I advised. I went to his office and we sat down for an hour. At first, I tried to take notes on my computer and capture everything he said. In doing so, it was difficult to establish a face-to-face connection with him. The computer blocked the natural intimacy we would have had while talking. I wanted him to confess the personal struggles he had experienced, but we never quite got to that point. This made me realize that if I wanted to truly empathize and connect with an entrepreneur's story, I'd need to do so without a computer between us.

In future interviews, I put the computer away and relied

instead on my phone to record the conversation. I asked entrepreneurs about their darkest days, their biggest sacrifices, their proudest moments, fights with parents, and friends or partners lost. I wanted them to be raw, honest, and reflective. I made observations of my own—from other founders and my own experiences—that provoked the dialogue.

Why did these founders confess some of the most intimate details of their lives to a complete stranger? The answer is simple. When I sat down with them, I listened to what they had to say and asked questions based on what they decided to reveal. I tried to get them to talk to me like a best friend and tell me what they were really feeling. I didn't want answers that were rehearsed. I wanted the truth. I was present, and so were they.

I wanted to piece together the story of how and why they became entrepreneurs. What did they do as kids that later developed into an entrepreneurial impulse? What role did their parents play with regard to them becoming entrepreneurs? How did their set of friends influence them to choose this path? The questions I asked forced them to reflect on their journey, which included many unexpected revelations: not speaking with parents for over a year; living in shelters during childhood; seeing their best friend killed; losing a brother; losing a father; growing up in poverty; and getting brutally bullied in high school.

Several entrepreneurs told me at the end of our conversation that the hour we spent together felt like therapy. A few even said the experience was cathartic. Some asked for the interview file because they wanted to listen to their self-reflections again. Others choked up and cried—both men and women—during our conversations. What they went through was hard. And I understood this.

As I sifted through the material, I started to see commonalities among all their narratives. A confession implies a sense of guilt or a feeling of shame or embarrassment. But this isn't the case with the confessions from these entrepreneurs. They are proud of what they have accomplished. They don't feel like they sacrificed anything. They did what they wanted to do on their own terms. The only crime they might have committed is bottling up their emotions because nobody wanted to listen or take the time to understand. Oftentimes it was a relief for them that they had the opportunity to share what they went through with me. Their confessions make up the true stories contained in this book.

Entrepreneurial Confessions has three main sections. The first part, Entrepreneurial Traits, contains stories that emphasize the specific traits that have made a particular entrepreneur successful. All entrepreneurs will be able to identify with these traits. For example, in Chapter 2: The Glory of Grit, I profile three entrepreneurs who share their steely determination to will their businesses off the ground and maintain their conviction for years even when the outlook was bleak.

In the second part, Personal Impact, I explore the relationships and experiences that become integral to a founder's journey. For example, in Chapter 9: I've Got Your Back, You've Got Mine, I profile Nikhil Arora, the twenty-seven-year-old founder of Back to the Roots, an organic food company based in Oakland, California. Nikhil and his cofounder, Alejandro Velez, bonded when they grew mushrooms out of coffee beans in college. They turned down lucrative jobs to pursue this obsession with only a $5,000 grant. In Chapter 10: Love Letters from Abroad, I share the experience of Neil Parikh, twenty-five, from Casper, an online sleep solutions company based in New York, who went from being a know-it-all millennial to witnessing real world problems in India. There he experienced the greatest generosity from those who have the least—kids who barely had anything came out in the torrential rain to offer him help.

In Career Models, the last part, I explore the different forms of entrepreneurship that I encountered. Instead of being organized by industry or the amount of funding raised, the section is organized by the kind of entrepreneurial model or path the entrepreneur embraced. For example, in Chapter 12: Accelerating Your Career through

Entrepreneurship, I profile thirty-four-year-old Ryan Bonifacino, a serial entrepreneur who decided to join a big company for the first time, at ALEX AND ANI in Rhode Island. In Chapter 13: "Hacking Your Way to Happiness," I look at Anton Cobb, thirty-one, a sales director at Hilton in Portland, Oregon, who started a nonprofit called hOUR-LUNCH, which asks the lunchtime business crowd to give up their lunch money to feed children in need.

Ultimately, this book is about you. While it's not designed to help you identify the right idea to pursue, teach you how to fundraise, or figure out how to get your first customer, what it does do is cut to the bone of what entrepreneurship is all about: you fulfilling your dreams. It forces you to ask yourself whether entrepreneurship is the right path for you, and if so, to consider what you will encounter on a personal level when you embark on your own business venture.

My hope is that reading this book will bring you closer to understanding what it feels like to be an entrepreneur. Remember, the highs and lows of entrepreneurship are more than just words on a page. The emotional toll of pursuing entrepreneurship is real. I can attest to that after a year of capturing, listening, and writing these stories from young founders. The pages you're about to read offer pragmatic tools to drive your business idea forward while also sharing the emotional strategies that have helped these entrepreneurs cope with the incredible demands of starting a business.

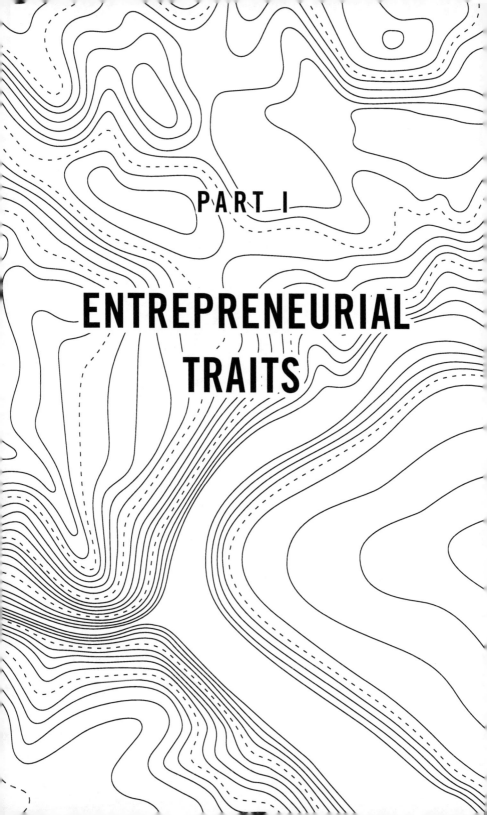

PART I

ENTREPRENEURIAL TRAITS

CHAPTER 1

ENTREPRENEURIAL ROOTS

THE TINKERER

Entrepreneur: Evan Daugharthy
Age: 29
Hometown: Overland Park, Kansas
Company: ReadCoor, a company that is leading the next generation of omics technology by delivering the first panomic spatial sequencing platform to a global audience of researchers, clinicians, pharma and diagnostics companies, and ultimately patients

Evan Daugharthy grew up on a rural farm in Kansas. His house was set about a half-mile from the main road where only a snaggletoothed tree marked the entrance to the driveway. There were no signs of modern life: no telephone poles, no stores, no people. Just Evan, his family, and their farm. It was as if time stood still for thirty years.

The farm had two sides that were divided by a lake. Evan and his family lived on one side where they tended to their livestock and baled hay. On the other side, they grew crops including soybeans and corn. Then there was the junkyard, which sat next to the crops, where Evan sourced equipment to disassemble and tinker with.

His grandfather owned several Dairy Queens franchises, so any decommissioned equipment was sent to the junk-yard. There were old compressors, cash registers, blenders, and ice cream machines from the 1940s and 50s. As an eight-year-old kid, Evan saw the junkyard as if it were a playground and headed over with his little pull wagon to load up on parts. He brought the parts back to his work-shop in the basement and got to work with his screwdriver.

Any machine that had a screw or a bolt was fair game for Evan to disassemble. "I was deadly with a screwdriver," jokes Evan. Whether it was an ice cream machine, a clock radio, a CD player, or even his grandmother's still-working Oldsmobile, Evan felt compelled to take contraptions apart. He wanted to see what was inside, take something old, and use it to create something completely new.

Evan didn't know how any of the parts or circuitry boards

worked. There were no how-to manuals and YouTube didn't exist yet. It didn't matter. He used the power of his imagination. Like many kids, Evan made forts, spaceships, and time machines. But two things in particular made him different than other kids. First, Evan's contraptions were very intricate with an array of levers, switches, and instrument panels.

Second, Evan documented what each part did with incredible precision. For example, one switch for his space rocket served to ignite the engines. Once Evan documented what it did, the part became functional in his mind, even if it didn't work in practice. He worked out the purpose for each part. He also noted how each part worked in coordination with one another. He worked out a sequence for when each switch had to be turned on—the timing was just as important as what each switch did.

What Evan loved the most was the process of building. Once he finished building a machine, he no longer played with what he had built. He wanted to go on to build something new and broke down the new machine so that he could reassemble a new one with the same parts. This process of recycling and reinvention was important to Evan. Each part in the old machine could be reused to serve as a part for a different machine. A blast-box switch could be reconfigured into the switch that marked the year on his time machine capsule. Parts were interchangeable in his mind.

The junkyard was a world where he was in complete control. Evan had a constant supply of projects and ideas and he enjoyed tinkering during his free time. At the same time, his love of machines was balanced out by his hatred of sports.

Evan's father had pushed him to become a great athlete just like he had been when he was in high school. This was torture for Evan, who disliked playing all sports, whether it was tennis or soccer. He cried. He yelled. He cursed. But the hours of practicing something he didn't like doing made him realize what he did like to pursue. Failure at sports at an early age gave him an appreciation for the intellectual pursuits he truly enjoyed.

"I would not change that experience," reflects Evan. "But at the time, it felt traumatic. I spent a lot of time with sports, and I just wasn't good at it. With any venture—intellectual, business, or athletic—there is a natural ability component to it and then there is a work component. With sports, I practiced a lot, but I was not gifted athletically. I am gifted intellectually, and I wanted to put in the work to get good at what was interesting to me. There is a zen quality in doing something over and over again until you master it to your ability. And now, I get to yield those benefits."

Evan's academic prowess powered him through college at the University of Pennsylvania and through his Ph.D. program at Harvard in bioengineering. He loved the purity of the sciences. His favorite place on campus was the bench in his science lab where he conducted experiments. His research findings lead to several publications in the scientific community, and he was on his way to becoming a professor. Entrepreneurship was never on his radar screen as a potential career option.

But at Harvard, Evan saw the difficulty of getting an academic job after completing one's degree. Professorships were hard to come by while tenure was even harder. For example, an acquaintance Evan knew who had landed a first-year professorship had been full of life and energy before she started her position. A year later, Evan bumped into her at an academic retreat and could see the stress built up in her face. Her energy level was low. The demands of academic life had taken its toll. She looked defeated as she went through the grueling process of securing a tenure position. She had another six years of this until her university made a decision.

Evan started to feel anxious. The only path that he knew was an academic one. This was his sole focus. PhD. Professor. Tenure. It was a very clear path. Now, the path didn't feel appealing. He started to become open to the opportunities around him—opportunities that had always been there, only he hadn't noticed them before. Evan simply became more receptive to what was around him.

The Church Lab that he belonged to happened to be very entrepreneurial and had invented a technology called CRISPR that revolutionized genomic research. They spun this technology out to the market and those working on it also helped commercialize it. When Evan talked with the CRISPR scientists, the difference in energy and passion that they demonstrated compared to scientists in academia was palpable. They had a passion and vigor for what they were doing and believed in a mission that was greater than themselves.

Evan started to believe that this was a path he could pursue, and now he had a template. His own research in systems biology could turn into a commercially viable project. He applied his knowledge of electronics to the field of biology to create a machine that sequenced RNA differently than anything else available on the market, providing new insights into the inner workings of cells. In mid-2014, he co-founded the company ReadCoor around this invention with his colleagues at the Church Lab.

"With electronics, I know how the circuitry works," explains Evan. "With molecular biology, nobody really knows how it works. I need to use my imagination. I need to develop tools in my mind that are handles, onto these things I can't see, which are imaginary parts of a complex system. The better my heuristics are, the more powerful my creative ability is on that creative medium. What I am most effective at is imagining all of the possibilities of what makes this black box machine, and it turns out that this skill is very important to invent technologies in this space."

The process that Evan used to build this machine was no different than what he did as a kid. Parts got reused from one machine to the next. Evan had to be flexible with his thinking in order to avoid getting stuck on one part's function, yet also specific enough to determine a concrete usage for each part. Imagination without specificity is not very useful.

He had bins full of parts. Bin A contained switches. Bin B contained transistors. Evan was able to integrate these common parts into something completely new; in this case, a machine that processed molecular samples accurately and quickly. Every single combination Evan tried was itemized and documented just like when he was a kid building imaginary contraptions. He was exhaustive about the building process and documentation so that each combination could be submitted as a patent.

Evan never stopped being the kid who built amazing contraptions from pieces of junk. The things he built as a kid were imaginary. The machines that he builds now use the power of his imagination to create something functional and beneficial. The output might be different, but the process remains the same. Evan, the time-machine inventor, is very much still a part of him, the scientist who sits at his bench and surveys parts to see what he can build next.

THE BOOTSTRAPPER

Entrepreneur: Spencer Fry
Age: 34
Hometown: New York City, New York
Company: Podia, an all-in-one digital storefront that makes it easy to sell online courses, memberships, and digital downloads to audiences

Spencer Fry could barely hear his mom call for him. He was sequestered in his wing of the house that he shared with his parents who were professors at Yale. "The wing was so isolated, not in a bad way, but it was more of a bat cave where I could do my own stuff and I wouldn't be interrupted," Spencer remembers. When he went over to see why his mom summoned him, she had the Yale IT department on the line. They had detected an unusual amount of bandwidth being consumed by their household and they wanted to know why.

Spencer shrugged his shoulders. He said he had no idea,

but in reality, he knew exactly what the issue was. He had set up an illegal file-sharing site for music. His efforts had netted him $50,000 in three weeks by forcing people to click on ads to get access to free content. And he had been able to do this because he had a broadband connection provided by the university, while others were still using dial-up. He knew what he was doing was illegal, but he was only thirteen. He figured nothing could happen to him, right?

Spencer rushed back to his room, pulled out the Ethernet connection, and smashed his hard drive. The next morning, he threw out the leftover pieces into different garbage bins to minimize any trace of his wrongdoing. That didn't dissuade Spencer from continuing to write software, though. In fact, it only encouraged him to keep doing it. He loved it.

"I immediately gravitated toward the Internet and computers. I remember the feeling of how much better situated I was than all of my friends. I went to a friend's house, and I could see how much better hardware and software I had. There was just a massive difference in performance and speed when I played Counter-Strike at my house versus somewhere else. The playing field was stacked in my favor, and I took advantage of it."

Spencer started his first business at age eleven when he

built a fan site for the game Myth. He placed banner ads online and charged $1 to $3 per click. He made $5,000 from that venture. He launched another business when he turned fifteen called TENKU.NET, a web-hosting company that ramped up to a hundred paying customers, each paying $10, by June 1999. Spencer was making money without spending a lot.

Shortly thereafter, the FBI called. Hackers had gained access to Spencer's servers and had used it as a beachhead to infiltrate FBI firewalls. Spencer had no choice but to hand over all of his files. It turned out that 60 percent of his customers had used illegal credit cards to purchase his service. His honest attempt to create a legitimate business backfired.

Spencer kept learning and developing his skills as he experimented. He started to build small communities around music and Internet news and made money by placing ads within them. Another venture he started at eighteen was a web-hosting business called Olternet, which he was able to sell for $10,000. Coming up with ideas for products and then building them was easy for Spencer. He was able to monetize what he had built in many different forms. It was second nature to him. He could make money when he needed to, but what he really wanted to do was build a company that scaled. It made no sense to Spencer to ask for capital when he could use his own, so he always bootstrapped his ventures.

After graduating from high school, he attended Yale where he spent most of his time incubating new businesses. During his freshman year, he and a friend invested $5,000 to start up a company called TypeFrag. The idea came out of their love for video games. One of their favorite games was Counter-Strike, which had an unspoken rule of not attacking players while they were typing into their keyboards and trying to communicate with teammates. Spencer wanted to create a better control panel for this specific problem, which he felt would enhance the entire game experience. The control panel would allow them to communicate through speech instead of typing and accelerate the team's play.

Spencer and his cofounder took three months to build a better control panel and launched it in March 2004. Nobody signed up for it during the first two days it was live. They were terrified that they had wasted so much time and had no results to show for it. Spencer went into action and tried to acquire users for their service. For instance, he offered a free TypeFrag service in exchange for free advertising on gaming sites.

After those first two days, they had one person sign up. A day after that, another two. Two days after that, another four. They were generating momentum boosted by the advertising. By summer, they were making $100,000 a month. Spencer and his cofounder ran this company for three years, and TypeFrag became a brand name in the gaming world. The logo even began appearing on the jackets of top gaming teams.

Despite their success, Spencer and his cofounder had disagreements over the direction of the company. At one point, his cofounder disappeared for a week. Spencer called him repeatedly, but didn't hear anything back. The silence was unnerving. He had to take action, so he consulted a lawyer who advised him to send a formal letter with an offer to buyout the company. It was a low offer, but if he didn't respond, Spencer could claim the company based on the buyout clause in their original legal agreement.

"That letter got him to respond. He was super pissed that I was trying to buy him out. We worked together for three years, and out of the blue, this buyout letter came, which infuriated him. Every time he called me, he yelled. I started to not pick up his calls. He then left me these voicemails. In retrospect, I might have handled this differently but I was young. He went MIA, and I was at a loss for what to do."

After going back and forth for five months, his cofounder came back with a higher offer than Spencer could afford to pay. He even solicited his friend's parents to back him, but he wasn't able to raise sufficient funds to submit a counteroffer. Spencer accepted his cofounder's offer on Christmas Eve. He was twenty-one years old and decided that having a ton of money was preferable to the stress of an erratic cofounder. He was ready to move on to something else even after an attempt to reconcile. Spencer was about to graduate, but it never occurred to him to get a corporate job. He wanted to continue building companies from scratch.

Since then, Spencer has started a few other companies. The most recent one is Podia, a software platform that helps content creators build their online businesses. What has remained consistent over the years is his love of building technology products. Spencer still experiences a childlike feeling of wonder when he releases a new product into the world. His biggest thrill is seeing users flock to his products. "It is like having someone compliment your jacket but at a higher level. It is the ultimate compliment that they paid for a product that I built."

For him, it has never been about the glory of being an entrepreneur. It's about doing something that he believes in, which gives him the greatest sense of fulfillment and independence.

"I have always maintained for the last fifteen years that I am an entrepreneur who builds businesses to feed my family, not to get famous or build a huge product. I am best known in the entrepreneurial community as a boot-strapper. I take my own money and build businesses from it with revenue from day one. This has given me the most control and flexibility over my own destiny in delivering a paycheck for myself and for my team."

What is different now is the maturity Spencer has shown in running his companies. Part of that maturity is reflected in the people he chooses to surround himself with, people he calls "old G's" who were tech entrepreneurs back then and are still his friends today. They get together every month at a restaurant where the conversation dives deep into personal issues: breakups with girlfriends; parents with cancer; trouble with employees; difficulty with fundraising. These are all topics that are on the table for discussion. Their discussions are a bonding experience, part group therapy, part problem-solving session.

"Before, I would try to have my hand in everything," Spencer explains. "I owe a lot of my maturity as an entrepreneur to knowing that you are going to get the best results when you get other people excited and let them shape their vision around the overall vision. I still want to structure the frame of the house, but I want my team to design the bedroom."

Spencer spent so much time tinkering with technology in his childhood bedroom. Now he's the architect of his own house. He takes the first step to draw up the blueprints. He identifies where the pitfalls are based on his previous experiences. And he rallies those around him to execute his vision.

THE MAGICIAN

Entrepreneur: Jon Jacques
Age: 24
Hometown: Glastonbury, Connecticut
Company: Applause, the leading live stream influencer network

One evening, Rick Thomas, a famous magician, stopped his show in Las Vegas to acknowledge a twelve-year-old magician named Jon Jacques. He had received a letter from Jon that explained how this young magician was working incredibly hard at his craft and doing 200 shows a year, an astounding number for someone his age. Rick asked Jon to stand up if he was in the audience that night. The spotlight searched for what felt like an eternity, but when it finally found Jon, he felt the intensity of the spotlight's glare and took a bow. Applause boomed throughout the theater. Jon never felt so happy in his young life.

After the show, Rick stood by the exit and thanked everyone for coming to the show. As Jon headed out with the crowd, Rick pulled him aside. They chatted for several minutes. He wanted Jon to keep pursuing his craft and not let any naysayers dissuade him from pursuing his dream. When Jon exited the theater onto Las Vegas Boulevard, he burst into tears—tears of ecstasy. Jon had put his heart and soul into magic since he began practicing at the age of nine. This acknowledgment was validation that he was on the right path.

It was Jon's parents who had originally set him on the path toward magic. They took him to Hank Lee's Magic Factory in Boston and loaned him $1,000 to acquire props and equipment. The $1,000 was a loan, not a gift. Jon's parents expected him to pay it back; they wanted to teach him the value of money. This forced Jon to practice magic seriously so that he could repay his parents by booking paid performances.

Jon shares, "My first effect was making a red ball appear inside a blue vase. I took the red ball, put it in my pocket, and had it reappear in this vase again. I watched how to perform this effect on my VHS tape recorder over and over again. I practiced the mechanics. I lived for the crowd reaction. I loved how the crowd reacted in amazement to this sleight of hand. I wanted to know what this felt like in real life."

He made $50 from his performance at a kid's birthday, a kid who happened to be the same age as him. Jon dressed up in a tuxedo. Everyone was excited to see a young kid with such bravado. They applauded after each trick and laughed when Jon goofed up. They were having a good time because Jon was having a good time. He was hooked on the thrill of performing in front of a live audience, which motivated him to do more shows.

Jon's reputation started to grow as a kid magician. During high school, he sometimes did up to eight shows over a weekend. He learned how to be incredibly efficient with his time. For instance, while some magicians took two hours to set up for a show, Jon needed only fifteen minutes. His efficiency helped him pack in as many shows as he could. His charm helped him in situations when effects went awry.

He once made doves appear at a birthday party. He had trained them not to fly, but because the room was flooded with light, once they appeared, the doves decided to take flight and landed where they pleased. They found their landing pad on the birthday cake. The cake was ruined, but everyone laughed because of the unexpectedness of the moment. "I told them they might want to cut that piece of cake out because of where the bird landed," jokes Jon.

At age fifteen, Jon performed in front of 8,000 people at Mohegan Sun, a casino and resort in Connecticut. By this point, he was on the path to becoming a professional magician and earning more money than his school teachers by performing magic on the weekends. But Jon was getting burnt out. By senior year, he started to turn down shows. He wanted to take a break. His parents, who had supported him throughout his young magic career, made a pact with him that he had to go to college. Jon obliged and ended up enrolling in Babson College, a school known for its entrepreneurial curriculum.

At Babson, Jon quickly developed a reputation as a great presenter because of his experience performing in front of large audiences. Instead of just presenting the facts, he turned each presentation into a show. Successful presentations also required an intense focus on the smallest details. "For me, it is all about the details of the presentation," explains Jon. "A lot of people gloss over that. I put in anywhere from one to three hours of preparation for every minute that I am on stage. Sometimes even more. I get pretty finicky with the details." Preparation in the details gave him the confidence to make the impact that he was looking for when delivering a presentation.

In one case, Jon helped an older classmate redesign a deck for a business-plan competition. The classmate, Alex Debelov, ended up winning the competition and used the seed capital he won to start his company Virool, a startup in the digital video space. Alex never forgot that moment. He was so impressed with Jon and how he had volunteered to help him that Alex recruited Jon to work for him after he graduated. It didn't matter that Jon had no experience in the industry. Alex wanted Jon because he knew he had the personality to succeed as an account executive. Jon gladly accepted the offer.

At Virool, Jon's role was to acquire new customers. He had to create demand for an advertising product that he had no experience selling. It was almost like a magician making things appear out of thin air. Jon shares, "I didn't have any contacts. I started from scratch. I hustled. I had to turn complete strangers into best friends so that they would feel comfortable authorizing deal sizes north of six figures. At one point in time, I was closing 20 percent of the revenue on my own and was the top salesperson. I did it by hustling." His experience building his magic business provided a template for success in becoming a top performer in selling Virool's ad product.

Jon also used magic as part of his sales presentations. Jon explains, "I used magic to my advantage. I had to show how my personality was different than everyone else so that potential clients would remember me. I walked into these presentations and went through the product content. Right before a meeting ended, I asked the audience if I could show them something interesting, which they usually obliged. I would perform an effect where I took the glasses off of one of their faces, and I would make them levitate. That had such a huge impact that word of mouth of spread about my presentations and started to travel within industry circles."

Once during a presentation at Red Bull, before Jon could even execute the levitation trick, one of the girls jumped out of her chair and said, "You are the guy who performs magic!" His reputation had preceded him. "I had CEOs of boutique agencies and executives sending me emails that said that this was the most compelling sales presentation they had ever seen in their fifteen years of working in the marketing space," Jon proudly recalls.

Magic helped Jon catapult to top salesman at Virool, but he wanted more. He was itching for a more creative freedom. On nights and weekends, he performed tricks on the live streaming platform Periscope. It gave him that butterfly feeling again of performing in front of a live audience. Initially, he simply live streamed from his bedroom. Eventually, Jon mustered the courage to go out onto the streets. Something was calling him back to his roots.

One night, Jon announced to his followers on Periscope that he was headed out to do street magic. His heart was pounding once he left his apartment building, but there was no turning back—he had fully committed to this experiment. Street magic was completely different than a traditional show. At a show, the audience knew who he was and came specifically to see him perform. In this case, he had to capture the attention of complete strangers.

He walked up to a guy who was with two women and asked if he could show them a trick. He asked the guy to hold his iPhone for his Periscope audience. Jon took five $1 bills and proceeded to turn them into five $100 bills. This trick was foolproof as Jon had practiced it more than a thousand times. Astonishment flooded the faces of the small crowd he had gathered on the streets, a typical reaction. But what he didn't expect was the kind of reaction he received from his Periscope followers. Comments started to flood in from his online audience while his three-person live audience was still caught up in the spontaneity of the moment. Jon was on to something.

Jon continued to do street magic. Sometimes those he approached didn't want to participate. The no's didn't dissuade him because he loved the feeling of performing live. It was different than before because he had both an online and offline audience. Jon had found his calling and continued to innovate in this new performance format. He quit Virool to focus on building his Periscope audience and became a top-fifteen influencer within three months.

One particular sequence of events changed the trajectory of Jon's entrepreneurial journey. Jon announced to his Periscope audience that any donations from his next performance would be donated to charity. He went to Times Square dressed in a suit and top hat. He performed in front of crowd of sixty people. He raised $30. He asked his Periscope audience how he should donate the money. They instructed him to set up a GoFundMe page, which then generated another $700. This random act of kindness was picked up by *Mashable*. It was the first time that anyone had raised money on Periscope, and *Mashable* tracked Jon's progress in raising and donating the money.

The *Mashable* article was shared more than 3,000 times and caught the attention of *The Ellen DeGeneres Show*. What Jon was doing aligned with what Ellen as a brand represented: a great personality, a fantastic entertainer, and a philanthropist who loved to give back. They came up with a show segment called "Magic Moments." In the closing episode, they broadcasted the story of a fourteen-year-old boy named Josh who wanted to be a magician. Just like when his parents brought him to his first magic shop, Jon did the same for Josh. He gave Josh $500 to purchase his own magic props to train with. This gave Jon a greater sense of purpose in his own path because he was giving back, just like Rick Thomas did in Vegas. Now it was Jon's turn.

Jon remembers, "That experience injected me with an emotional high that brought me back to when I was nine years old and visited my first magic shop. This kind of giving will always be a part of our culture. We want to help make the world a better place by giving in a way that has been never done before and make people smile along the way."

This was when Jon started to think about himself on a larger scale and beyond just being a performer. He had had his time in the spotlight. It was time to help shine a spotlight on others and help other influencers with a significant audience through live streaming. A network of influencers created more scale for big brands to invest advertising dollars in. Jon started his agency, Applause, as a way to represent these influencers at scale.

Jon's journey as an entrepreneur started with his love for magic. Magic was his foundation, and it powered all of his experiences. It stayed with him throughout his time in college and at his first startup. Magic allowed him to rediscover the joy of performing for a crowd through the live streaming format. He reinvented himself each time but still remained true to himself. Magic will always be a part of Jon, but now his mission is much larger than himself.

CHAPTER 2

THE GLORY OF GRIT

COUCH DUDE

Entrepreneur: Alex White
Age: 30
Hometown: Ithaca, New York
Company: Next Big Sound, the leading provider of online music analytics and insights, tracking thousands of artists around the world

Alex White was known by his roommates as the "couch dude." After graduation, he moved into a large house in Lincoln Park, Chicago, with a bunch of his recently graduated friends. His room was the living room couch. His friends let him stay for free because he had turned down a full-time offer to focus on his startup idea, Next Big Sound, instead. Next Big Sound had raised $25,000, but Alex wanted to be conservative with his personal expenses. So he asked his friends if he could stay with them for free while he got this company off the ground. He converted a small kitchen pantry into his closet. This was where he kept his clothes, his sheets, and all his personal belongings.

While he had no privacy, he got used to it and adapted his budget to accommodate this lifestyle. Alex remembers, "I was borrowing one guy's gym membership and was grocery shopping once a week. I spent $20 on groceries and $40 on beer every week. Those were my two limits. I knew that with $60 a week, I would be okay in the short term, but I asked myself how long could I go? My only other expense at the time was my cell phone."

Alex simplified his living down to the bare minimum. He was obsessed with making Next Big Sound, a big data analytics company, a transformative force in the music industry. Music had always been a part of Alex's life. His father was a cello teacher who encouraged him to play a musical instrument. In middle school, Alex started with cello, and then in high school, transitioned to playing guitar. He soon began writing his own songs and recording his own music. In 10th grade, his music career crashed at a school talent show before it even had a chance to get started. The anxiousness and nervousness that Alex felt before, during, and after his performance was not something he wanted to feel again. He decided he'd be better matched to opportunities on the business side of music.

At Northwestern University, where he enrolled in 2004, he cobbled together music and business classes. Through these classes, he met a few students who had had internships at Universal Music the previous year. This lead him to secure his own internship there following his freshman year. Yet when he got to Universal Music, he found himself just stapling weekly CD sales reports together. Alex was willing to do anything to work his way up the ladder and gain a position where he could influence the music that became popular in America. His most strategic move was to ask an assistant if he could get fifteen minutes with Pat Monaco, an influential music executive at Motown Republic. It was a big ask framed in an innocuous way. Pat ran sales and distribution for the company, so he was extremely busy. The assistant agreed to keep Alex apprised of an opening in his calendar.

Finally, toward the end of the summer, Pat's assistant alerted Alex that Pat had a small window of free time. The advice Alex received in those fifteen minutes changed the entire course of his career trajectory. Alex explains, "He was eating lunch at his desk, and I came over and pulled up a chair. I asked him how he got started in the music business. I expected him to say, 'I started as an intern and I worked my way up.' That was the opposite of what he said. He started a distribution company that was bought by Universal. That was the moment when I realized that I needed to start something in the music business in order to end up in the corner office, and that was the first time I ever considered entrepreneurship."

That conversation gripped Alex for the rest of college. He wanted to be a record mogul more than anything. The first iteration of Next Big Sound was a fantasy site where users could track how well bands they signed performed through a point system. Alex sketched out the idea in his notebooks. He thought about it all the time. But he told nobody for two years until he shared it with a friend who he thought of as a worthy cofounder. Alex started to describe it, but because he hadn't rehearsed it, it all came out in a jumble. His friend was pleasant and acted interested, but didn't commit to joining. Alex was not dissuaded and was determined to find another cofounder.

The second person he approached was David Hoffman, a classmate of his who was a year younger. Alex was impressed with David because of the way he broke down complex problems. He also had web design and programming skills. They agreed to meet one Sunday morning before winter break at Einstein Bros. Bagels. The fact that they had complementary skills encouraged them to work together for an entrepreneurship class the next semester. However, they still hadn't settled on an idea.

Alex wanted to pursue Next Big Sound. David had his own startup ideas. So Alex decided to back down from his desire to focus exclusively on Next Big Sound in order to get David to work with him for the class. Alex remembers calling David during winter break, "Let's do one of your ideas. I want to work with you. That's the most important thing." During the course of the class, though, Alex was relentless. He slowly convinced David that Next Big Sound had the most market potential and was worth exploring.

After the class ended, Alex, David, and Samir, another classmate who joined the group, went out for beers to celebrate. Alex saw this celebration as the beginning, not the end, of their journey. "I don't want this to be over with just this class," he told his classmates, "I am not going to take classes this spring quarter and I am going to devote myself to this full time. Who is with me? And what will it take for you guys to actually do this?"

The answer was money. David and Samir decided to forgo their summer internships if the team could raise $30,000 by June 1. On June 2, they raised $25,000 from an investor down in Champaign, Illinois, which allowed the team to build the first version of the site. When fall semester started, David and Samir went back to school, while Alex moved onto the couch in the house in Lincoln Park. He stayed on that couch through spring 2009 when

Next Big Sound was accepted into the Techstars program in Colorado.

"When we moved to Boulder, we moved into a four-bedroom house, and I got my own door and desk, and my mind was blown," Alex recalls. "But we only received $18,000 through the program and that would barely last us through the end of the year. We would have moved to Timbuktu if someone had given us the money. We were just grateful for another crack at the bat."

Alex took every opportunity to maximize the company's runway for success. This included preventing David and Samir from defecting to a safe corporate job if their parents pressured them. He set a date for all of their parents to come out for one weekend and meet their investors. It was a "parent's weekend" for their startup. The goal was to showcase how the business they were working on was legitimate and real.

Parents, investors, and employees all convened at one of the investors' houses on a Saturday night. Each investor stood up and gave a speech about how impressed they were with the maturity of the team, despite the fact that they had just graduated from college. Then Alex gave a toast. He recalls, "That was the moment that all of the parents got that their kids were doing something really special and that the investors were seasoned and world class." Afterwards, Alex went to each parent and told them to call him if they had any concerns. He never received a follow-up call after that weekend.

The team continued to follow their vision of making data accessible and useful to the music industry. In summer 2012, they moved to New York, and shortly after, they signed Sony Music as a client. As a Sony music executive, I saw the value they provided because I knew that Next Big Sound data helped to track the performance of Sony's artists and songs. Data was becoming more prevalent at music labels, which traditionally valued gut feelings over statistics. Across the next three years, Next Big Sound's momentum continued as they signed up more clients and eventually became an acquisition target for Pandora.

The acquisition was the culmination of a gritty, seven-year journey of long workweeks and even longer weekends. "This couch story, the recruitment of David and Samir, the parent's weekend," Alex reflects, "I think back to what we went through to bring it to this point, and there were so many times that this thing could have died. It was only July 2015, after the deal was closed and the wire transfers had gone out, that was the first time that I finally exhaled. I started with an idea and got it all the way across the finish line that only few people cross and even fewer people cross with a successful exit."

When I asked Alex what's next on the horizon, he says he is still dedicated to making Next Big Sound's data an even more integral part of the music industry. Having Pandora's infrastructure and resources will help bolster their ability to execute that vision. His enthusiasm, though, is tempered by a tiredness that I could hear in his voice.

"There is no part of me that wants to start another company. It was fucking hard," Alex says. "I talk to a lot of entrepreneurs who are not in the headlines. They are firing employees, flushing their 401ks, losing their spouses. And it is brutal. And nobody talks about them. That is when you get the separation of people wanting to stick it out and willing to sacrifice their salary, location, and relationships and those that are in it for a quick win."

A HIGH TOLERANCE FOR PAIN

Entrepreneur: Abhi Lokesh
Age: 30
Hometown: Palm Harbor, Florida
Company: Fracture, a company that revolutionized the printing of pictures right onto glass

On Saturday morning in November 2015, I met Abhi Lokesh at Fracture headquarters in Gainesville, Florida. When Abhi started to tell me his story, there was a heaviness in his voice. He reflected on what he and his company had endured to survive. Only stopping to take a breath, he proceeded to share his story for forty-five minutes straight. I could feel the total determination that it took him to keep his company alive for the past seven years.

The story of Fracture starts with Abhi's relationship with his cofounder, Alex. They met through a mutual friend in a social entrepreneurship class at the University of Florida. The class offered them an opportunity to apply the skills they had learned in a real-world setting. Through a connection they had on the ground in Swaziland, they learned about the HIV/AIDS epidemic ravaging the tiny African country. Their nonprofit idea was to source art from socially-conscious artists from around the world, produce digital copies, sell them online, and donate all profits to charity. The idea never took off, but their friendship did instead. They won a $10,000 grant to spend the summer of 2008 in Swaziland, implementing an agricultural initiative focused on improving the lives of those with AIDS. They bonded while living and working together in a remote part of Africa that was isolated from all the comforts they knew back home.

Abhi explains, "One of the reasons we felt so connected to each other was that each of us was the link back to the life we knew. We would talk to each other about things that we could relate to. It was a different life and a different world. We did the most basic tasks together, such as washing and hanging laundry to venturing into the capital in a mini-van from where we were stationed. As the summer wore on, we spent more time talking about this new idea called Fracture and less about Swaziaid, the original reason why we went out there."

In 2008, Facebook was just starting to scale and Twitter was becoming more mainstream. Abhi recognized the success of these businesses, but he wanted to make a physical product that had a blue-collar, old school, hard knock vibe to it. He knew how resourceful Alex was and that he could make almost anything. The idea they came up with was a product that would allow consumers to print photos directly onto glass. They took the time-tested business of printing photos and brought it into the digital age.

A few hundred dollars got them started with building a prototype once they returned back to school. Abhi remembers, "When Alex brought over that first prototype, it looked great. It was something tangible. Alex can do this. I can do this. We can do this. We can build stuff. We had something real."

In order to continue building more resources, they needed to raise investment capital. Abhi went to his father and asked if he could pitch Fracture to his investment club. The club had been formed to pick stocks, not startups, but Abhi knew that access to this group of investors could provide him with the quickest route to capital.

A few days after he pitched the club, Abhi received a phone call from his dad. They were going to give him $60,000 to start the business. Abhi was ecstatic. But looking back at that moment, he now realizes how fortunate he was. Abhi shares, "They didn't know what they were doing. You couldn't ask for less informed investors in terms of consumer goods e-commerce startups. The only thing that carried them through was their love for me and my reputation. In fact, we were all playing it cool, but none of us knew what we were doing."

While the concept of printing onto glass was straightforward enough, executing the idea was a lot more difficult. It required integrating software and hardware components. Abhi and Alex didn't anticipate the complexity of what they were tackling. They were in over their heads and had to rely on grit alone to survive. Poor decisions almost sunk the company before it started.

Abhi admits that when they first started, "We didn't build a good team. It was Alex and myself. We needed another founder who was software engineering focused. What I think was the biggest weakness of Fracture was Alex taking on so much that he was literally connected fundamentally to every system in Fracture. When you are a company that needs to scale—that is the worse thing that can happen. Alex was Fracture's greatest strength but also its greatest weakness."

They also tried to build all of their systems from scratch. "One of the biggest mistakes we made in terms of a business model was that we wanted to do everything by ourselves," Abhi shares. "We started every system we have from scratch—all of the hardware, software, marketing, and finance. We built everything ourselves. I don't know what more we could have taken on to make this a harder challenge for us."

The sheer amount of work required to get the business off the ground caused tension between Abhi and Alex. All of the building fell to Alex who started to resent Abhi. When he sensed Alex was angry, Abhi could feel Alex's eyes burning into the back of his head. It made Abhi buckle down on making the business a success even more because he felt obligated to showcase what Alex had built to the world. But Abhi struggled and was lonely in figuring out how to keep the company afloat.

"Nobody told me how to do it, especially coming from a scientific background where you have a manual and a standard operating procedure or curriculum or a textbook for everything," Abhi reflects. "It was really hard not having somebody to talk to who was not Alex and could relate to me. The saying that it is really lonely at the top, as a CEO, I felt really, really lonely. I almost missed someone telling me what to do because I felt like nothing I was doing was right. It certainly wasn't reflected in the bottom line because for a while, we weren't going anywhere. And yet somehow, we kept slugging it out. We never gave up, kept fighting and pushed that rock up that hill, millimeter by millimeter, inch by inch. And it was brutal."

At the end of December 2013, Fracture had a profitable quarter after four years in business. Finally, they were trending positively after so many quarters of losing money as they made key hires. But the coast wasn't clear yet. Their expenses had skyrocketed and they were losing money every day, with a cumulative loss of several hundred thousand dollars. "I didn't know what just happened, but we almost lost all of our money. We weren't frivolous, but we also weren't as lean as we could be," recalls Abhi. He had to take control of the expenses or risk losing control of the entire company.

"Day in and day out, I listed out every single expense and checked every bill and bank account to see when it would cash. If I didn't know what was going on, I would just hammer it out until I knew exactly to the cent how much we were spending on a monthly basis and how much we were making. That was the level of diligence that not a lot of people would go through unless their lives were on the line. It was about how willing I was to look at numbers, detail after detail, until I was positive everything added up.

New life has been infused into Fracture since it scraped

by those lean times. Their cost structure is more sound, while their new hires, starting with their chief marketing officer, began driving top-line growth in early 2014. They haven't looked back since.

The difference between the survivors and the quitters, Abhi explains, is this: "My tolerance for adversity and pain is quite high. It wasn't always that way—I was very weak in the beginning, and I have had a lot of dark days. If another person had one of those dark days, they would have folded. But I've gradually built up this well of resolve and self-belief. I really do believe that I can do whatever needs to be done regardless of what is thrown at me. You can beat the hell out of me, and I will still keep coming back."

BRIDGING EAST AND WEST

Entrepreneur: Andrew Chau
Age: 35
Hometown: San Francisco, California
Company: Boba Guys, a company that serves the highest quality boba tea in the world, a brand that stands for quality, transparency, and giving a damn

In his early teens, Andrew Chau biked over to his parent's Chinese restaurant in New Jersey most nights. He headed down to the basement where the food was prepped, got on his stool, and started to peel the string beans off their stems, slice potatoes, and prepare wontons. It was monotonous work. He'd be down in the basement prepping food for four hours straight. He learned that jobs are not sexy, but he tried to make what he was doing as enjoyable as possible.

Andrew explains, "I would fold the wontons onto a tray and stack them up. I wanted them stacked so that each row was the same number of wontons. It has to be perfect order. I do think, looking back, that I was probably made for what I do now." Today he runs a network of premium bubble tea shops, Boba Guys, based in San Francisco where his obsessive attention to detail makes the operations run smoothly.

Hard work has been a consistent theme throughout Andrew's life. It didn't help that he is restricted by a severe case of rheumatoid arthritis. The condition froze parts of his body to the point where when he played tennis, he could no longer grip the racket. There were nights where the pain was so bad that Andrew couldn't sleep. The Chau family moved to California in Andrew's mid-teens to seek better medical treatment so that he wouldn't have to live in such pain.

He was accepted to University of California, Berkeley, where he enrolled as a pre-med major until he decided to switch to communications his sophomore year. He came home one weekend to let his parents know about his decision. It was 10 p.m. on a Saturday night. His mother was just winding down by playing the piano in the living room. Andrew mentioned to his mother that he was going to study communications. Her heart was set on Andrew being a doctor. The conversation got heated as both went back and forth in a mix of Chinese and English. "It was an emotional conversation. I cried. I yelled at my mom. I said things that I didn't mean," recalls Andrew. Frustrated by the conversation, Andrew stormed back to his room and slammed the door.

In the other room, Andrew's father was getting ready for bed as he had to get up at 4 a.m. to start his morning shift as a Muni bus driver. The commotion drew him out of his bedroom. Andrew heard his parents arguing in the living room and then a knock on his door.

His father opened the door and walked over to him, placing his hand on Andrew's shoulder. He never showed any physical emotion, not then, not now. But it made a deep impression on Andrew who always saw his father as emotionally reserved.

"In his broken English, my father said we came to America. It is freedom. You happy. You choose," Andrew recalls. Then, switching to Cantonese, his natural dialect, my father continued, "I didn't come here to lose freedom because I forced you to do something that you didn't want to do. I choose freedom, and we choose freedom for our children. That was probably the most animated that I had ever seen my dad."

The emotional weight of that conversation took a toll on Andrew. He didn't speak with his mother for two months. She was still upset about her son not pursuing a medical degree. But Andrew knew himself. He was an extrovert. The thought of burying himself in the library and the hospital for the next decade was stifling. Instead, the path he chose led him to marketing roles at several companies, from Walmart to Leapfrog. It was at Timbuk2, a designer bag company, where Andrew met his cofounder Bin, and they conceived of the idea for Boba Guys.

Andrew and Bin first bonded over ping pong during a stressful work day. That relationship extended out of the office during lunch time. They tried every single lunch spot within biking distance of their office based in the Mission, a bohemian neighborhood in San Francisco. That was their time to talk work but also spitball ideas for a possible startup. They naturally gravitated to technology because they were in the heart of Silicon Valley. But it didn't feel right. Their conversations had a broader, more philosophical feel to them.

"We thought we could make a business around the purpose

of bridging cultures. What cultures? The most obvious one was East-West. When we talked about different ideas, food was one of the few ideas that could bridge cultures. Media was the other. I didn't want to make content for a living. Food was it. Every time that we talked about the idea, we brought up bubble tea. We thought that bubble tea could bridge cultures. We had the mission before we had Boba Guys."

There was already a huge food movement happening in the Mission. They knew Danny Bowien before he became the celebrity chef helming Mission Chinese. Danny's rise as a chef who made Chinese food accessible to American tastes was a trajectory Andrew and Bin felt they could follow with boba. Neither had any food or retail company experience. But they felt they had enough grit to figure it out themselves.

Their first order of business was to figure out the recipe. They watched a few YouTube videos and started to experiment with not only the different brands of milk, tea, and tapioca, but also with the ratios at which they were mixed together. Other questions came up such as the temperature of the water, when to add the tapioca balls, and the amount of sugar added. What was originally conceived as a straightforward recipe became a complicated formula with many different combinations that they captured in a spreadsheet. What was important was achieving a level of quality that matched their vision.

Andrew recalls their comprehensive, three-month testing period: "If we were going to achieve our mission of bridging cultures and wanted to achieve a certain kind of high class and be premium, we needed to get rid of Coffee-Mate. The water ratios were really different when we used creamer so we had to get our proportions correct with the milk we decided to use. Another vector we needed to test was the chewiness of the tapioca ball. We tested boiling it at various time intervals: twenty-five, twenty-eight, thirty, thirty-three, thirty-five, and thirty-eight minutes. The longer it boiled, the chewier it became. Did customers care about really chewy versus really, really chewy? We ended up at thirty minutes, which fairly weighted operational efficiency against customer satisfaction."

Once they had an acceptable product, they wanted to test out whether consumers would enjoy it. Their way of beta testing food was a pop-up shop. They were friends with a lot of restaurant owners because of their lunchtime, culinary excursions, and the owner of a Japanese restaurant offered them a rent-free space. Pop-ups are a popular way for existing restaurants to create buzz while helping to support the area's culinary ecosystem. This is what Danny Bowien first did before opening Mission Chinese so that he could test out his food concept. Andrew and Bin's series of pop-ups around the city were a smash hit with customers who queued up to taste high quality boba.

That experience gave them the courage to look for a lease in the area. They bypassed a real estate broker and opted for a more direct approach. Every store they walked into was an opportunity to secure a space. It didn't matter if it was a Chinese restaurant or a locksmith. It turned out that the owner of a bubble tea shop that Andrew and Bin frequented during lunchtime was willing to transfer his lease to them. After some negotiation, they agreed on a transfer price, but that was only the first step. The landlord still needed to be convinced before he would grant them the right to continue on with the lease.

"The landlord was in his sixties. I had to convince him we were legitimate. He didn't know we didn't have that much experience," Andrew explains. "I pointed to our hot pop-up only two blocks away and let him know that we were going to be his best tenants. He agreed and handed over a six-page lease, handwritten on lined paper. That was the way that he did business. I retyped it and signed it. And we then worked to open up our store, and on our first day, lines were out the doors. We, in fact, became his best tenants and increased his property value."

Both Bin and Andrew were willing to roll up their sleeves and do what was necessary to open their first store. That mentality carried them to opening three more stores, two in San Francisco and one in New York. Despite their growth, they never lost sight of their original mission of bridging cultures. Quality, transparency, and giving a damn are their key values and help filter their decision making. For example, they declined an investment from a prominent venture capitalist because the infusion of cash would have compromised their values.

A significant moment in the brand's trajectory was a commercial they filmed for the Nissan Rogue. The ad targeted Asian Americans but the spot ran nationally. The brand picked Boba Guys because this was a product that was relatable to an Asian American audience but still had mass appeal. The exposure was great for Boba Guys. But the real reason they decided to participate in it was that the commercial represented what Andrew and Bin originally intended to do—bridge cultures.

"We knew the commercial was cheesy," jokes Andrew. "There was super Asian-style editing, music, and copy. But we liked it, and what was really cool was the impact that it had on our non-Asian friends. They read about what we stood for but never really understood that. Watching the commercial and seeing us in it changed how they saw our culture. We wanted to be bold among the Asian American community not known for being bold, and we were able to be bold through our food."

Mainstream press, including *The New York Times*, *The Wall Street Journal*, *GQ*, *Vogue*, and *NPR*, have covered how Boba Guys is driving the bubble tea movement. This press is not accidental, but a result of the fact that Boba Guys stands for something more than high quality bubble tea. The brand represents a cultural ideal that bridges many cultures together—not just East and West—over a delicious drink.

CHAPTER 3

THE PARADOX OF RISK

THE OPPORTUNIST

Entrepreneur: Amanda Slavin
Age: 31
Hometown: Las Vegas, Nevada
Company: CatalystCreativ, an experiential marketing agency with an expertise in marketing, events, and design

Amanda Slavin and her boyfriend were standing outside a hot, new Miami club on a Saturday night. The line to get into the club wrapped around the corner. They were not on the guest list, but Amanda walked up to the doorman with a cool and calm demeanor. She looked him in the eye with both respect and confidence. "Hi, it's just me and my boyfriend. We're great people. We're not going to cause any trouble." It was kind and direct, not pretentious or nasty. Most of the time, Amanda got in without any trouble, and in this case, the doorman let them pass right through.

Amanda's hustle did not go unnoticed. She regularly got friends into clubs in New York and London with ease using the same technique she applied in Miami. One close friend even suggested that she go into club promotion so that she could get paid for delivering a certain number of people to the club each night. What she disliked was the exclusivity of clubs, which granted access to some, while restricting entrance to others. She wanted everyone to have a good time and found her calling when she started hosting events in New York City. It was the start of her journey as the founder of CatalystCreativ, an experiential marketing firm for brands.

Before Facebook, Amanda was the walking Facebook of her high school. She knew everything about everyone, from who they were dating and what their hobbies were to what jobs their parents had. She loved connecting with people and bringing them together to have a great time. That feeling and energy was what had powered her since she had been young. In first grade, for example, she facilitated snack exchanges with her classmates.

But Amanda didn't always intend on throwing parties to make a living. She had been working on both her bachelor's and master's degrees to become a teacher when her boyfriend's fraternity brother introduced her to a tech entrepreneur; he suggested that she use her hustle to throw parties for venues. Her first party was at Cellar Bar in the Bryant Park Hotel in Manhattan. She had to deliver fifty people to the venue to earn a commission. She set up a Facebook group, texted them, emailed them, and followed up with everyone she invited.

"I had to invite two hundred people to get fifty people," Amanda remembers. "I invited as many people as possible, and even if they said yes, I would assume no because they would drop off, whether they might have double-booked themselves or had a work deadline that they had to stay late for. I was studying psychology because I was planning to be a teacher, so I would go person by person and think of the right incentives for them to come whether that be free drink, the cool vibe of the venue, or the people who had already confirmed."

The success of that first event snowballed. What started out as just one event turned into requests from six venues. They needed her services to throw events for different occasions like anniversaries, birthdays, and major holidays like Christmas and New Year's Eve. She was making extra cash on the side while getting her degree to become a teacher at the University of Connecticut. Everyone thought she lived in New York because she was always planning parties. The truth was that she was only there during the weekends because the rest of the week she was at school.

After graduating in 2009 during the recession, Amanda found that her classmates were having difficulty finding suitable positions. She decided she would take a different route when the owner of the Paige Hospitality Group, a restaurant and hospitality business, offered her a job at his company. He was impressed with the quality and quantity of her events. "I was not in school for communication and events. It was all organic. I was good at what I was doing and had built up a rolodex of people who would come. The owner saw that as an asset. I ended up becoming the director of events and marketing for his restaurant group."

Amanda thought about opening up her own event planning company, but she felt the risk was too great at that point. "I was the type of person who needed a paycheck so that I could cover my rent and have a foundation to build off of." She received some valuable advice to use this job as a launching pad since the company was going to open up new restaurants and night clubs that she could have a direct hand in developing.

The Paige Hospitality Group was a small company with big ambitions. It created an opportunity for her to have a large impact over the course of her three years there. She started off running marketing for one property and then, because of her strong performance, she took over marketing for all the properties. While her job consumed her, it didn't stop her from saying yes to other opportunities. One of them was Summit at Sea, a voyage that brings the brightest young minds together on a weekend cruise.

Summit at Sea was a ten-day commitment in Miami, but that didn't stop her from saying yes as she had vacation time she never used. It turned out to be an experience that transformed her life. Amanda explains, "I met people outside of my normal sphere, which was banking and nightlife. One guy was building an irrigation system in Cambodia, while another was rebuilding a community in Africa. I saw Gary Vaynerchuk speak, who was so dynamic and crazy. He reminded me of my personality. Where were these people all my life? I felt so connected to these people. They were my kindred spirits."

One of the key people she met on that trip was Tony Hsieh, CEO of Zappos, who was also an investor in the Downtown Project in Las Vegas. He invited her to come visit Vegas and learn more about the initiative he was building there. After arriving, there were some mishaps (he didn't remember who she was), but after a few days, they reconnected when he invited her to lunch. The night before their one-on-one meeting, Amanda read Hsieh's book *Delivering Happiness*. She wanted to be prepared.

When they met, Tony put her at ease. He wanted to learn more about how she could help build Las Vegas into a city with an identity beyond gambling and gaming.

At that point, Amanda was at a crossroads. She was still at Paige Hospitality Group where the owner was about to make her an offer to become a full partner in the organization. Her experience at Summit at Sea catalyzed her entrepreneurial ambitions. She loved her life in Manhattan, but there was an allure to starting something new. She always said yes to new kinds of opportunities. Why stop now? Here was an opportunity to work with a billionaire investor who had grand visions of how to catalyze a local community. She agreed to start a company with Tony Hsieh called CatalystCreativ to develop an event series that she and Tony developed for the Downtown Project.

To kick it off, Amanda wrote down the names of the thirty people who would participate in the first Catalyst week. She knew them all from her years of throwing events. They came from impressive backgrounds. One was the executive producer of *Batman*. Another was the head of marketing at Gatorade. She emailed hem and all of them agreed to come for an entire week.

"That week transformed all of those people's lives," Amanda recalls. "Every single person who attended said that there was a part of their lives that was transformed.

From there, they shared their experiences with other people who then started to ask when they could attend."

Since then, business has grown organically. People have clamored to be a part of Catalyst events. Sensing an opportunity to develop beyond the original vision, Amanda expanded the concept to design experiences for brands targeting specific kinds of consumers. She transitioned her business from a series of workshops to a full-fledged creative agency using experience design as their distinct strength.

Risk is the flip side of opportunity. Amanda never saw her moves as risky. She worked hard to put herself in positions where she could meet the right people and showcase her skills in the right environment. Turning down an opportunity was the biggest risk she faced. What led to her success was saying yes and seizing opportunities that came her way even if they were uncomfortable at first.

Amanda explains, "I have always said yes. I think of them as opportunities. I am pretty practical about taking that leap. My brain works quickly. When I get offered something, I think about risk and opportunities and make a decision with a cumulative review within ten seconds. I think that I have been strategic with the moves I have, which have not made them seem as huge risks because I saw them adding to my foundation as a person."

Entrepreneur: Aman Advani
Age: 31
Hometown: Atlanta, Georgia
Company: Ministry of Supply, a company that engineers high performance dress clothes that fit well, look sharp, and most importantly—are insanely comfortable

In high school, Aman Advani noticed he had a sweat problem. It wasn't excessive, but it was uncomfortable enough that he noticed. It didn't help that he grew up in Atlanta, Georgia, known for its hot, sticky, and humid summers. For junior prom, he taped cotton balls underneath his arms to absorb the sweat and avoid unwanted attention from his date and friends. Aman probably didn't sweat more than the average person, but because he was self-conscious about it, he decided to do something about it.

After graduating from Georgia Tech with an industrial engineering degree, Aman joined Deloitte Consulting. He wore the classic corporate wardrobe: crisp button-down shirt, pressed slacks, and quality leather shoes. Looking good made Aman feel good, which allowed him to focus on delivering high quality work. He was often on his feet for sixteen hours a day. After a long day, the first thing he did when he came home was take off his shoes and rip off his socks. His feet ached, and Aman didn't get any support from his dress socks, which were flimsy. The socks didn't absorb his sweat, so that by the time he got them off, it was like flinging a damp towel into the laundry.

These moments triggered memories of when Aman was in high school running to class or to his extra-curricular activities. "There was no greater sensation than putting on a pair of Thorlos, a high-end, performance running sock. When I put my first pair on, it was a magical feeling. I looked forward to wearing these socks. Why couldn't I have the same sensation at work when I was wearing these crappy Gold Toe socks?"

Aman had tinkered with product ideas as an adult, but he didn't realize that entrepreneurship might be something he was interested in. There wasn't an entrepreneurial ecosystem in Atlanta. His ideas ranged from designing bags that slung over the shoulder better to building contraptions to keep pants from wrinkling. Working on socks was just another category he tackled, but it ended up being more serious than his previous pursuits. He even put up a sock blog called Eight Socks, where he reviewed the quality of different socks. The momentum he gained from the blog was what inspired him to start his own business.

One day he walked into his parent's house with a bag full of socks ready to test. His mom was sitting down, hemming a pair of his pants on the sewing machine. Aman took out his socks and asked her if she could cut out the soles of the Gold Toe socks and replace them with the soles from Nike DriFIT Socks. She was somewhat puzzled but obliged. She had seen Aman tinker with ideas before, and she thought that this was no different. Aman had very specific instructions for binding the urethane tape using heat from an iron. This gave the sock more structure, which in turn, would give his foot more support. He then took his prototypes and started to think carefully about who he could share his idea with.

Aman was at a respectable consulting firm, where sweaty feet and bad odors were not regular topics of conversation among his colleagues, much less his friends. He wanted to talk about what he had invented but wasn't sure how to proceed. He needed to find someone who could handle the topic of conversation, but also give him constructive feedback. That turned out to be John, a work colleague, who had become a close friend. John and Aman had been staffed on several projects together where they worked late into the night. Their friendship grew as their late night conversations turned personal and they talked about how they planned to break out of consulting to pursue their own ideas.

"We often joke how that was a meaningful moment," recalls Aman. "I showed him when we were at a client site in Texas. I was wearing one of the prototypes. I pulled out my other prototypes to show him. I asked him if he even cared about this? He then went on to tell me how much he hated the same thing. He started to bleed out his heart about what he hated about his socks. Specifically, how his socks would quit when they lost the elasticity around the tube, which caused the sock to slump down. He said that somebody needed to solve that problem. I saw someone who cared as much as I did."

Aman felt compelled to write a business plan that captured how this high-performance, workwear sock could transform into a full-fledged brand. It was called Beneath, which Aman envisioned including all sorts of undergarments from underwear to bras. He applied to business school with the express purpose of working on this problem. He got accepted to MIT Sloan in the fall of 2011.

Up until his business school acceptance, Aman didn't risk very much. He had worked at a prestigious consulting firm and graduated college with a highly-valued degree in engineering. Poor sock absorption and construction was a problem that he was personally invested in. Business school could have opened the door to working at a sportswear apparel company like Nike or Adidas, who have the resources to solve this problem. But Aman saw the path of working at an established sportswear brand as a greater risk than trying to attack the problem with his own passion and drive.

"I could have spent fifteen years working my way up to the point where I had some impact on product development," explains Aman. "And then at that point, I would launch a line of dry-fit dress socks. That to me didn't feel the best route to get there. I would have been stable. I would have finished school. But that was riskier than doing what we are doing now. Plus, getting a job at Nike isn't easy. The presumption that I would work my way up to that role with that kind of autonomy was not a given."

Aman continues, "The biggest risk was the market. I identified this as a problem. There was a white space opportunity, which meant there was room for this idea to exist. Why not go capitalize on the opportunity now? My thought process was that a corporate job was more risky because it was not guaranteed that I could work on the problem now. In this case, I could work on the idea now and see if I could create a new category of clothing. Viewing it in this way, it helped dispel the idea that entrepreneurship and risk are synonymous."

The first day of school Aman met Kit, another MIT first-year classmate who had been assigned to his core team. Like many business schools, MIT assigns students to work in a group for the first semester to promote teamwork. Aman shared his sock idea with Kit who loved the concept. In fact, she wrote her business school essay about starting up a performance workwear company. As the semester progressed, they became extremely close. They worked on problem sets together and a business plan for their startup concept.

Aman and Kit both tapped into the resources of the MIT Venture Mentoring Service (VMS) and started to develop their idea, from manufacturing to design. MIT established VMS to connect and coordinate startup activity across its different schools. Through the Martin Trust Center for MIT Entrepreneurship, Aman and Kit learned that another team in the engineering school was also independently working on performance workwear. "What were the odds that there was another team working on form meets fashion?" recalls Aman. The other team developed a prototype for a high-performance dress shirt that wicked away sweat at the source. Instead of seeing them as a competitive threat, Aman embraced the opportunity to join forces.

He was transparent from the start about his intentions. "I shared everything with Gihan and his team. I heard that they were doing some awesome things. Gihan then told me about this wicking technology that they were going to leverage in a dress shirt. It helped regulate body temperature better. I remember being like, holy shit. I finally met other people as equally passionate about this problem as I was." They came together and formed a new venture called Ministry of Supply.

Ministry of Supply decided to launch their high-performance dress shirt for a Kickstarter campaign in June 2012, the summer in between their first and second years of business school. They raised close to half a million dollars, far surpassing their original goal, but the market momentum they had generated was compromised by their commitment to school. A decision had to be made to stay or leave school. They decided to leave school to pursue building the company.

This was a big decision for Aman. "My family was not rich. There was no safety net. If we had failed early, I would have had the option to go back to MIT, which was not a bad plan B. It made taking that risk a lot more palatable. I didn't want to think about a plan B. I felt like I made a rational decision where the ceiling was high and it was a problem that I deeply cared about. The con was the opportunity cost of doing two years of something else, which at the time was consulting, which I already knew."

Was the risk worth it for Aman? When I visited Ministry Supply's headquarters in Boston, the office was bustling. Racks of clothing littered the hallways. Aman never envisioned himself as a fashion kingpin. As a kid, he preferred to blend in instead of stand out. But now his fashion is about solving a problem with purpose. Aman and the team often get emails from customers proclaiming how Ministry of Supply's dress shirts and socks have transformed the way they feel at work, which always elates them. It makes the risk they took to start this venture worth it.

WHY NOW IS THE BEST TIME IN HISTORY TO START A COMPANY

Entrepreneur: Spenser Skates
Age: 28
Hometown: Cambridge, Massachusetts
Company: Amplitude Analytics, the number one product analytics platform built for the modern product stack

During spring semester of his senior year at MIT, Spenser Skates asked twenty of his friends to start a company with him. All of them rebuffed his offer except one. Curtis, one of his classmates, was interested in starting a company but didn't want to do it right after graduation. Instead, he accepted a job at Google in San Francisco and told Spenser that he was willing to revisit the conversation in a year.

Spenser knew he didn't want to start a company alone. "It is so hard to do stuff on your own," he explains. "Having a cofounder who could help shoulder the moral weight of a startup was important to me. There was someone else who could check if we were headed in the right direction as a company and could share in the workload."

So after graduation, Spenser joined DRW, a hedge fund based in Chicago, as an algorithmic trader. The company recognized Spenser's elite programming ability—he won Battlecode, a prestigious competition held at MIT. The objective of the competition is to determine which player can write the best artificial intelligence program and win a game of strategy. Winning put Spenser on the radar for hedge funds looking to recruit talented engineers who could apply advanced analytics to the stock market.

The job was intense but very lucrative. Still, Spenser resisted the urge to get comfortable with the trappings of material success. His free time was spent engaging Curtis in side projects on nights and weekends. For instance, they worked on building a product that helped locate everyone's whereabouts after graduation. While this idea had the most momentum out of all the ideas they came up with, the activity of working on it was more of a way to keep the dialogue open between them. Spenser feared that after a year, Curtis might want to postpone starting a company for another year. Working with Curtis was a way to steer him out of Google and into a startup venture where they could work side by side.

Spenser had decided he wanted to start a company by using a framework adopted from Jeff Bezos, founder of Amazon, called regret minimization. The method works like this: project yourself into the future and determine what regrets you might feel based on the decisions you're making today. That projective mindset helped Spenser make decisions at MIT when he switched from biology to nonprofits to programming to finance and finally to entrepreneurship. The constant switching scared his parents who worried about the seemingly capricious decisions he was making. But internally, Spenser was looking at his future self and seeing someone unhappy in each particular field, so he made the decision to change his path. This was his way of minimizing the risks of pursuing entrepreneurship.

He embarked on a quest to understand entrepreneurship by reading books like *Talent Is Overrated* and *Founders at Work* and by talking to at least fifty founders. "I was very risk averse, and I wanted to get as much data as possible," he explains. The yearlong process revealed three key insights.

First, he came to the conclusion that if he committed to a startup idea for at least two years, there would be a worthwhile outcome. The best-case scenario was the startup idea might gain market momentum and lead to liquidity potential. The worst-case scenario was the company would fail to get off the ground and leave him worse off financially. Even in this scenario, Spenser saw the value that he would gain from the experience of developing a business and building up a lot of skills and connections that could serve him well in future endeavors.

Second, investing two years into his first venture could

help inspire him for the journey ahead. The two years was the minimum amount of effort he needed to invest in a business in order to put himself in the best position to succeed. But the journey wouldn't end after two years, even if he had to shut down the business. It would only be the beginning because Spenser figured he needed to commit to seven to ten years before the company could be a success. "If it was going to be such a long journey, I needed to take the time to build the inspiration and get a full picture of what I was committing to because this was going to be brutally hard along the way."

Finally, Spenser found his purpose in pursuing entrepreneurship. "One of the classic tropes is that entrepreneurship brings a lot of money but not happiness," Spenser says. "What is one of the things that will bring my future self happiness? One of the consistent themes that I saw was this idea that serving other people brings you happiness. I questioned whether I would be happy if I ended up having the biggest company, was in the press, and was making a lot of money. I came to the conclusion that I would be most happy if I could serve other people. If I build a company and can serve people—my employees, customers, and investors—really, really well, I expect the older Spenser will have the least amount of regrets."

About nine months into his hedge fund job, Spenser began to get restless. He feared that Curtis was not going to quit Google because of how rich the stock options were. Google used these options, which vested over a specific period of time, to lock in top-flight talent. Curtis wasn't going to leave on his own. Spenser would have to pry him out by moving to San Francisco and putting pressure on him through proximity. So Spenser quit his job, gave back his signing bonus of $45,000 because he had stayed on the job for less than a year, and got on a plane and moved in with Curtis.

The first four months were not easy. At first, Spenser slept on the couch. Later he bought a mattress and moved into Curtis' bedroom. While Curtis was at work, Spenser was left alone in his apartment to work on their idea. But it was hard to motivate himself. Spenser recalls, "I played StarCraft all day, and then Curtis would come home around 6 p.m. and then I was like, 'Shit, I need to get some stuff done. I am going to look so bad. I am not making him excited about leaving and I am wondering if he believes in me enough to leave after seeing me like this and not super motivated.' I tried to use that to motivate myself and when Curtis came home, we would work on stuff together."

The pressure of proximity eventually did convince Curtis to quit Google and join Spenser to start the company that became Amplitude Analytics. As Spenser states, "He is the best cofounder I could have asked for." Since starting the business, they have been heads down in execution mode. They have built the company up by fundraising, acquiring customers, and hiring employees. Their journey is not yet complete. But Spenser is still the same guy who slept on Curtis' couch and convinced him to start a company. The slight difference is that Spenser is more appreciative about what his success has meant and how fortunate he has been.

"I still don't feel qualified to be an entrepreneur," Spenser says. "The only difference between me and someone else is that I made the choice to do this four years ago. Whenever I think things are down or not going well, I always think, for people our age, not long ago, you would get drafted to go fight in Vietnam. You talk about risk, and that is a much riskier outcome because you are risking your life. Whenever I come into a risky situation, I put myself in the mindset that I have it so good, nothing that could happen could bother me at all. I have such a good standard of life even though on a cash basis, I am very poor. I have been poor for the last four years of my life but I still feel very rich."

CHAPTER 4

THE INTIMACY OF SELF-REFLECTION

DROPPING BREADCRUMBS ALONG THE WAY

Entrepreneur: Adam and Ryan Goldston
Age: 30
Hometown: Los Angeles, California
Company: Athletic Propulsion Labs, a unique sportswear brand that sits at the intersection of technology, performance, and fashion and enables athletes to maximize their potential in all aspects of life

"Hey Adam, just confirming that we are still good to meet today at noon? Look forward to meeting you!" I emailed Adam Goldston on the morning of our scheduled conversation when I arrived in Los Angeles. "Sounds good. One quick thing, we don't let competitive brands into our office," Adam replied. "Shit," I thought to myself. I was wearing my low-cut, white Nikes. I quickly surveyed my options given limited time. I found a Target nearby and purchased a hideous pair of brown shoes with the intention of returning them. "This better be worth it," I muttered under my breath as I headed to the Athletic Propulsion Labs (APL) office in downtown Los Angeles. My conversation with Adam and his brother Ryan turned out to be one of the most impactful for me during my entire journey.

When I arrived, Adam greeted me and escorted me to their showroom. Ryan Goldston, his twin brother, soon joined. I was sweating because I was somewhat intimidated in their presence. Both of them were imposing figures. They played collegiate basketball and football, and clearly kept in shape. Adam had more flair with chains draped around his neck and a beard that rivaled NBA basketball star James Harden's. Ryan was more clean cut in comparison, but the intensity behind his quiet demeanor could still be felt.

Any sense of nervousness soon melted away as the brothers proudly showed me their collection of shoes. They started with the first pair of basketball shoes that had launched the brand. As we walked through each season, they went into intimate detail behind when they launched each collection of shoes, why they launched it, and what it had meant for them. They felt more than just pride. Their showroom served as a way to remind them how far they had come since their first official collection. They ended the tour with their most recent collection of women's sneakers that marked their entry into the category. It was a huge milestone for them as their brand originated out of their love of basketball and now extended into a completely new category.

We sat down at the table in the middle of their showroom. Like all conversations, I asked where they traced their entrepreneurial roots. They proceeded to share a story about their father, Mark Goldston, who was an executive at a sneaker company. He brought home a pair of sneakers for Adam and Ryan when they were five years old. He hadn't brought the shoes as a present, but rather to see how they reacted to them and if any modifications were required. The key feature he was testing was the flashing lights that were embedded at the back of the sneaker.

Adam recalls, "We both ran to the bathroom and jumped on the counter side by side. We flipped off the lights. 'Ryan, can you see my lights?' Ryan replied, 'Yeah, can you see mine?' I said 'Yeah.' We could see each other's lights, but we could not see our own lights. We told our dad that he had to move the lights to the side of the shoe so that we could each see our own lights. He called the factory in Asia and told his guys that they had to figure out a way for them to move the lights from the back to the side of the shoe. Keep it the way it is for the adults but for the kids, we need to make that change. They moved the lights to the side of the shoe, and they sold millions and millions of pairs of sneakers. That was where we like to think our sneaker obsession started and how we got started in the business."

Playing basketball was an intrinsic part of Adam and Ryan's identity growing up. What they lacked in height they made up for in grit, preparation, and precision. They were particularly obsessed with jumping as high as they could. Jumping higher gave them a competitive advantage so that they could add lift to their jump shot or soar above taller players for rebounds. Their strenuous workouts didn't translate into higher vertical leap. In fact, working out did the opposite as it put more wear and tear on their body. Once, Ryan tore his hip abductor during his training regimen. Inventing technology to add more inches to their vertical leap was a way for them to compete more effectively at a collegiate level.

School was the laboratory where they invented APL's technology. At first, they ordered small springs that could fit into a casing. It sounded simple in theory but it was a complex process of figuring out which springs fit into a casing that would energize, not deaden, the impact upon jumping. They started out in their dorm room at USC but soon went back to their parent's house because they had more workspace there to play around with the different variables. It was a four-year odyssey to figure out which type of springs and casings produced the optimal vertical leap. Even though they were unable to use this technology as collegiate athletes, Adam and Ryan were determined to commercialize the product to give other athletes a competitive edge.

The brothers graduated from college on May 15, 2009, and faced a dismal job market. Ryan had several investment banking offers but declined them to focus on this venture full time with his brother. Three days later, they moved into their first office, which was only 60 square feet. They soon received their first samples back from the manufacturer. Ryan remembers, "They were the worst things that we ever got. What the fuck were we going to do? How can we get from this to something that we could sell? If we put our name behind something, we wanted to be proud of it. We couldn't release this or something remotely close to these first samples. It looked like a death trap."

What the brothers did have was their core technology in place. They also had their own grit and determination, traits they developed from years of athletic training. So they got to work. Even though they were not designers, they sat in front of their computers and figured out a way to articulate what the shoe should look like to their factories. After two more rounds of tweaking, they got it to a point where the shoe design matched what they envisioned. The design was just as important as the technology because it represented their sense of style.

About half way through the conversation, I stopped Adam and Ryan because they kept referencing exact dates. The day they graduated. The day they received their first samples. The day that they launched their pre-sale. They referred to so many specific dates, which was unusual in my mind. Adam explains, "We remember every moment, and we value every moment. And if you can recall that certain time, and remember where you were, it helps a lot going forward because it lays a strong foundation for the future. That foundation makes it easier to plan for the unpredictability ahead."

Ryan adds, "Once you graduate college, everything becomes a blur. The days become weeks, the weeks become months, the months become years. And you lose perspective of when stuff happened. You start to think to yourself, 'Man, I've been working on this forever.' Remembering those dates helps to keep a timeline in my head and lets us remember those moments. This was where I was, how I felt, and what date it was that makes us appreciate more the journey leading up to today. It's like leaving breadcrumbs along the way to find the trail back home."

They pointed to a story they read about Michael Jordan,

arguably the greatest NBA player in history. He had been rummaging through his old belongings when he was selling his house and came across letters that he wrote to his parents back in college. After reading them, Jordan commented that he could no longer identify with the person he had been in college. That comment stuck with Adam and Ryan. They didn't want to lose their own sense of identity five years into their journey. "If you lose a line of communication with yourself, then you've got no way to go back and feel what it was like to be in that moment. It just becomes another story instead of something that can help with your decision making," comments Adam.

October 19, 2010, was the date the NBA banned APL's Concept 1 shoes and their patented Load 'N Launch technology for "providing an undue competitive advantage." The sheer volume of orders for the shoes crashed their website. "Within ten minutes, our lives had changed," remembers Ryan. "It became the number one news story in the world. It became the second most searched term in Google. There were a million articles in ten days. We sold nine months of inventory in three days. That month was crazy. We didn't sleep. It changed the trajectory of our lives."

That date was easy to memorialize. But other dates that year were just as important. On June 17 they approached David Stern and Adam Silver at the NBA playoffs game.

They presented to the NBA's competition committee on July 28. On October 8, Adam and Ryan posted social media messages on Twitter about the brainstorming session they'd just had with each other and how they felt something big was going to happen.

I met Adam and Ryan on November 30, 2015. Through listening to the lows and highs of their journey, I gained a greater appreciation for my own journey. Before then, I remembered time in the context of years. I was living day to day, getting up, going to work, returning home, going to sleep, and then repeating the cycle. It was a routine. After this conversation, I started to reflect on my own experiences more and anchored myself to key moments—where I was, what I was feeling, what time it was, who was there. Time started to slow down.

I reflected on all the moments that had brought me to today: The day that I moved out. The day that I quit my job. The day I traveled to Colombia so that I could spend a few months living and writing. Regardless of the book's outcome, the personal outcome was that I had started to live more fully. I embraced moments that I might not have before. Adam and Ryan, through their own journey, taught me to enjoy the small moments and everything in between, which is why theirs was the most impactful conversation during my journey.

THE HUSTLER

Entrepreneur: Rodney Williams
Age: 33
Hometown: Baltimore, Maryland
Company: LISNR, the leading global provider of data-over-audio solutions that power the connected world

Sitting in a corporate training class, Rodney Williams typed furiously on his computer. His notes had nothing to do with the training, which was supposed to coach employees for another organizational change at Procter & Gamble, the manufacturer of world class brands like Tide, Old Spice, and Secret. Rodney had joined the corporation's marketing department two years prior in 2009. As a marketer, he was seeing a dramatic shift in how his millennial peers were consuming media, from television to digital platforms. For example, he had just learned about an audio technology that facilitated ID metadata exchange for content recognition.

It was in this class that Rodney had his moment of inspiration. "I just opened up my laptop, and I did a brain dump," Rodney recalls. "I was typing everything out. What could it do? How does it do it? How would we sell it? It was a jumbled mess but I sent it to my best friend who had startup experience. He replied back that my notes were all over the place and it made no sense. I kept cleaning it up and sending it back to him. By the third day, it made sense to him. I went over to his house to continue the dialogue."

That was the beginning of LISNR, a communication protocol that sends data over audio to enable proximity data transmission, second-screen functionality, and secure authentication. For example, the technology could help marketers target their customers more accurately or encrypt payment information at the point of sale. But LISNR was still just an idea on paper at that point. The technology didn't have investors or even a name yet. All Rodney had was enthusiasm for an idea that he would not let go of. He knew very little about startups, but he had the hustle to make something happen. He had been doing that his entire life.

Rodney was a marketer as well as technologist who had three technology patents. He understood conceptually the technology he wanted to build, but he needed an engineer to actually build it. So Rodney asked a friend with a deep technical background for references, and his friend suggested he talk to Chris, a software engineer who happened to live across the hall in Rodney's apartment building. Rodney didn't skip a beat. He sprinted down the hall and knocked on the door. When Chris opened the door, Rodney quickly introduced himself and pitched his idea right there in the hallway. Chris was a little perplexed at first with this stranger knocking on his door, but the idea intrigued him enough to think on it for a day.

The next day he called Rodney and said he liked the

idea but wanted to see more validation. Chris suggested they enter into StartupBus, a national startup competition on the way to the annual South by Southwest Conference (SXSW), and if they won, he would be the technical cofounder. They won the competition for their region, which prompted them to start LISNR in earnest. Rodney didn't quit his job immediately, as he explains, "I wasn't going to leave until I had funding." Within two months, Rodney lined up investors and signed up two beta customers before he quit his job at P&G at the end of August 2012.

In many ways, the story of starting LISNR is the story of Rodney becoming aware of his own identity and personal narrative. Growing up in a Jamaican household in Baltimore, Maryland, everyone in his family had had a steady job as well as a side hustle. His father was a contractor but fixed things on the side; his mother trained as a nurse but owned her own hair salon. Rodney was also a hustler. At age seven, he brought in magazines to his mother's hair salon and charged her customers to read them. In school, Rodney sold penny candy out of the coatroom. He had success with these creative ventures but wanted to apply his hustle beyond the local community.

Rodney recalls, "I used to watch *Lifestyles of the Rich and Famous* when I was eleven. I wrote down the type of person that I wanted to be, like lead a company, and things that

I wanted to do, the opposite of what I saw my family do. This hustle mentality was a good thing. I wanted to build a business that could sustain generations. I didn't have a lot of family in education. I wanted to find a path to learn, and I wanted to build a blueprint, and I wanted to inspire people. I methodically tried to chip away to be that person. I did that really early."

Education provided an avenue for Rodney to expand his horizons. Recognizing that Rodney had special talents, his parents sent him to private school, where he was suddenly surrounded by classmates who came from families with more privileged backgrounds than his. It didn't make him envious or jealous. Instead, it piqued his curiosity to see the trappings of success beyond entertainers and athletes. It was then that he realized he didn't know enough. "This was when my hustle went from making $10 to how I can hustle to learn," Rodney says.

He enrolled at West Virginia University, but "within thirty minutes, I experienced a rail slur," he recalls. "The guy across the hall from me had up a Confederate flag. That was a first tough week. When I went after pursuing this education, I never would return back home. I embraced it for what it was. I started to make friends who came from different environments and relate to them on a human level being insightful, smart, and respected."

Rodney graduated with two degrees from West Virginia University (WVU). He then went on to secure two more master's degrees, one for integrated marketing communication from WVU and one for business administration from Howard. At WVU's graduate school, there was one particular class covering entrepreneurship that had a powerful impact on him. Every week, an entrepreneur led a discussion with students about the challenges of building a startup. That was an eye-opening experience. "I saw people from every different economic status and ethnicity, but they all had the hustle, and all had an idea that they believed in, and they all tried to fight it and tried to figure it out," Rodney says, "and that sparked something that stayed with me."

He started a promotional marketing agency in college to bridge the gap between what his financial aid covered and what the tuition actually cost. At first, he just organized parties on his own, hiring a DJ from New York and then charging a $10 cover for entry. He amassed an impressive list of emails from the people who attended the parties, so he then went to local businesses and sold them access to market special offerings to his list of students. But this was just a school hustle. Rodney had larger aspirations, and he felt the need to see more and continue his education after school. That led him to apply to P&G, the largest consumer products company in the world, where he landed a marketing role.

"If I wanted embrace my own culture but also identify with a wide range of employees, I needed to learn their language, which is why I went to P&G," Rodney explains. "For example, if you always listen to hip hop music, you really can't have an intelligent conversation about any other genre. It is the same in leadership. If I didn't learn how to lead in different environments, that would make it hard for me to relate to a team."

While he was working at P&G, he continued his education by reading voraciously. He didn't just read startup and technology books, but also biographies of people like Ned Turner and Reginald Lewis, whom he admired because they were all about the hustle. They were rough around the edges like him but had gained the experience they needed to become leaders. He identified with them because his ambition was to lead a successful company at a high level.

Rodney spent four years at P&G before he had his moment of inspiration to start LISNR. Even today, his desire to continue learning hasn't stopped. When his investors seriously questioned his ability to grow LISNR beyond its initial vertical in music, he saw that challenge as an opportunity to learn. He took the investors' point of view and cataloged all of the negatives that might have caused them to doubt his leadership ability: youth; lack of tech expertise; poor communication; stubborn mindset. Whether or not these concerns were valid, they provoked doubts that hindered Rodney's ability to run his company.

He decided to hire someone who had experience in scaling a company to the next level. Making a significant hire would restore investors' confidence in growing the company and up their trust in Rodney for being able to recruit someone of that magnitude. Figuring he had nothing to lose, he cold emailed about twenty executives at competitive companies and asked for thirty minutes of their time. He ultimately hoped to recruit one of these executives, but just getting a meeting with them was the goal. Most of them did in fact agree to meet with Rodney. One, Eric Allen, a respected technology executive, even agreed to join Rodney's board.

Rodney saw the calming effect that Eric had on the board because of his experience in the space. After the first board meeting, he approached Eric with the idea of having him become the CEO of LISNR. Rodney asked him right then and there after the meeting. He wanted to strike when the energy was fresh, even though he knew Eric was already leading a $250 million business unit and earning more than $1 million annually in compensation.

"I felt like it was game six in an NBA playoff series with me shooting a three-pointer from half court with us down by two with only a few seconds left on the clock. I was at the game, but this was a long shot. We were a company out of Cincinnati. We had only raised $3.5 million, while he had a comfortable, well-paid job already. But, like I always say, if you are doing something great, people will gravitate. I asked him if he would consider coming on. He paused. He said it wasn't a bad idea. We went back and forth on terms. He saw my relentless energy for this product. When I got Eric on board, the entire dynamic changed on the board and they were now willing to put in more money for our next financing round. I am glad it happened. The story could have ended up a lot differently."

Throughout this time, Rodney has stayed true to himself. "I might have gone to school to clean the edges and learn to talk to anyone and be relatable. But I am still kind of me. I never changed," Rodney concludes, "I am not your Harvard guy, not your MIT guy. I like poindexters, but I am not the poindexter guy. When I go to speak and talk to people, I encourage them that they don't have to change their appearance or change who they are to be relatable or to excel in business. Some people think they need to fit a certain type to be successful in business. I am inspiring that group because I carved my own path to get there."

LARGE SCALE IMPACT

Entrepreneur: Tim Hwang
Age: 25

Hometown: Potomac, Maryland

Company: FiscalNote, a software, data, and media company that uses artificial intelligence and big data to help organizations build and execute effective, data-driven government strategies

"I've been interested in making large-scale change in a short amount of time." That was the first statement that Tim Hwang made when I asked him where he traced his entrepreneurial roots. His answer caught me off guard. Most entrepreneurs typically say they trace their desire of becoming an entrepreneur to a person or a specific experience, but not to a philosophical statement. Never once did I encounter a statement of such conviction, vision, and magnitude. There was something really different about Tim, and I was eager to learn more about what drove his sense of mission.

Tim got involved in politics at age sixteen when he was one of the first field organizers for President Obama in 2008. At age seventeen, he ran for public office on the board of education in Maryland. He won and inherited a $4-billion budget and the responsibility of managing more than 20,000 teachers and 200,000 students in Montgomery County. His interest in politics was driven initially by how he perceived himself as a kid.

"One of the things that I hated when I was really young,"

Tim explains, "I thought about my identity as an Asian American and what it meant. My parents wanted me to be a doctor or lawyer, and that felt to me like that was just another extension of being part of the rat race. Politics was the most perfect thing that I could have done. It is so diametrically opposite of being a part of the pack. You are really sticking your neck out there when you're running for office."

Tim took on a huge amount of responsibility at an age when most high school seniors were thinking about the next stage of their life—college—and not how to impact the next generation of students with policy decisions. He had to give up his own schooling in order to make decisions for schools countywide. Politics was the arena that he thought he could make the biggest impact. "Campaigns are a lot like startups," Tim says. "They have a terminal outcome. Little money, high energy, and late hours characterize what it is like to work on a campaign, all guided by a pure mission."

Running for office was one half of the equation. The other half was actually governing. The most public part of being an elected official is giving speeches. Sometimes Tim would talk to a few parents in a roundtable discussion, while other times he'd be addressing a few thousand teachers. He quickly became comfortable with public speaking because he was constantly in the public eye giving his point of view.

What separated him from other politicians was his intimate and detailed knowledge of education issues. Not only did he keep up with current affairs and read *The Washington Post* and the *DC Gazette* front to back every day, but he was also intimately familiar with the details of education policy. "When I talked to parents, I had to get down to the nitty gritty. Your tax rate is at this rate, which is currently going to this program, which is not working because of these key performance indicators," Tim explains. "Knowing the facts and being prepared more than allowed me to make up for the perceived lack of experience because of my age."

What he found surprising was the complexity of so many different stakeholders and how their interests coalesced—or not—around a particular policy decision. Navigating through the various stakeholders required a calculus of aligning incentives with those who were most impacted. This came to a head at a county council meeting when there was a $400-million budget deficit. Massive protests erupted outside as different groups of firefighters, police officers, and teachers lobbied to stop their budgets from being cut. The council members had a heated discussion, but Tim was able to channel all of the emotion into focusing on the facts. Together, they combed through each line item in the budget and were able to close the deficit without raising taxes.

You might say he received a lifetime of experience in that

one term. After his term ended, he could have chosen to continue on with a career in politics or go back to college, head to law school, work in government, run for governor, and become a cabinet member in the future. But his plan pivoted heavily when he saw how companies in Silicon Valley were making large-scale change by reshaping industries in a matter of years, not decades. This fascinated him and he thought it was something he wanted to explore.

Tim had demonstrated entrepreneurial instincts even before he was in politics. He started a tutoring company when he was fourteen. What irked him was the egregious prices tutors changed students to teach subjects like Algebra 1. Prices were being driven up by tutors who had graduate-level degrees, but Tim felt that students who had aced the course a year or two ago could teach more effectively. He undercut the going tutoring rates by 80 percent and enlisted his friends as tutors. And all of the profits were donated to charities that give school supplies, clothing, and bedding to the homeless.

Once his term expired on the board of education, Tim had the chance to pursue entrepreneurial endeavors at a larger scale. He didn't head to Silicon Valley right away. Instead, he enrolled at Princeton where he hoped to enjoy the normalcy of being a college student. But normalcy soon felt like complacency. By the summer of his junior year, Tim and two high school friends headed out to Sunnyvale, California, where they rented an affordable room at Motel 6. They recruited two others to join their team, so eventually five guys piled into that room, two on each bed and one on the floor. Every morning, they had to open the door to let out the steam that filled up the room from five guys taking alternating showers.

"We worked insanely hard. The team was coding like crazy, waking up at 9 a.m. and going until 1 a.m. in the morning," Tim remembers. "I was cold calling customers and pitching investors. Coming from D.C., we knew there was this problem with all of this information in government with nobody trying to organize it. Four months into it, product wise, we built a major prototype, a search engine that aggregated all legislation across the country and a predictive algorithm, which could predict the outcome of legislation with 95 percent accuracy. Investors piled in very quickly after that because they saw the promise of being able to deliver political and legal analytics and how big a business that could be."

This was how FiscalNote was born. The team moved back to D.C. to be closer to their customer base. Tim spoke about the company's journey as if what happened was meant to happen all along. It was what he was destined to do.

"When a job interviewer asks you, 'Where do you want

to be in five years?' 99.9 percent of people don't really know what they want to be doing," Tim says. "I have a crystal-clear view of where I want to be at ten, fifteen, and twenty years. I then work backwards—five, six, seven steps for me to get to that point. I am competitive with myself and competitive compared to the titans of history. It helps benchmark my progress against, for example, Richard Branson, who started his first company at nineteen, opened his first record store at twenty-one, and started seven companies before thirty."

Tim has an inner drive that pushes him forward. His biggest fear is not failure, but mediocrity. "I am not afraid to fail. More than failing, I am afraid of being mediocre at a lot of things," he concludes. "Being part of the rat pack is like a drug to a lot of people. To do the whole thing—school, college, job, and retirement, and then death—doesn't appeal to me. Living this way is both boring and annoyingly bad. Failing will not be because I didn't turn in my project to my boss on Friday and I got fired for this thing that I didn't do. I don't know where the drive comes from, but I don't want to be like the rest of the group."

CHAPTER 5

THE POWER OF PERSPECTIVE

ALWAYS ON, REGARDLESS OF AUDIENCE

Entrepreneur: Brian Wong

Age: 25

Hometown: Vancouver, Canada

Company: KIIP, an in-app mobile advertising solution that uses proprietary "moments" methodology to create meaningful customer interactions and generate highly targeted, custom audiences

Every January, more than 100,000 attendees descend on Las Vegas to see the latest in technology at the Consumer Electronics Show (CES). In 2014, I was hanging out at the Sony exhibit toying around with the newest gadgets. I looked up and saw a young, skinny Asian kid with glasses doing the same. But he wasn't alone in checking these devices out. He was with the president of Sony Electronics America, Philipe Molyneux, who, surprisingly, was giving the kid a tour. That kid was Brian Wong.

Brian and I became friends after working together when Sony Music embedded his mobile advertising technology into our marketing campaigns. Brian was always "on," regardless of who he was with or where he was, because he was the biggest champion for the technology he had invented. Watching him at CES with a high-profile executive was what I expected. That was, in my mind, Brian being Brian as he seemed to be everywhere in the press. I soon gained a greater appreciation for what drove the buzz around him and why the press gravitated toward his larger-than-life personality.

Growing up in Vancouver, Canada, Brian was a precocious kid. He skipped several grades and entered college at fifteen. He started a web design firm the following year when he found himself sidelined from ice hockey, a game he had played all his life, with a knee injury. His mobility was limited, so he had to find another way to channel his energy. Brian and a friend decided to start a web design company together because they had complementary skills. Brian knew design, while his friend knew how to code. They charged their first client $500, the second $2,000, and the third $10,000. They made money, but more importantly, they learned how to run a real business, and that business soon became their top priority.

As a kid, Brian had always wanted to work in the Bentall Centre office towers, Vancouver's business district, and be a "badass motherfucker." These skyscrapers served as his reference point for both power and success. But when he traveled to Singapore, his perspective changed. He saw how a small parcel of land could generate billions of dollars in economic value.

When visiting Asia as a teenager, Brian was always introduced to his relatives as his father's son or his mother's son. They didn't look at him the way we do, as Brian Wong, the entrepreneur. His parents had a successful accounting business, and he was exponentially proud to be their son, but he wanted more for himself. He didn't want to live in their shadow or limit his success to his hometown. He wanted to be part of a world that he could grow into, instead of one that he would quickly outgrow. Silicon Valley was the answer.

His web design business, Aer Marketing, allowed him to experiment with new ventures. He used the firm's resources to create a tool that allowed users to follow top influencers by category on Twitter. It got 50,000 downloads in one week, topped off with a story in *Mashable*. The app was Brian's ticket to something bigger. He emailed startup founders and investors in the Valley with the *Mashable* link attached. That was his resume, and he used it to get hired at Digg, a link-sharing news network, in a business development role.

At Digg, Brian was responsible for engaging top-tier publications like *CNN* and *The New York Times*. He received media training and learned the art of staying on message. He first began to appreciate the power of the press when he had an internship at 1-800-GOT-JUNK. Making junk sexy was hard. But Brian saw firsthand how press can change everything when the company pitched and secured placement for their junk removal services on the television show *Hoarders*. This product placement was the perfect integration of the company's services with the concept of the show. Brian realized that if junk could be made sexy, anything could be.

Unfortunately, after six months at Digg, Brian got laid off. He lost his visa and had to return to Vancouver, only returning to the Valley on a tourist visa. It was during this period that he came up with the idea for a mobile gaming and advertising platform called KIIP. The concept was to integrate in-game rewards from advertisers when a player leveled up. Brian felt that the clutter of display ads at the time were ruining the user's gaming experience. He thought he could improve the gaming experience by delighting players with in-game rewards. He created a new advertising model around this insight.

At nineteen, Brian had a smart business idea. He knew he had a great story. He was a young founder in mobile advertising, which at the time was a new category. Others in his position dismissed press because they didn't understand it or were afraid of it. Not Brian. He maintained the reporter relationships he had cultivated from his time at Digg, and turned up the volume on his own personal narrative. "There are people who I meet who don't want to boast about their accomplishments, but if you are in front of a reporter from a major fucking publication, you need to tell them every goddamn thing that is exciting about you and your company! You need to highlight a few things that you need to repeat over and over and over again."

He balanced his enthusiasm and energy with a softer touch when interacting with reporters. He researched their stories and genuinely complimented them on their work. He fostered and made bona fide, personal connections. Brian put himself out there in a way that was authentic to him. The press came to him because he understood how the game was played. When Michael Arrington sniffed out a story about Brian securing funding from a top VC company, his company was profiled in *TechCrunch*, and later in *Fast Company*, *Bloomberg Businessweek*, and *Forbes*. He landed on the cover of *Entrepreneur* magazine. He was everywhere that he needed to be. But it wasn't out of hubris. It was out of a need to embed his company's product in the media and marketing ecosystem.

Brian's ability to attract good press doesn't mean the process of growth has always been smooth. He has surrounded himself with people who will tell him what they really think:

"'Brian, you are loud, you are cocky, and you swear too much. You don't listen that well, and you always are distracted, and you cut people off.' I got all of that," Brian says. "There are certain things that you know you can change, and you try your best to change them, and there are certain things that you know you can't. Accept that and move on because you can't please everyone. Get yourself to a point where you are good enough that most people will want to work with you. Leave it there."

Even though Brian projects an outsized personality to the outside world, he maintains a certain sense of calm when managing his company. One cardinal rule is that he "never ever flips out." Not even in the most explosive situations, like when he was sued, when his company almost ran out of money, or when a key executive hire left after a week on the job. He is able to maintain a measured disposition even when things go haywire. Brian understands that employees look for stability, and an explosive founder creates unnecessary fear and tension in the workplace.

Because Brian essentially grew up in the spotlight, he has learned when he needs to turn up his personality and when he needs to dial it down. Nobody taught him how to manage his persona, but through trial and error, he learned it on his own. If he crashed and burned, he chalked it up to a new learning experience. If he was successful, he examined why he had been successful, so that he could achieve the next milestone.

His best piece of advice to other entrepreneurs is for them to get to know themselves better—both strengths and flaws—through introspection. "There are some entrepreneurs who are so blind to their own faults, and they end up crashing and burning." His grounding allows him to adjust his personality according to different situations without losing himself in the process. He can be Brian, the Ultimate Pitch Man when talking on national TV. And he can be Brian, the Inquisitive Young Founder walking the halls with the president of Sony Electronics. But he can also be Brian, the Guy Grabbing Dinner with a Childhood Friend when he's back home in Vancouver.

Brian doesn't change from moment to moment. He admits that would be exhausting. Instead, his personality is adaptable to many situations, and it is never forced because these are all different but true aspects of who he is. He is able to gain strength from each of these interactions so that he can be a better leader for his company. His personality is what makes him a successful founder, CEO, manager, and friend because he understands his audience and what different people need from him.

SELLING A KIDNEY TO RAISE MONEY

Entrepreneur: Lisa Fetterman
Age: 29
Hometown: Shangdong, Jinan, China
Company: Nomiku, a company that harnesses the secret weapon of sous vide with elegance and intuitive features, allowing anyone to cook mouthwatering meals worthy of a top chef's kitchen

I knew my conversation with Lisa Fetterman was going to be different from the outset. She was forward, funny, and a little quirky but in a refreshing way. "I hate my fucking life when I have to do something the same way every day. It just sucked. When I got my first proper job at Hearst, I couldn't believe what people did *ad nauseam*. I saw that people would be there for thirty years doing this. How could you? It is so far removed from being human." As our conversation went on, she made me chuckle on several occasions with her unique brand of humor. She dropped references to Yoda and a Notorious B.I.G. song, and shared the awkward moment when she met her husband at the gym.

You would never guess that Lisa was a shy, nerdy, overweight kid with glasses growing up. She never cared about how she looked because she was living inside her own world. That made her an easy target for bullying. "People wanted to pull me out of my world even though they didn't do it in the nicest way," she says. "They would tease me and lock me into a conversation I could never win." She coped by recounting these incidents to her friends in a funny way. Soon she realized that humor could be a defense strategy for diffusing tense situations.

As a ten year old, Lisa watched an interview with comedian Drew Carey on TV. He explained that he only learned to be funny after he went to the library to read books about how to be funny. This was a revelation to Lisa. "Fuck, I could do that. I love to read. I love the library." And that was what Lisa did. She planted herself down in the library and read all the books they had on comedy. Being funny isn't just about the content of your humor. It also depends on your cadence and how you deliver the punchline. She tested her newfound insights on her friends and was encouraged when she made them laugh.

She started to incorporate humor into all of her social interactions. Bullies no longer bullied her because she could embarrass them in verbal sparring matches with quick-witted one-liners that crippled even the harshest of verbal attacks. Humor was also a way for her to connect with others more deeply and make people feel good about themselves. Lisa felt good when people laughed at her jokes. So humor became an intrinsic part of her personality. She couldn't erase it today if she tried.

At college, Lisa decided to study journalism. She loved the idea of meeting new people, interviewing them, and then writing a story about them. After college, she joined Hearst, where she hoped to bring her creativity to the media world, an industry in transition. It sounded exciting on paper, but in reality, her day job was little more than checking to make sure the technology worked. She was bored. Her creativity was never embraced. She left after four months. To support herself, Lisa bartended at night and pursued a new media journalism career during the day.

Working freelance created the flexibility to pursue other hobbies. She found her therapy in cooking. She loved the instant gratification of making something and then eating it. But she wanted to expand her knowledge beyond just home cooking. Her curiosity lead her to kitchen jobs at fine dining establishments such as Jean-Georges and Babbo in New York City. It was during this time that she came up with the idea to commercialize an industrial piece of equipment for home use. This kind of idea had been brewing for quite some time as Lisa had developed a passion for cooking as a young kid and worked in restaurants both during and after college.

Lisa's entrepreneurial journey to creating Nomiku began when she met Abe at the gym. She recounts the story: "People ask me all the time if I ran game, girl? You got moves? I just stared at him. I was twenty-two. He was so strange, unapproachable, and really tall. His head would often scrape the ceiling when he did his exercises. We talked a little, but the gym people saw there was potential chemistry. The trainers both reached out to us separately to take a yoga class. When we arrived, we were the only two in the class with the instructor. That was awkward! He really tried to do all of the yoga moves to impress me. We talked after class and decided to meet."

The night of their first date, Lisa pitched Abe her idea for the first home sous-vide machine. She loved the food she could make with an industrial-sized sous-vide machine, but buying one for home use was cost prohibitive. Without hesitation, Abe agreed to try to make a home version. He didn't have a culinary background, but what he did have was a Ph.D. in plasma physics and astrophysics from Princeton. A new entrepreneurial venture was born at the same time as their future marriage was hatched.

Lisa and Abe moved in together two weeks after that first date. As Lisa explains it, "It went pretty fast. What made me say yes to that? It just happened. I was staying in his apartment a lot. I think I should just move everything there. It just felt super chill. We didn't have to talk about it." Abe proposed to her six months later.

Together, they were partners in life and business. They taught others how to solder their own sous-vide machines through Maker's Classes, a network of do-it-yourself studios across the country. This process of teaching helped them refine their own product development ideas to help them gear up for mass production. They went to China with a prototype, but came back saddled with $28,000 of debt. They were so close to launching the product, but didn't have the funds to cross the finish line.

"We were sitting in a train station. I remember eating something and watching all of the trains pass by even though we were supposed to get on. I didn't get on it because I was so catatonic, driven by my own depression at the time," Lisa recalls. "I couldn't taste the food because I was super sad and down. I then had a great idea. I was going to go back to America and sell my kidney for $18,000 because that is how much I could get according to Google. I would then come back and finish the prototype with that money. Abe said no to that idea. I then said let's take out another credit card and go on to vacation in Thailand. And that is what we did."

That detour led them to look up a former student from their Maker's Classes who lived in Thailand. Their friend,

Wipop, took them out to breakfast and they told him about how they were struggling with the design for the prototype. It turned out that he had an industrial design degree from Rhode Island School of Design, the best industrial design school in the world. Lisa asked if he wanted to join their team and he accepted as Nomiku's third cofounder. Wipop's added expertise was a breath of fresh air that reinvigorated the team, and Lisa and Abe went back to China with more conviction and purpose. "That move was a Hail Mary, what's up?"

With a working prototype in place, Lisa and Abe now needed funding to ramp up production. They turned to Kickstarter at around the same time they were planning their wedding. To save money, they roped their wedding videographer into shooting their Kickstarter fundraising video to explain their product. Lisa's maid of honor planned the majority of the wedding, while she and Abe worked to get ready for mass production. They got married, went on their honeymoon, and launched the Kickstarter campaign the day after they got back. The couple hasn't looked back since.

Throughout the process of launching and now running Nomiku, Lisa hasn't compromised on who she is as a business leader, a wife, or a new mother. Her sense of humor shines through it all. "Having a company in general is so hard," Lisa says, "Adding not just one baby, but now two babies into the mix is a level up. It's like triple black diamond skiing on one ski while you have both babies in one hand and the company in the other." Lisa has successfully navigated all of these complexities with her own brand of humor and without sacrificing who she is.

CHARTING YOUR OWN PATH

Entrepreneur: Baldwin Cunningham
Age: 28
Hometown: East Hartford, Connecticut
Company: Partnered, a platform that provides sponsorship management solutions

Baldwin Cunningham moved effortlessly from one person to the next when I met him at Forbes' Under 30 Summit held in Philly in October 2015. We were introduced through a mutual friend, and his energy was infectious. I told him more about my project of interviewing young founders, and he said, "I'm in." Then he was off to meet more people. I saw him on several different occasions during the conference, but always with a different person. He was on the move, meeting new people and creating opportunities to talk about his business Partnered. He was social with a purpose.

Baldwin's parents moved to East Hartford, Connecticut, from Jamaica. He had four older sisters and a four-year age gap separated him from his youngest sister. When he was a kid, he was left to his own devices as nobody wanted to play with him. He was forced to find his own fun and immersed himself in different groups. Early in his childhood he found The Boys & Girls Club. Later on in his early teen years, he boxed in the Police Athletic League. In high school, he starred as running back of the football team. But he never defined himself by what he was doing. Instead, he defined himself by how he associated with different sets of people.

"Stereotypes created buckets, which was weird to me," Baldwin says. "In class, I talked to everyone from athletes to nerds to the musicians. I was curious to learn from everyone, and I created a comfortable environment for my classmates to talk with me regardless of what background they had. I communicated with both introverts and extroverts. My angle was that I could find the commonalities with people to have an interesting conversation. That was my mindset from day one."

Baldwin attended Springfield College where he majored in finance. That led him to pursue a summer internship his junior year at a major financial services firm. Baldwin recounts, "The firm offered me a job after the internship concluded. I turned the offer down as I decided I did not want to pursue that kind of career. The guys I was working with—the senior partners—were not happy at all. They were the most miserable people I saw. I did not want to spend fifteen to twenty years of my life pursuing this goal without the guarantee that I would be happy. This was not the direction I wanted to go in with my life."

This experience contrasted with the happiness Baldwin saw on people's faces while they vacationed in Martha's Vineyard, a small island off the coast of Massachusetts. During his freshman year of college, Baldwin's friends rented a house on the island for the summer and invited him to join them. Since he has an insatiable curiosity to seek out new people and experiences, he accepted the invitation.

Baldwin recounts, "Why not move forward with this new experience instead of doing the same things everyone does during the summer in my hometown? Martha's Vineyard was one of the happiest places to be because people were on vacation. I saw wealth at a magnitude that I have never ever seen before. I wanted to understand what people did, and I didn't meet too many people on the island who were in finance. Everyone had different paths to achieve this level of success."

Baldwin went back to Martha's Vineyard every summer during and immediately after college to be with his friends in this shared house. After graduating, Baldwin applied for an internship at an experiential marketing agency, What's

Up Martha. He was hired along with twenty other interns. Two weeks into the internship, the agency decided to host an event on the beach for one of their clients. It was disorganized at best. Baldwin picked up a football and organized an impromptu contest to see who could throw the farthest. He set up a line of girls and guys. The winner won a t-shirt and a pack of beer. Suddenly, the event was organized. People lined up to wait their turn to throw the football.

The agency recognized Baldwin's social talents, and he was soon put in charge of more events. He realized that his social instincts for creating fun experiences was an employable asset. The company also recognized his talents and anointed him director of marketing. But this was not a full-time role as his agency only had work during the summer. But this role put Baldwin in a position to collaborate with other agencies looking for marketing activations on Martha's Vineyard. One agency, Zehnder Communications, was so impressed with Baldwin's ability to connect deeply with consumers and clients that they offered him a role as account lead with Firefly Vodka in Austin, Texas.

At first, Baldwin was skeptical. He didn't have any friends in Austin and he didn't know where to live. So he reached out to David Boyle, the commencement speaker at his graduation. David's story appealed to him because David was a millionaire on his own terms. He ran a security company and a wine company. People wrote him off at college, but he ended up being more successful than all of his peers. Baldwin identified with his story because he didn't want to conform to someone else's narrative. He wanted to write his own. David told him that this was an opportunity he should take, so Baldwin packed his bags and moved down to Austin.

Baldwin shares, "This was one of the biggest pivotal moments for me as a person. My friends were all skeptical about me moving down to Austin. I didn't know anybody, and I didn't have any friends. Where was I going to live? I determined that those were are all of the wrong questions. What about all of the positives about doing something so completely outside of my comfort zone? But nobody talks about that when something new is in front of them. I went down there and met tons of new people. It shifted my cultural understanding of what happiness was and how to achieve happiness."

Once there, Baldwin saw a different kind of happiness than the happiness of being on vacation in Martha's Vineyard. He saw a culture of following one's passion. For example, bartenders and baristas were happy because they were able to pursue their passions, whether that be music, painting, or writing. "In most places, passion fell secondary to the pursuit of financial wealth. It made me start to question myself. What do I want to do? What am I doing? Why is this person happy? Why am I not completely happy? Most people would think I was happy, I just graduated from college, and I was making some good money working for three alcohol brands. Was this who I was though? I didn't want to be pushing alcohol all my life."

Austin was the first entrepreneurial community Baldwin ever experienced. He sized everyone up and saw that he was just as smart as any of them. The difference was that he felt like he could out hustle everyone else. He built up his confidence to compete on this new playing field. Baldwin recounts, "I met a lot of people who were building things. They were just doing it. That was the real difference between an entrepreneur and not an entrepreneur. They were trying to make it happen versus the person who was building up steam to take that step forward. I wanted to be taking that step forward instead of working for someone else."

In his role, Baldwin struggled to figure out how to spend his marketing dollars efficiently across different local events. There was too much clutter to sort through. There had to be a better way for sponsors like himself to reach those looking for partners who could reach consumers in an engaging way. Armed with this insight, Baldwin enlisted three friends from the Austin area to build a platform to connect people seeking sponsorship dollars for their events with people wanting to invest as sponsors. The team launched Sponsorfied (which eventually evolved to Partnered) in 2012 at South by Southwest, the music, film, and technology festival, where they had 250 events sponsored through their platform. That was sufficient evidence for Baldwin to quit his day job and see if his idea had legs.

He and his team moved to Silicon Valley to raise capital. They applied to Y Combinator, a prestigious incubator program, and got in. They were committed. During the first six months, though, Baldwin struggled with his own identity in this new environment. "I tried to be like every other entrepreneur. I would wear my Patagonia vest to every venture capital meeting. I created this perception about what I thought a successful entrepreneur was. In reality, I saw there was no cookie-cutter model. If there was a cookie-cutter model, everyone would do it. I met people who were black, white, Asian, and they were so true to themselves. I had to be as well."

The turning point for Baldwin was an interaction he had with Garret Camp, founder of StumbleUpon, a web discovery platform, and cofounder of Uber, an on-demand car service. Garrett asked Baldwin to come in and offer his advice on some early Uber marketing initiatives. "I thought to myself, what? This guy succeeded over and over again. Why did he want to hear from me? He could hire experts and analysts. He recognized that I thought differently, and that was the moment where maybe how I was thinking was right. This was when I came into my own. This was me. This was who I was. I was going to make the right moves. I was going to try hard. I was going to do whatever it took. Yes, I could learn from everyone and acknowledge that everyone's path was different, but that moment was when I could be Baldwin."

Growing up, Baldwin didn't have role models he could look up to outside of basketball and music. They were flashy industries that didn't appeal directly to his calling. There were no successful-black-entrepreneur tech stories that he could follow. He had to create his own narrative: summers in Martha's Vineyard, the Austin entrepreneurial scene, and now Silicon Valley. He purposely downplays race because he wants to be measured by his accomplishments. And while he sees himself as a role model, he wants to earn the title of role model first by exiting this company. It will help inspire the kids who grew up like him—with very little means—to find the confidence to take the first step as an entrepreneur.

CHAPTER 6

ADVERSITY AS FUEL

THAT BARK – THAT'S THE DOG IN ME

Entrepreneur: Ali Gates

Age: 30

Hometown: Harlem, New York

Company: Claim it!, a social video platform for giving away, selling, or buying anything, anywhere

Ali Gates was in the middle of working out when he got the call. "Be at Ruth Chris in Times Square at 10:30 p.m.," they said. He had no time to go home and change. So he rushed over to the steak house with his workout gear covered only by an army fatigue jacket. He wandered to the back where Al Harrington, the former star forward for the New York Knicks, was sitting in a private room with his family. Harrington's assistant ceded his seat to Ali, who took a deep breath and launched into the pitch for his tech startup.

It was 2008 and Harrington, basketball player turned businessman, had his own sneaker line, Protege, exclusive to Sears and Kmart. When he wasn't playing, he was always on his phone making deals. At that time, Harrington's deal flow was endorsements. Technology was not on his radar screen until Ali came to him with his idea and asked for an investment of $20,000. The idea was to build a technology platform for a reality TV show. A few days after their Ruth Chris meeting, Harrington agreed to make the investment.

They shot the pilot for the reality TV show and built a beta version of the tech platform to broadcast the pilot. Nobody wanted to buy the concept. Despite this setback, Ali befriended Harrington because he wanted to learn from him. In private, Ali sat silent as he listened to Harrington making deals on his phone while he was caravanned around in his Escalade for appearances. When Harrington arrived for an appearance, he would put on his public face and give the fans all of his attention. He gave away tons of free shoes during these appearances, and this was what kickstarted the idea for Ali's company Claim it!

Ali's journey up to this point had not been easy. His parents divorced when he was ten. This sent his father into a downward spiral. Ali went from living in a brownstone in Harlem to alternating between single occupancy homes and shelters with his father and brother. Ali remembers, "There was a period of time for three years where we were on welfare and lived in shelters. We bounced around. At one time, we lived with my father's girlfriend who had three kids in a studio apartment. I will never forget when five of us were sleeping in one bed."

During his early teenage years, Ali also suffered from severe acne and eczema which lowered his self-esteem. Ali recounts, "During the summertime, I wore tube socks up to my knees. I would wear hats so that people couldn't see the scars on my face. I would wear long sleeve shirts to cover up my skin condition during the summer, even when temperatures soared past 90 degrees. My skin was ruined because I scratched it all the time. I would bleed at night. My brother would yell at me to stop scratching."

Basketball became the outlet he used to express his physical aggression. He finally made a friend named Alphonso who played basketball with him every day and that made Ali feel normal for once. "Alphonso and I had this partnership where we played basketball every day. We never played with anyone else. We played one on one. That was my hobby and my friendship that allowed me to be social. He changed my life."

In high school from 2001 to 2003, Ali took an after-school computer class three times a week. At the time, this was the only class that taught programming in Harlem. He was one of only two students to take advantage of it. This was where Ali learned to code and build websites. He did not have many material possessions but realized he could use technology to create wealth for himself. His aspirations were high. He wanted to be the next Bill Gates. He had his fair share of doubters who said he couldn't be like that because he was a kid from Harlem. This only fueled Ali to prove them wrong.

Ali enrolled in college and he worked at Duane Reade for $250 every other week so he could support himself. It was a steady paycheck that covered his basic needs. In his free time, he built technology products such as 5th Avenue Sports, a search engine that allows a user to find any sports statistic. He built a voice messaging app. Every time he built a product, he tried to commercialize what he built. He hustled and looked to sell his technology products for hundreds of thousands of dollars but was never successful in selling anything. That was just the way he thought that business was conducted. Ali jokes, "I asked myself why I wasn't rich yet. It's because these businesses had no real value."

Even though he hadn't flipped a technology product into instant wealth, Ali collected a rolodex full of powerful contacts. "I have to be a dog. I have to bark. I am aggressive. I communicate well. I am driven. That is the dog in me. I would shake money out of people. I'd fight. If I can't get money out of you, I wanted to get time and contacts. I created this list of people who are advisors to me who believe in my potential," Ali explains. Even with these powerful connections, Ali still had to tend to his basic living needs. In 2006 he took a job as a technology director at the Public Schools Athletic League. It was a dream job because it married his interest in sports with technology.

But the experience was also so corporate. He hated wearing a shirt and tie. His peers didn't embrace him. He wanted to innovate, but everyone told him to wait his turn. "Ali, you are still young. Have patience," they would say. Ali lasted there for two years. He wanted to work on his own startup ideas, so he quit.

He was living with his girlfriend then and they discovered she was pregnant. They couldn't pay rent for several months and were eventually evicted. His girlfriend left him. It wasn't a proud moment in his life. Ali recounts, "During that time, I had thoughts of suicide. I was depressed at the highest level. Mentally, I was at a bad place."

For the next eight months, he bounced around friends' homes, shelters, and the streets, trying to reconcile what had happened. He was depressed. This was one of the few times he reached out to his mentors for help. They loaned him money to move back into his apartment and stabilize his life. He vowed to become a better person, a better partner, and a better father.

While Ali was homeless, he still had the mental fortitude to develop and test his startup idea. At his previous job, he had developed relationships with corporate sponsors who wanted access to their athletes. He continued to work with them after he quit as he was their main point of contact. Red Bull, for instance, continued delivering product to Ali, so he directed the driver to send the pallets to his last apartment instead of the school. After the driver left, Ali went to the corner store to sell the cases. He made $1,000 from this effort. This hustle led to the insight that brands wanted to trial-run their product. They had the budget for it. He knew what he was doing was illegal, but it served as the inspiration for how to build a legitimate business around free product trials.

Ali iterated on this idea for several years to find a business model that supported free trial products from brands like Red Bull and Nike. He took several jobs to sustain himself. This allowed him to get back with his lady and raise their daughter together. He never let go of this particular idea. He remembered the fan craze Harrington created whenever his Escalade pulled up for an appearance. People loved free stuff. Why not give away free product away from a truck? People could claim their prizes from the truck in person after first securing them online. Brands like Red Bull and Nike were spending money online to access these millennial tastemakers.

Ali created an ad-supported business model that had a call to action for consumers: watch a series of brand ads for the opportunity to claim a series of prizes. Upon winning a prize, the consumer shows up at the Claim it! truck to pick up their winnings. The business was born in 2014 with seed capital from the relationships he had cultivated in previous years.

I met Ali in his Harlem offices. Just like when he was a kid, he rode his bike over to meet me. He had a big smile on his face and greeted me warmly. He teared up on a few occasions while recounting his story. I could tell it wasn't an easy journey for him, but he never gave up. He continued to claw and scratch. He beamed with pride when he showed me his offices. His face lit up even more when he talked about the future of his seven-year-old daughter who reads much better than he did at that age. Ali knew he was on to something, but it was his life's journey that first enabled him to find this path. Now that he is on it, he will do everything in his power to make it successful—for himself, his team, and most important, his family.

ENTREPRENEURIAL DETOX

Entrepreneur: Daniela Luzi Tudor

Age: 32

Hometown: Ploiesti, Romania

Company: WEconnect Health is a relapse prevention platform for those recovering from alcohol and drug addiction and provides outcomes data in real-time throughout the healthcare system to improve treatment.

On her third week in rehab, Daniela Luzi Tudor finally felt more stable. She had admitted herself into a rehab center in Seattle but started to feel anxious because she needed to leave the center in a week. Her insurance only covered twenty-eight days. How was she going to maintain her sobriety post rehab? She had a schedule of regular support meetings she could attend. But what about those times in between? In her darkest moment, she saw the light of a digital business opportunity.

Daniela grew up in communist Romania. Her father moved her family around a lot, first to Germany, then to Portugal, and finally to the United States, which had been his goal all along—he wanted to give his family a better opportunity to succeed. Daniela was very close to her father. They fished, went to the movies, and strolled through the park when she was younger. He treated her like an adult, telling her stories about communism. He wanted a better life for her—a life in America.

Daniela's father was an engineer by trade but had an entrepreneurial spirit. He cut out articles from *Wired* and *Inc.* magazine to share with Daniela. He wanted to give her the tools to achieve her dreams: not working for a company, but starting her own. At the same time, Daniela's father never wanted her to forget her heritage. They took a trip back to Romania shortly before Daniela entered college. They visited the family's hometown, historical sites, and vacation spots. This cultural foundation helped shape her future identity.

Like most college students, Daniela enjoyed casual drinking and recreational drugs in social settings. She was part of the Greek system and had a boyfriend who belonged to a popular fraternity. One Saturday, after arriving back on campus after a quick trip home, she received a call from one of her boyfriend's friends at another fraternity. He asked her to sit down in her sorority's room during the call. She sensed something was wrong and demanded to know why. Her boyfriend was dead, he said. He had overdosed the night before from a combination of alcohol and Percocet.

Daniela was in shock. That same weekend her boyfriend had told her that he loved her. It was so sudden. She didn't know how to respond. She went back home to gather herself. When she came back to campus, she went to his fraternity house knowing that she would never see him again.

Daniela remembers, "I felt numb. I didn't want to deal with it. I didn't want to believe it. That week was hard. What was weird was that I didn't cry when normal people cried. I didn't cry at the open casket or at the service afterwards, but I would break into a complete panic and start crying while playing a board game. I didn't feel like a normal person and act like what normal people would do under such circumstances."

Daniela took a quarter off from school at the prompting of her school counselor. The school also suggested grief counseling, which she refused. She thought she could handle it. This was the beginning of Daniela's cycle of addiction. She woke up every morning, made herself a cup of coffee, and poured vodka into it to help numb the pain.

Her budding addiction served as the backdrop for her entrepreneurial activities. While in college, she co-founded a night club promotions company called Lush Life Entertainment. After graduation, she moved down to Los Angeles to start a company called Soundstrokes Art. The concept was creating live paintings at music festivals based on the visual waveforms produced by the music. She was passionate about music and loved how technology could create music experiences at scale. The entrepreneurial lifestyle suited her need for career independence while helping to feed her alcohol and drug addiction.

Soundstrokes Art was in business for two years. During her last six months at the company, Daniela's addiction began hurting the business. She was showing up late to meetings and stopped following up on her to-do list. Every night was an excuse to stay out late and party because, she rationalized, it was a way to network with new DJs or artists. Her entrepreneurial lifestyle demanded it. But she was spiraling out of control. "Towards the end, the quality of who I was with mattered less. Sometimes I would end up in situations that not in a hundred years would I want to be in. In one instance, I found myself in an underground gambling bar that was run by the Armenian mafia. My actions were insulting to the sacrifices that my parents made to get me here."

Her cofounder confronted her after she noticed Daniela's work was slipping. She sat Daniela down on the couch in their office. "Look, I love you. But the drinking and partying, you may want to take a look at your behavior." Daniela's cofounder did not accuse her of being an alcoholic, but was forceful enough to suggest that something was wrong. Daniela came up with a solution. She would stop drinking for thirty days to prove to everyone that she didn't have an addiction problem. She stayed sober until day twenty when she snuck wine into her house. Nobody knew, so when day thirty hit, they popped a bottle of champagne to celebrate the occasion.

This public display of fortitude allowed Daniela to return

to work with vigor. But in reality, she was still out of control. Everything started to fall apart. She didn't uphold her work commitments. Recklessness in her personal life interfered with her professional responsibilities. She knew she had to get help and moved back home to Seattle, which signaled that she was finally ready to start over again.

She moved into an apartment, purchased a car with the help of her parents, and got a job. She wanted to live a normal life, but she didn't treat the root of her addiction problem. She was finally forced to confront her addiction when she was arrested for a DUI and missed her arraignment. She was thrown into a holding cell and detoxed on the cold floor, shaking uncontrollably with shame, fear, and exhaustion. Daniela remembers, "The feeling was like every cell in my body wanted to escape." When she came out of that state, she recognized her cellmate as someone from her high school. He said that she was the last person he thought would end up in jail.

It only got worse after that. Her father was in tears when he bailed her out. She had only seen this look on his face once before when he had picked her up after she had disappeared for a few days in college and gone binge drinking. She felt his disappointment ripping through her body. He had sacrificed so much to provide her with a better life, and she was throwing it all away. She had to get help. She locked herself in her parents' house for three days until she could get a bed in the local rehab center. She was done pretending she didn't have a problem, so she confronted it head on.

That first day in rehab they took away all of her possessions. Daniela was scared. She cried for the first thirty-six hours. She was alone but realized that she was in a rehab center with other people going through a similar experience, suffering from the same chronic illness. The population wasn't old homeless men as she previously thought. She met Travis, a few years younger than her, whose first question was, "What's your DOC?" meaning her drug of choice. She went through her treatment and was given books to read like *Under the Influence*. Daniela learned about the neurological and physiological cause of addiction. Understanding it helped her gain a deeper perspective of how to treat her condition. Slowly, she began to feel more in control of her life.

By the third week of treatment, Daniela felt lighter in mind and spirit. She stopped physically craving the substances that fed her addiction and wanted to continue her progress after leaving the rehab center. Her entrepreneurial instinct kicked in as she wondered what kind of resource could help her stay clean. Always-on accountability minimized the chance of a relapse. She found out from her counselor that a digital companion app didn't exist, so she decided to build one.

Daniela didn't build the app right away because she wanted to stabilize her life first. She got a job, but one that allowed her to moonlight on her app idea. She worked up the courage to bring the idea to a weekend startup event. She was nervous. This was the first time she was going to announce publicly that she was a former addict, a person in long-term recovery.

Before Daniela went on stage, she went into the bathroom and practiced in front of the mirror. Another woman walked in while she was practicing and she grabbed the opportunity to present to her. Daniela explains, "I asked if I could practice on her. I went into my pitch, and she just gave me a blank stare. I thought to myself that my idea must be crazy, just a really stupid idea. Why am I doing this? She paused for a long enough time before she told me she thought the pitch was great. I thought she was just lying to be nice."

It turned out that the woman's silence was due to the fact that she was still grasping at the gravity of the moment. That same woman ended up joining Daniela's team for the weekend to work on the idea. She revealed that she had to hold back tears after Daniela told her story. The woman had received her degree in neuropsychology because individuals close to her suffered from addictive conditions. She also complemented Daniela's skillset perfectly because she had the technical skills that Daniela lacked.

That woman became Daniela's cofounder for pala-linq, which was later renamed WEconnect Health.

When I was in Seattle in November 2015, I watched Daniela pitch her app to a local tech meet-up. She did it with confidence and pride. She did it knowing what she had gone through and the struggle all addicts in recovery go through on a daily basis. That determination and tenacity guided Daniela and her team to build a product that could reduce the chance of relapse while in recovery. Since that November, WEconnect has raised more than $5 million in funding, grown to more than thirty employees, and gained product distribution in treatment centers and health care systems across the country.

Daniela doesn't run away from her past anymore; she learned to confront and embrace it, just like she did with her cultural heritage when she went back home to see Romania for herself. Daniela's entrepreneurial journey is as much a journey into the future as it a journey into the past. This entrepreneurial path is not just a professional career for Daniela. It's also a mission to help others break the cycle of addiction and find a thriving life in long-term recovery.

KEEP PUSHING HARDER

Entrepreneur: Sherrard Harrington

Age: 24

Hometown: Washington, D.C.

Company: Fanzee, a social advocacy software platform that enables organizations to plan and distribute content through brand advocates

"Hey man, come and pick me up." Sherrard Harrington didn't detect anything unusual in his friend Josh's voice. It was like any typical Friday night that he and Josh hung out. Sherrard told him he'd be late because he was finishing up watching a basketball game. Thirty minutes later another phone call came in that would change Sherrard's life forever.

Josh had been his best friend since they were nine years old, growing up on the streets of Washington, D.C. Sherrard met Josh when he came to his aid in a fight. They'd been inseparable ever since. Josh practically lived at Sherrard's house and Sherrard's mom treated Josh like a son. Josh lived on a tight budget throughout high school and often didn't have enough money to eat.

Sherrard grew up in a rough neighborhood. Every time he left his house, he had to look over his shoulder. He was always at risk of being mugged or worse, shot. Josh helped mitigate that risk. Sherrard explains, "Growing up in the neighborhood that I grew up in, there was always a funny guy who made people laugh. Josh was that funny guy.

Most of the drug dealers who lived in my neighborhood never messed with us because Josh made them laugh. They paid him money just to crack a joke. That was how he supported his life without his mom giving him that much money. Because I was Josh's boy, none of the drug dealers touched us because they looked at us as a tandem."

One day, when Sherrard came home, he saw his mom trying to catch her breath because she was jumping around with such excitement. After she calmed down a little, she told him that she had won tickets to *The Oprah Winfrey Show*. Sherrard was immediately suspicious. He asked for the callback number to retrieve the tickets. It turned out to be Josh's phone number. Josh had pranked Sherrard's mom into thinking she won free tickets. His pranks were always in good fun, even if it was at the expense of Sherrard's mom. Besides, it was Josh who kept Sherrard safe.

The call that changed Sherrard's life that Friday night was from another friend named Tyrone. Tyrone was frantic. He explained that Josh had been shot in the head. He was bleeding out. Sherrard told Tyrone to stop playing. Sherrard knew Josh was a prankster. He thought that Josh was playing another one of his practical jokes. Sherrard hung up the phone. He turned to his cousin who was watching the basketball game with him, "He can't be serious, right?" Sherrard waited another fifteen minutes and called Josh's phone. Josh didn't answer. He called Tyrone. Tyrone implored him to get down to where he was. Sherrard knew then that something was wrong.

When Sherrard arrived, there was yellow tape everywhere. The police had cordoned off the area. Josh had already been whisked away to the hospital. When Sherrard got to the hospital, he saw Josh lying there. His head was swollen. He'd been shot straight in the head. A big bandage covered his head wound. There were tubes down his throat. He had already been pronounced dead, but the hospital was preserving his body because he was an organ donor. Josh had been murdered. Sherrard cried. If only he had picked Josh up when he had called, none of this would have happened. "That was the moment," recalls Sherrard, "that I had to go harder. Anybody that told me that I can't do something, I had to go ten times harder than I did before." He used this experience as fuel to power him in sports and in entrepreneurship.

Sherrard's only sanctuary from the streets was football. He tried out for the varsity team in 9th grade. He didn't make the team. The coach said he had a bad attitude and wasn't ready to compete at a varsity level. Sherrard went home and sulked. Instead of quitting, he used this as motivation to get better. He pinned a picture of the coach to his wall. He visualized the coach telling him that he wasn't good enough. It fueled him to train harder. He pulled up training videos on YouTube, and he modeled his workout regimens to help improve his footwork and route running.

Every morning before school started, he went to the local basketball courts near his house. It was winter time when the temperatures fell below freezing. Sherrard bundled up in a jacket and sweats—and a parachute. He ran sprints with the parachute attached to his back to improve his speed. "I was out there looking like a fool working on my craft. All of my friends thought I looked crazy, but I didn't care. But I was going to make that football team the next year." Sherrard even sought out training advice from players who went on to play college football. He wanted to get better at all costs.

His hard work was rewarded when he made the varsity team his sophomore year. He became a two-way starter on both offense and defense. They won the state championship that year and the two years after that. This success led to Sherrard being invited to the high school combines to showcase his skills for college football teams. He wasn't the most highly recruited athlete out of high school, so he had to continue to prove himself against the elite competition. He studied films of all the other players who would be competing against him. That hard work paid off. He outperformed everyone on the big stage. He came away with many awards at the combine and an influx of scholarship offers came his way. In the end, he decided to enroll at the University of Colorado.

When Sherrard arrived on campus, he experienced a huge culture shock. In his neighborhood in Washington, D.C., the crime rate was sky high. There he had to constantly look over his shoulder to make sure nobody was trying to rob or hurt him. In Colorado, it was different. People smiled at him, and he smiled back. He didn't have to worry about his safety anymore. Now he could focus on how to build a productive life for himself.

During his freshman year, he fractured his hip in the weight room. He wanted to get back on the field to compete but the fracture limited his mobility and speed, which is what he needed as a top-flight cornerback to cover agile wide receivers. The injury ended his football career. He was devastated. Football was all that he knew up to that point. The coaches and athletic director were supportive. He was able to keep his scholarship, but Sherrard had to redirect his energies toward a new purpose.

Sherrard knew that he didn't want to work a regular nine-to-five job. Football instilled in him the belief that he could do something bigger than just himself. He had seen the worst of the worst—his best friend killed by gun violence. He wanted to give back to his community and serve as an example of someone who made it in an industry other than sports or music. He couldn't do that in a regular job. He had to start something himself.

He googled "Entrepreneurship Colorado" and found out that Boulder had a huge entrepreneurial community. He used the school's entrepreneurship center as home base. He reached out to everyone in the community that the school put him in touch with and also with those he found through his own research. He met with hundreds of entrepreneurs, such as Tim Enwall from Misty Robotics, Jason Robins from Draftkings, and Adrian Tuck from Tendril. In these meetings, Sherrard was never nervous. He had experience interacting with coaches who appeared on nationally televised football games, so this was just another meeting for him.

He was also a voracious reader. While his friends were out buying clothes and shoes, he invested in a book collection. His friends would call him different nerd names like Steve Urkel for reading books. He wasn't the norm. But he had this drive that came from his football days to succeed at any cost. As Sherrard explains, "Football prepared me for the grind of entrepreneurship. I saw people quit when things got hard, but I was willing to go the extra mile to accomplish things. Football gave me discipline. I had to wake up every day at 5 a.m., work out between 5 - 7:30 a.m., at 8:30 a.m. I had film study, then from 10 - 2 p.m. I had class, and then it went on. I had to be very efficient with my time and grind through every day."

To gain real-life experience, Sherrard joined a startup

called Musikfly, a blogger submission platform. The startup failed, but it proved to be an amazing learning experience. Through it he learned about user acquisition, managed product development, raised capital, and became more fluent in the language of entrepreneurship. After this experience, Sherrard co-founded Marvel Capital Group, an investment group, as a senior and raised $500,000 in capital to purchase real estate. This investment company was acquired in October 2014.

In February 2015, he co-founded Fanzee, an enterprise marketing service that manages influencers. Sherrard secured investment from several angel investors, celebrities, and athletes, and he continues to build momentum for Fanzee in the marketplace.

Even to this day, Sherrard feels the spirit of Josh running through him. Something clicked in him when he saw his friend lying motionless in a hospital bed. He decided he had to push ten times harder to succeed in life. First, it was football. Now, it's entrepreneurship. He pushes because he has seen what success looks like, and he wants to achieve that success not just for himself, but also for his community.

He sees resilience in his community because they have seen the worst of the worst and still they have survived. Resilience is one of the ingredients it takes to produce great entrepreneurs. But his community lacks role models who might provide them with a different point of reference. Sherrard wants to be that role model for the next generation of "Sherrard Harrington 2.0s."

As Sherrard concludes, "I am going to keep pushing. There is that same mindset in sports as in entrepreneurship. There is no limit to what I can do. I am going to continue to reach out to anyone and everyone. If they say no, I am not afraid to keep grinding. Keep pushing like early in my days. Find out what they like and don't like so that I can get more traction so that I can come back to the table. It is similar to how I reacted to my coach in the 9th grade when he told me I couldn't join the team. I'm going to keep coming back even if they tell me no."

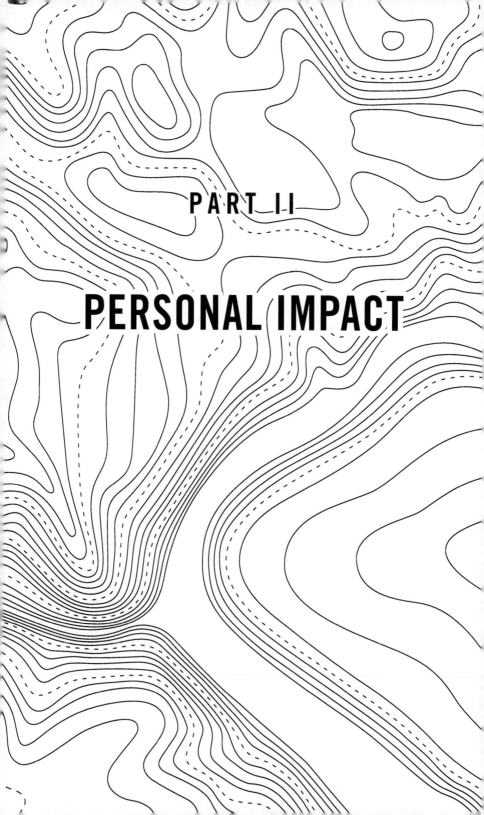

PART II

PERSONAL IMPACT

CHAPTER 7

ALL IN THE FAMILY

I NEVER WANTED TO BE AN ENTREPRENEUR

Entrepreneur: Suneera Madhani
Age: 30
Hometown: Dallas, Texas
Company: Fattmerchant, a payment technology company with membership-based wholesale pricing that makes payment processing simple, powerful, and fun for business customers

Suneera Madhani threw her phone against the wall. The senior team had rejected her proposal. They didn't want to change the way they had been doing business for decades. Payment processing generated lucrative returns. There was too much risk in changing the per-transaction model to a subscription service. Suneera saw an opportunity to make the market more efficient, but senior management didn't want to listen to her recommendation.

"Merchants were being nickel-and-dimed by big banks. This needed to stop. I asked my bosses to run with a subscription model in Orlando. They hated the plan. They told me it wasn't going to work. That was the final straw. I said screw it, I'm going to do this myself. That was when I quit in 2013, and I was going to figure this out. I was solo, by myself, female entrepreneur, in the payment industry. I don't even know how to find Mr. Visa and get this started. But I didn't want to continue to feel the way that I had felt for the last seven years in the workforce."

Starting a company was never something Suneera wanted to do. She quit because she was so exasperated at the response she got from senior management. She wanted to create value for the company. But they wouldn't let her. She hated the feeling of being told she couldn't do something more than the uncertainty of creating a future for herself without the corporate structure. That motivated her to take action and leave the safety of her corporate job.

"There is type A and type B," Suneera explains, "I am type A to the A to the A to the A. It is just innate in me. Things get under my skin a lot. I get agitated a lot. I am not distracted at all. I am so focused on one thing. It is the one thing that I want. It is innate in my biology that I need to do something about it if someone tells me no."

Suneera called up her brother, Sal, two years her junior, to let him know what she planned to do. She wanted his advice because she respected his business acumen. He was excited and offered his help. Emboldened by his encouragement, Suneera worked on a business plan for a subscription-based payment processing service. She entered it into the National Women's Business Plan Competition. She had the basis of the business plan from her previous job. The idea remained consistent, but now she was pitching to a new audience. She won the competition. This gave her the confidence to push forward. She incorporated her company Fattmerchant in April 2014 and signed up beta users. Press started to cover her company and story.

In November 2014, *Fast Company* wrote about how Suneera was disrupting the credit card industry. Her phone started ringing non-stop. Customers wanted to sign up for the service. Investors were calling to put money in the company. Suneera needed help because she was overwhelmed with the response. She turned to her brother again and asked him to help field calls.

Sal took two weeks of vacation and flew from San Francisco, where he was living, to Orlando, where the company was based. That was when things clicked for Sal. Previously, he had only advised his sister because he already had a prominent role at a fast-growing startup. The frenzy of activity in Orlando opened his eyes to the potential scale of his sister's business. He loved the excitement of seeing the company grow. The energy at Fattmerchant was different than his startup job, which he had joined later in the company's life cycle. Here, he was on the ground floor growing a business. In January, Sal made the decision to join his sister as cofounder.

Suneera and Sal had never worked together before, but they quickly realized they were perfect complements to each other. They had an underlying respect for each other that went beyond their sibling relationship. As Suneera explained, "I have learned so much from Sal. I am impressed every day by being an older sibling and watching my younger sibling be ten times smarter than me. As a cofounder, that is what I need with everything that I am not. I told you right before, he is patient. He is analytical. He is more financial. He keeps us focused and ensures that we are going down the right path."

Sal responded in kind: "Suneera is a very passionate person and celebrates the moment more. She is great at inspiring people from a leadership standpoint, something that I look up to because I see how the team responds so enthusiastically to her. I am more of the disciplinarian, while she is more of the cheerleader who tells everyone not to worry after I leave."

At first look, Suneera and Sal's upbringing might have foreshadowed their future as entrepreneurs, but in reality, that wasn't always the case. Their father was an entrepreneur whose business interests ranged from gas stations to call centers to pizza stores. Their family moved frequently to accommodate these business interests.

Suneera hated the lack of stability in her upbringing. She wasn't able to establish any consistency at school because her family always had to move. She went to ten different schools in twelve years while she was growing up. She was forced to make friends quickly. By the time she cultivated a new circle of friends, she had to move on to a new city and repeat the cycle all over again. Suneera decided her path to personal and professional happiness was a corporate job.

Sal, on the other hand, saw his father's various ventures as learning opportunities. For example, he eagerly took on responsibilities that his father handed over to him. "At thirteen, I went to my father's store to do the accounting every Saturday. When I was fifteen, I went to Sam's Club every day after school to fill inventory for the pizza shop we owned. Afterwards, when I returned to the shop, I signed off on people's paychecks. It was interesting writing

a forty-five-year-old person's paycheck when I was fifteen."
Sal loved learning how to do new things because he was
always looking for the next big adventure.

Suneera and Sal never planned to start a company together.
They were siblings who each carved out their own unique
identities. Suneera was a planner. At school, she prepared
for each test as if the stakes were life or death so that she
could get a perfect score. During middle school and high
school, Suneera's main extracurricular activity was sing-
ing in the choir. Sal, on the other hand, grew up playing
multiple sports, including lacrosse, football, and track.
He received good grades, but he was fine not getting the
highest score on a test if that meant he could devote more
time to practicing sports.

Suneera shares, "We were two different people with two
different personalities. He was extroverted, while I was
introverted. He was always good at certain subjects, while
I was good at others. He was more of a risk-taker, where
he had a million scars from playing sports, while I never
broke a bone in my body. We had a yin and yang kind of
balance that then extended into our professional life."

The values that they shared as siblings are reflected in the
values they founded the company on. For example, one of
the company values is "Best Damn Experience," which
reflects a commitment to deliver a great experiences not

only to customers, but also to investors, their community, and to each other. This particular value reflects Suneera's personality; she brings out the best in everyone she works with regardless of level or position.

Another company value is "Get It Done," which is about rolling up your sleeves to get the job done. Working at a startup is not a nine-to-five job, and even if it's not in the job description, there is an expectation at Fattmerchant that everyone needs to pitch in. That might mean getting ready for the next investor meeting or opening up a new office. This value reflects more of Sal's personality since he is about getting to the core of an issue and zeroing in on how to accomplish it regardless of the obstacles in his way.

The third value, "Transparency," is core to their business model since their product brings more transparency and predictability to the payments and fees that small businesses incur for processing credit cards. This has allowed Fattmerchant to save businesses 30 to 40 percent on processing fees. Transparency also extends to the visibility that Suneera and Sal provide to everyone in their organization about what is happening with the business. They hold all-hands meetings on a weekly basis and host company retreats quarterly.

In late 2017 at one company retreat, Suneera recalls, "Sal

and I took a step back and saw another thirty new hires who were being immersed in the Fattmerchant culture for the first time with the core team members. This wasn't about doing business. It was about team building and getting us to work together on something that is larger than all of us. We are now supporting more than seventy-five families, which is a huge responsibility. I had to pinch myself because I couldn't have imagined something like this when we first started four years ago."

Suneera and Sal's values have set the foundation for Fattmerchant's 500 percent growth year over year since its inception in 2014. In 2017, they processed more than $1 billion in merchant transactions with the goal of reaching $10 billion in merchant transactions by the end of 2020. To fund that growth, they have raised close to $10 million in venture capital from prominent investors.

"I didn't go to CEO school to learn how to do this," Suneera quips, "But I've been able to manage having so many things thrown at me while we try to maintain this torrid growth trajectory."

The business of running a startup was all-consuming for Suneera. In mid-2017, she had her first child while she was in the middle of raising capital for the company. "It's been a huge balancing act of being a brand new mom and running a business," she shares. "I want to continue to grow my family and also my business, and I want to show that we as women can do that."

What has kept Suneera grounded, motivated, and inspired is her relationship with her brother.

"As siblings, I trust my brother innately," Suneera explains. "Even if we fight as siblings, it is different than any relationship, as I can trust my brother wholeheartedly and never feel judged for not knowing the answer. It is amazing to have this now as an adult as my business partner because at the end of the day we are always going to look out for each other and our company as it's truly one team, one dream."

ARE YOU SERIOUS, MOM?

Entrepreneur: Vicente Fernandez
Age: 26
Hometown: Miami, Florida
Company: SportsManias, a leading platform that delivers real-time, personalized sports content from leading local and national writers, featuring an industry-leading emoji keyboard

Vicente Fernandez was exchanging the usual catch-up pleasantries with his mom over the phone until she dropped an idea on him out of left field. "Vicente, I think we should start up a sports technology business." He was a sophomore at the University of Chicago at the time and was thinking about securing a summer internship. The last thing on his mind was starting a business, much less with his mother.

"Mom, what are you talking about? This is crazy. You are not even a sports fan!"

But because he both loved and respected his mother, who was also an accomplished entrepreneur running her own advertising agency, he knew that he had to take his mom's idea seriously.

Vicente marinated on the idea. He loved sports. Growing up in the Miami area, Vicente was an avid fan of all the local sports teams. Every morning, he ripped open the *Miami Herald* to pull out the sports section. He devoured every article and memorized all the stats of his favorite players. He also played sports throughout high school as well as football in college. Sports played a huge part in forming his identity.

When Vicente moved to Chicago to start college, he continued to pledge his love for Miami teams, but being thousands of miles away, he had to do so online. He'd go to one site to read about the Miami Heat's playoff victory, then another site to catch up on the Hurricanes' recruiting strategy, and finally a different stie that analyzed the Marlins' recent trade to acquire more minor league talent. He had to cobble together a mishmash of sites in order to satiate his needs and find out the latest on his favorite teams. He started to realize there was an opportunity for centralizing this type of browsing behavior. His mom was on to something.

Vicente's mom, Aymara, was always working. She started her career at Crispin Porter, a prestigious advertising agency, and jumped around to different agencies to take on more responsibility. She started her own agency, Aymara & Associates, in 1995 to focus on the Hispanic market, which she felt was underserved by her clients. One of the highlights of her career was working with the world-class Michael Bay, who directed the film *Transformers*.

Aymara enlisted Vicente in all sorts of projects. At first, it was to get his feedback on specific slogans, copy, or designs for her campaigns. She wanted his fresh, raw perspective. As Vicente got older, Aymara brought him on set for her shoots, and he even stood in as an extra in some of the commercials. This allowed Vicente to see his mom in action. She was very particular about what she wanted for the set design, the wardrobe look and feel, and the actor's movements. She conferred with the director during shoots, watching intently what transpired on set in front of the camera. It was important for her to be in the details because those details translated into the larger vision of what her clients wanted.

In 2011 Aymara saw a shift in the advertising industry and marketing budgets moved from television to digital. Vicente's mom felt the pinch; the quality of what her clients demanded no longer matched up to the dollars they were willing to pledge. They wanted the same level of quality or higher, only at a lower cost. Recognizing this dynamic, competitors swooped in to undercut her firm on price. It was time for Aymara to consider a career transition.

Live sports was the one sector that Vicente's mom found was immune to the shifting landscape. Broadcast networks actually commanded a higher premium when deciding rates for advertising during games. She saw her son as one of the consumers driving this shift. He loved watching games live, which was matched only by his obsessive tracking of everything online before and after the game. When she approached her son, it was strategic. She saw the potential in the sports market for a digital business, and she believed her son could identify that gap in the marketplace.

"I have always loved my advertising agency," Aymara recalls. It wasn't work. It was something that I absolutely loved, and I got paid handsomely to have fun. This line of work was my lifeline. I was the sole provider. I knew that Vicente could take on the role. At the time though, I didn't realize how complex and sophisticated this would become, more than we had ever imagined."

After that initial conversation, Vicente's weekly calls with his mom quickly turned into discussions of the business opportunity in the digital sports business. Originally, the business idea was to create a sports enthusiast social network. That idea eventually morphed into a centralized digital hub to track local news on favorite sports teams. Vicente had the insight that local newspapers and beat writers craved a national audience but lacked the ability to scale beyond their local market. Aggregating all of this local content could create an opportunity for publications to gain access to a new audience if Vicente and his mom could acquire users who wanted a centralized content hub. The idea for SportsManias was born.

Vicente was more than ready to start the company with his mother. Everything about his college experience screamed sports. He was the sports editor for the school newspaper and he started a sports club that brought in executives from the sports industry to speak on campus. That summer, in between his junior and senior years, Vicente and his mom built the beta version of their product. His mom was still running her agency, and Vicente worked out of her office to be closer to his cofounder. They didn't have any experience in the tech industry, which turned out to be a blessing.

They organized an initial meeting with patent lawyers to see if they could protect their idea. The conference room was impressive, encased all in glass with a corner view that overlooked the water. His mom started off the presentation while Vicente closed. The lawyers were stoic until Vicente explained how they wanted to tap into sports beat writers and give them a national platform for their content. The lawyers, who screened hundreds of patent proposals, thought they were on to a good idea. This meeting provided early validation that that they were on to something.

Later, Vicente realized that meeting with a patent attorney wasn't the most useful next step to building a tech company. Executing the idea was more important than patenting it and securing proof of concept was the ingredient they needed to attract investment capital. Patents are useless without a working product and users who give feedback on it. But what that meeting did was give them confidence. Negative feedback from a venture capitalist might have crushed them and halted their progress. This was the initial wind that lifted their sails.

Another turning point was when Vicente and his mom presented to the second in command at Time Inc., a huge media conglomerate that considers *Sports Illustrated* one of its crown jewels. Vicente commanded the room. He knew the product inside and out, and he related to these executives even though they were thirty years his senior. By the end of the meeting, they were close to signing a syndication deal. Vicente's mom was so proud to see her son rise to the occasion when many at his age might have faltered under such pressure. That was a moment that she could truly appreciate as both a mother and cofounder.

Now, when Vicente and his mother meet with media properties or investors, they always have a slide about their team. Vicente points out that his cofounder is also his mom. This typically elicits a round of chuckles, as most think it is both unusual and cool that it is a mother-son team driving the business. Family has taken on so much more meaning for both of them. SportsManias is a business that they run together out of Aymara's former agency office. They have had tremendous success, hitting number one in the App Store in seventy-eight countries, including the US. That success is only magnified because they get to work together as mother and son.

"My mother has always done what she has done," explains Vicente. "But I see it differently now than I did as a kid. I live at home. From the moment we wake up to the moment we sleep, we are working. I am twenty-three years old. I can handle this. This is the time when I can go through the fire and beat myself up. But it has been incredible to see my mother balance her work and family."

Vicente continues, "I have an eleven-year-old brother. She wakes up and takes my brother to school. She comes to the office and works the entire day. She goes home and makes dinner. She does the laundry. She helps my brother with his homework. She washes the dishes. I am just working all this time, and when she is finished, she comes and joins me on emails and brainstorming until we go to sleep. The cycle repeats itself every day. Wow. Seeing it from start to finish with the way that she works is incredible. For me, it makes me feel that I need to give it everything I have."

A TRUE FAMILY AFFAIR

Entrepreneur: Tina P.
Age: 30
Hometown: Bucks County, Pennsylvania
Company: Happenings Media, a network of digital magazines that provide entertaining, informative, and interactive hyperlocal lifestyle content paired with engaging live events in communities across America

Tina P. and her husband Chris woke up to the rushing sound of water flooding into their basement studio apartment. Hurricane Irene had caused the river in their town to overflow, forcing the evacuation of its residents. Tina grabbed her computer and raced out, along with Chris, to find shelter at a friend's third-floor apartment. The next day, they moved back to Tina's parents' house for a week, while the damage to their apartment was being repaired.

As it turned out, the flood was caused by a rare combination of hurricane and human error at the town's water facility. But to some of Tina's family, this seemed like yet another consequence of her leaving a safe corporate environment for lofty entrepreneurial endeavors. She would never have been in a basement apartment if she hadn't left her old job.

A couple years earlier, Tina and her sister Angela had gone into business together and started a jewelry box business for young girls called BeMe. The product line was diverse, catering to girls interested in a variety of things such as music, soccer, and ballet. At the time, Tina had a lucrative job at a hedge fund, but she quit to focus on the business idea full time, as did her sister. Tina and Chris had moved into the basement of Angela's house in Pennsylvania. The lines between their work lives, their family lives, and personal lives became blurred. Sensing the need for more privacy and independence, Tina and Chris secured a studio apartment after living with Angela and her husband for almost a year. Then they took refuge in Tina's parents' house after the flood.

Tina's parents had questioned her decision to start a business and quit her job. She had worked so hard to get to that position and was a rising star. The company even sponsored her MBA. Quitting her job felt like a step backward. Moving out of her comfortable Westchester apartment and into the basement of her older sister's home was a harder blow to stomach. From their perspective, Tina and Chris were giving up something real for a pipe dream. They wanted to bring them back to reality.

The week after the flood was intense and the pressure from her parents to give up her entrepreneurial ambitions was stronger than ever. Tina and Chris left the house once their apartment was outfitted with new carpeting. She was frustrated.

"It felt like all the trust that I had earned throughout my childhood and young adult life was being disregarded— that people assumed absolutely no thought had gone into making such a big decision, which certainly wasn't the case," Tina remembers. "It was already so hard to start a business with the ups and downs of that. I couldn't handle both anymore."

Tina took solace in the fact that she and her sister were in this together. They hadn't always been this close. Angela was three years older than Tina and as kids, that gap often made the two sisters feel worlds apart. As they grew older,

Angela became more protective. They both went to Fordham University in the Bronx, New York, and overlapped there for one year. Angela offered Tina career advice and even planted the seed that Tina should date Chris, who was just a friend at the time.

Tina worked on BeMe for three years on nights and weekends before she had enough savings to quit her day job. After long days at work, Tina would head down to Chinatown to source their product and spend the evenings exchanging emails and compiling sales forecasts. She invested her bonuses in purchasing inventory. Tina called Angela frequently to talk about how to evolve the product. They traveled to trade shows together. They showed up at Irish step-dancing competitions to sell their product. It made sense for them to live together to reduce their overhead and build a closer working relationship.

Tina knew her sister well, but working together required a different dynamic. "You have this older sister/younger sister dynamic growing up, and if you have that as partners in a business, that would be a problem," explains Tina. "From the beginning, there was a mutual respect. There was trust that we were doing the best things for the business and for each other. Our strengths are different, and we default to each other on those areas that we are each good at."

BeMe consumed most of their time. It was a business

that grew steadily but slowly. There were major barriers to entry that they had to work through in consumer product goods. On the side, Angela involved herself with community events in Bucks County, Pennsylvania. She set up a website and published what was going on around town. Angela and her website started getting noticed around town and local merchants appreciated the online publicity that the site was generating for them. Watching the site's popularity grow and seeing her sister get access to some fun perks compelled Tina to start writing for the website too. "I had always enjoyed writing, and this seemed like a fun thing to get involved in." Viewership on this website grew organically, and local merchants asked to advertise there without even being solicited. Tina and Angela had a media business even though they did not treat it as a business.

A reporter from a local magazine reached out to cover their story as sisters starting a business. Tina and Angela arrived prepared to talk about BeMe, but the reporter was more interested in talking about the website, to which they responded that this was just a hobby. The reporter laughed. That was their eureka moment. They had been focused on creating a demand for BeMe, when one already existed for their "hobby." In the process of trying to publicize their business, they built a platform where local businesses could clamor for online attention in their hometown. The sisters figured what they did in Bucks County could be replicated in other cities. They sold BeMe and instead focused all of their efforts on building Happenings Media, a local media and events business, one market at a time.

The path to discovering their business wasn't obvious. What was obvious to Tina, though, was that she needed more separation between work and life. Running a startup was all consuming and the sisters had different approaches to unplugging. Being one stairway away from each other made that balance increasingly difficult. Tina knew they would all benefit from clearer lines of separation between her business with Angela and her life with Chris, and the business had grown enough to make the move feasible.

Tina always supported Chris' desire to become a beer brewer. He had quit his lucrative finance job to work the line at a brewing plant in New Jersey. When a higher level job opened up in Miami, he moved down there and Tina moved with him. She opened the Miami office for Happenings Media. It was important for Tina to have success with her startup. It was equally important to have success as a couple and support Chris' interests while still pushing forward her own.

"Chris loved his career in beer but in his current role, he felt so unsettled," recalls Tina. "There was no opportunity to move up. A job opportunity came up in Miami. When he got the offer, there was no question. It was the right move for him to pursue. He said to me that he wouldn't take it if it was something that would hurt my business. I told him no, we will figure it out. We moved down to Miami over Christmas 2014 for him to start his job on January 9th. There were times that it was hard on me, not being around our sales team or not being close to clients. But it was the right thing to do for us, as a couple, to help us grow."

Tina had her two closest partners, Angela and Chris, by her side while building her business, and eventually the rest of her family began to see the potential in it.

Part of that challenge came down to a generational gap in understanding her career change. Tina and Angela ran a digital business, but her parents hadn't grown up in a digital world. At a time when Facebook was largely confined to college campuses, starting a digital media business seemed completely insane. "I really do not think they had any idea what we were doing all day," Tina recalls.

What finally helped crystallize the potential of Angela and Tina's business for her family was an event they hosted in their hometown. There, her parents were able to see firsthand, away from the computer screen, what Tina and Angela had built. 300 people showed up because they followed the website and were genuinely interested in the event and the entertainment that was planned, not because they had been invited by family members. Movers and shakers from the local business community were there. This was the big moment that helped bridge the generational divide.

Tina's father was, in fact, her biggest cheerleader growing up. "He would tell me, go for the idea. You can do it. When I came home with a TV script idea in middle school, he sent out the script to all these TV executives to show me that anything could be done. When I had an idea to create a rollerblading workout machine, he entertained actually sourcing an architect." That enthusiasm was infectious. He himself was an entrepreneur who had left behind a thriving corporate career to open his own law practice. He balanced an enthusiasm for entrepreneurship with the pragmatism of raising his kids. He wanted to instill the same discipline in his children, who were now starting families on their own. What he didn't realize was that he had sparked a strong entrepreneurial passion in them when they were kids.

Starting a business with family isn't easy. Those who might be closest to you—husbands, wives, fathers, mothers, siblings—all have their own perspectives on the risks involved in starting a business. And day-to-day decisions about running a business might not seem important when loved ones don't want to support the venture. In the case of Tina and her sister, they showed fortitude not only in growing their business, but also in withstanding the pressure from their family to pursue a different path. All in the family is really all encompassing. It isn't just about the business. It's about the network of people who are closest to the entrepreneur and can make life easier or harder when they're doing one of the toughest things imaginable: starting a business.

CHAPTER 8

THANKS, MOM AND DAD

KING OF THE FIXIES

Entrepreneur: Austin Stoffers
Age: 28
Hometown: Los Angeles, California
Company: Pure Cycles, a company founded with one mission in mind: to get more people on bikes

Torrential rain flooded the streets and water poured into stores. Austin Stoffers was fourteen and on a trip with his dad to India. He gleefully jumped from table to table, watching his dad pick out furniture. Three shopkeepers literally held Austin's father above the flood water inside the store so that he didn't get wet. More importantly, this gave his dad sufficient visibility to see the furniture and select pieces for his retail store back in Los Angeles. Most exporters might have waited for the rain to let up. Not Austin's dad. He was determined to make use of his limited time so that he could ship a full container of goods back to the States. "When he had his mind on accomplishing a goal, he would go for it. He was never one to turn back," Austin says.

His dad grew up in a small town in Iowa and dropped out of high school when he was fifteen. He bounced across the country from Florida to California and got drafted to the Vietnam War. He saved up money overseas by acting as a loan shark. When he received his monthly pay, he lent the money out to other soldiers who wanted access to cash immediately. Then he made money off the interest. He didn't go out spending it because he wanted to save money so that he could start a business that would fulfill his childhood dream of becoming a millionaire. When he returned to California, he even lived in homeless shelters to save every penny he could. He could have afforded an apartment, but he chose that lifestyle to preserve his savings.

The import-export business idea came to him when he traveled down to Mexico on a surfing trip with his buddies. He saw local artisans selling furniture on the side of the street. He purchased these goods and brought them back to sell in Los Angeles. His success fueled him with confidence. He went down to Mexico more frequently, not to surf, but to acquire more furniture and was eventually able to open up a store. After a few years, Austin's dad ventured out beyond Mexico. He traveled overseas to Asia to source unique items from countries such as India, Vietnam, and China. He built a successful import-export business with three retail outlets in the Los Angeles area.

Austin always had a special bond with his father. The basis of their relationship was their mutual love of business. "Most kids my age were playing sports with their dad. It was never like that with me and him. By choice, we talked about entrepreneurship and business, and that was what he liked and that was what I liked." Austin soaked up his father's knowledge on those overseas trips. For example, he learned how to negotiate from watching his father in action. His father focused on items that he didn't want to shift attention away from the things that he did truly want. Showing interest translated to higher prices. This strategy gave him greater flexibility to negotiate better prices with vendors who were more eager to sell when he threatened to leave because nothing interested him.

In watching his father in action, both overseas and at home, Austin always knew that he wanted to start a business. But he didn't want to go into the family business. He wanted to start his own. The only commonality was that he wanted to start a business where he could measure progress one sale at a time. The idea came to him when he was at University of Wisconsin. Austin saw everyone else taking corporate jobs, but he and his friends wanted to be their own bosses. They'd been his best friends since kindergarten. They talked about starting up businesses as often as they talked about girls. They cycled through many ideas until one finally stuck.

As kids, Austin and his friends rode bikes together all the time. When they got to college, they went to the local bike shops and were surprised that a cool-looking bike cost more than $1,000. These bikes had all the bells and whistles, which were features that the bike enthusiast wanted, not the average college student. They spotted a market opportunity to deliver an affordable, design-friendly, single-speed bike targeted to college students.

After conducting their research, Austin and his friends went into action. It wasn't hard for Austin to take action after watching his father do it for so many years. It was natural for him to go through the process of identifying an overseas bike manufacturer, giving them design specs, and placing an order for bikes. Finally, it was his turn to apply what he had learned and experienced first-hand from his father throughout the years. They made a purchase order for 160 bikes for $30,000 and invested their own capital into purchasing the initial order of bikes. They didn't ask their parents for that capital because they wanted to prove that they could be successful without their help. They also didn't want money to interfere with their personal relationships.

A huge container arrived in January during winter break of their senior year when they were back in home in Los Angeles. Austin and the team recruited all of their buddies to help unload the bike inventory. His dad owned an abandoned house where they locked up the bikes. Now they had to sell them. His dad was supportive but somewhat skeptical. He figured that they could sell these bikes on eBay if nobody wanted to buy them or a have a party with their friends to get rid of the inventory. But Austin and his friends were more optimistic. They were confident that they could sell the bikes by the end of the year. Their expectations were exceeded as they sold out in two weeks.

Similar to when his father was in India going from vendor to vendor, Austin went door to door to all of the bike shops in the Los Angeles area. He loaded bikes into his car and trotted in his product when he found a new store. He was initially terrified but overcame this fear as he went into each store with a growing sense of confidence. He had a product that was delivering a market need, and he was able to connect with the owners of these mom-and-pop shops because his father was also a small-business owner. His big break came when a dealer in Santa Barbara placed an order for twenty-five bikes. Austin received the call when he was at dinner. At the time, they were running their business using their cell phones out of the abandoned house. Bikes were packed into the house. Moving required awkwardly maneuvering around the space. After two weeks, they could move freely until the next shipment of 600 bikes arrived.

Austin and his friends received feedback from the stores that had purchased from the first shipment of bikes. They took this feedback and incorporated it into their product design for the second shipment. In addition, they made the decision to switch factories. It was a risk to switch, but they saw the new factory's hunger to grow with them. Aligning incentives helped them improve product quality and scale up when the market embraced their product. The market did indeed embrace it, as they quintupled their order volume, expanded their distribution outside of California, and received several investor inquiries. The factory owner was happy. He even named his first child after Austin.

Today, Pure Fix Cycles is the number one brand in the single-speed category of bikes called fixies. In 2017, Austin and his cofounders evolved the brand name to Pure Cycles to reflect the team's aim to become the number one lifestyle bicycle brand globally. Throughout this growth, Austin has maintained a super close relationship with his father. "My dad is the most important person in my life, hands down. I can tell him anything. I can talk to him about anything. We can bounce ideas off each other." Austin used to be the one going to his father for advice; now his father comes to him for advice. His father doesn't make any major decision without consulting Austin first. He respects what his son has accomplished at such an early age. Austin's dad is a father, a friend, an advisor, a mentor, and now a business peer to Austin.

Pure Cycles' office is in a space that originally belonged to Austin's father's business. Austin took over the space when they needed more room for their inventory, which happened to be at the exact time his father started to scale down his furniture business. When Austin shared this detail about his father, he paused and acknowledged the moment. His father came a long way from humble beginnings, and Austin was now there, in his father's original warehouse space, to continue his family's legacy of entrepreneurship.

MOM'S DELI

Entrepreneur: Loren Rochelle
Age: 30
Hometown: Ocala, Florida
Company: NOM, a platform that provides advertisers with the singular solution to create, manage, compare, real-locate spend, and make real time-decisions to optimize video buys across social media platforms

"Deli, deli, deli." Loren Rochelle smirked and blurted this phrase out every time she had to go to her mom's deli. She spent a lot of time there when she was growing up in Florida and had to occupy herself as her mom was busy running the entire operation. Though she disliked being there because there was nothing to do, the upside was that she got to spend time with her mom. She'd crawl over to her mom and wrap her entire body around her mom's leg. Her mom would try to shake her off, but Loren always refused to let go, clinging on for dear life.

Loren's mom, Lynn-Ann, did everything at the deli, which sold fresh subs and pre-made goods such as sausage, pasta, and sauces. At lunch and dinnertime, she was behind the counter taking orders, making subs, and operating the cash register. Outside of these hours, Loren's mom was prepping the food. Her specialty was making Italian sausage. At night, she'd season two big pig butts and then ground them into bits of meat. She didn't own a machine that could case the sausages because it was too expensive. Instead, she negotiated a deal with the butcher at the local supermarket chain to use his machine. She found creative solutions to problems like this because she was relentless, but in a charming way.

On top of running the deli, Lynn-Ann was also a single parent raising two kids: Loren and her brother. Because she'd had Loren when she was a teenager, she hadn't had the opportunity to attend college. She opened a deli to support her family because she loved cooking. They were relatively poor, but Loren never felt that way. She was able to pursue what interested her both in school and outside of school. Her mother was always there to support her despite her busy schedule and limited resources. For example, she served as the leader of Loren's Girl Scouts troop and regularly drove Loren to gymnastics. Loren's mom wanted to give her the best possible chance of succeeding in life by letting her explore who she was.

In high school, a teacher pushed Loren into art and design classes, which she ended up loving. The classes sparked her creativity. She continued to pursue this interest in college at the Fashion Institute of Technology. At the same time, she always had this feeling that she wanted to run a business but didn't know what kind. What she did know was that creativity had to be at the center of the business. After college, she set out to explore different options that might lead her to an idea.

Her first job after school was as an executive assistant for a graphic design company. This was during the middle of the recession in 2008. The founder was on the brink of bankruptcy and had to lay her and other staff off to survive. Loren pre-empted him by offering to help rebuild his business and lower her already meager salary to $300 a week. He agreed, so every night she went home and learned how to code. She built him a website. She published articles about their business. She built out all of his social media profiles. She networked like crazy. Her efforts started to pay off as the firm acquired new clients through different marketing channels. And she gained confidence that she could build a business by rebuilding his.

Loren fell in love with digital marketing and tried to get another full-time job, but no company was hiring. She decided to hire herself by starting a jewelry company called LoveBirds. Friends began complimenting her on the jewelry that she made by hand. Soon, a hobby turned into a business.

Of course, she gravitated toward the marketing side of the business. She created a website, secured editorial features, walked in cold to jewelry boutiques, and organized photo shoots. What she disliked was the core of the business, which was making the jewelry itself. It wasn't enjoyable anymore because she only ever wanted it to be a hobby. But what this business gave her was a case study to showcase to startups in the digital marketing space. She soon got a job as a marketing manager for a startup called RedBlack that built e-commerce stores for large media publications.

By 2010, Loren saw that YouTube was exploding with more than just cat videos. Brands were starting to spend heavily in the space to create videos and a marketplace was developing. She jumped into the fray by joining another startup called Feed Company, which helps expand the reach of branded videos. Originally, she thought the startup created the videos. Deep into the interviewing process, however, she discovered that the business focused only on video distribution. "Fuck it, I was going to do it. I thought it would be a great learning experience," Loren says. It turned out to be the place where Loren found her niche for launching her own business.

Loren moved on to two other startups afterwards. With each move, she learned something new. And at each startup, she noticed there was something broken that needed to be fixed. The CEOs of these startups didn't want to fix their problems. So each time Loren left. At the last startup she worked at before starting NOM, she came to a crossroads. She now had the experience to start something on her own and the confidence to do it. However, she was acutely aware that she needed a partner to help scale the business. Loren's strength was sales and marketing, and she recognized she needed a technical partner to build the product.

That cofounder turned out to be Brent, the CFO at Channel Factory, where they both worked. He noticed that Loren was lost in her own thoughts at a board meeting one day. He could tell that she had one foot out the door already. After that meeting, he invited her to have coffee with him and laid out all the reasons he thought they should start a business together. When he had finished making his case, Loren told him yes immediately. That was the conversation that led to the birth of NOM, a video distribution platform.

Loren recalls, "Prior to my conversation with Brent, I had already been planning on leaving the company to go off on my own. I had been planting seeds and having conversations with my contacts to go into companies as their independent hired gun. When Brent propositioned me about the business, my face lit up. I was already putting the pieces into place, but the right cofounder was my missing link. Here the perfect cofounder was ready to take the leap with me. It was the only thing keeping me from starting a legitimate entity so I felt like it was fate, which is why I said 'yes' immediately."

Recognizing that their departure could crater the company, Loren and the CFO recruited replacements and put processes in place to keep the business running. At the same time, they went to work on building their own business. It wasn't easy. The investor community rejected them. Friends doubted them. They didn't have a stable income and lived off savings for the first year. Despite the struggle, they kept fighting. They developed a great product that allowed advertisers to purchase, optimize, and measure the success of their video content across social properties such as YouTube, Facebook, Instagram, and Snapchat. They brought on new clients. They established a reputation for great customer service. All of this translated into a successful first year in business. They have continued to follow this recipe and expect to close out their second year with double-digit growth.

Throughout this entire process, Loren's mom has been her biggest cheerleader. Like any proud parent, she is the first one to blast out any positive news about her daughter's accomplishments. What is special about their relationship is that it has evolved into a true friendship and admiration for one another. "My mom is a super badass. She is a woman who doesn't need anything. She does everything for herself and everything for everyone else. She will help everyone else before she helps herself. "

The deli experience, once a point of consternation when Loren was a kid, is now a point of pride. Seeing her mother at work was a formative experience that Loren can now look back on and appreciate. Although her mom may have just scraped by, she never compromised on delivering quality service and products or taking care of her family. No matter how tough business conditions get, Loren knows she has the fortitude to push forward because of what her mother went through to give her a better life.

Entrepreneur: Ben Jacobs
Age: 30
Hometown: Los Angeles, California
Company: Whistle, the smarter way to keep tabs on your pet's location and activity levels when they're living it up at home, in the park, or on the run

Ben Jacobs' mom, Barbara, went through the list of tactics they needed to execute well in order to make the event successful. Were the sign-up sheets in place? Were the tables positioned correctly for the greeters to welcome guests? Were the balloons high enough so that nobody would accidentally pop one? Barbara owned an event company in Los Angeles, and she roped Ben in as free labor on weekends. The car ride over was filled with anxiety. Barbara verbalized all of her thoughts as they approached the event space.

As an extrovert, Barbara was wired for the frenetic pace of the events business. Once they arrived at the venue, she hit the ground running. Food had to be prepared and delivered on time. Drinks needed to be served. She focused on all the production details to ensure guests were enjoying themselves. She operated on the principle that the smallest of details could have the greatest of impact.

Meanwhile, Ben was put to work. He did not sit idly by

observing. He filled in wherever his mom needed him. He washed dishes whenever the kitchen was short-staffed. He greeted guests at the door and signed them in to keep track of who attended. Ben had to keep up with his mom's frenetic pace since she was running around at these events. Nights ended well past midnight, but his mom didn't relent until the last guest left. The car ride back home was a chance to unwind and relax after being on for the entire night. This was Ben's introduction to startup life.

Ben recalls, "I was free labor for my mom. I wore "Barbara Jacobs Events" t-shirts. It was tactical catering—serving as a waiter, setting up tables, or tearing down structures. Whatever needed to get done. I felt a sense of pride in helping out with the events. In event management—hospitality, restaurants, and hotels more broadly—I got to see my mom touch the customer in a very real way and adjust her actions because she was getting feedback from customers so quickly."

As a single mother, Barbara was involved in other aspects of Ben's life besides running an all-consuming events business. She was his basketball coach even though she didn't play herself. She got Ben his first dog, Bear, a purebred, black German Shepherd, who they took out to Rancho Park. When Bear passed away, his mom got another German Shepherd, Kramer, named after the Seinfeld character. Just like the TV character, Kramer was a klutz and slid on the wood floors in Ben's house. Ben loved his dogs, and these early experiences informed his understanding of how he could positively affect the lives of animals.

Ben's second startup exposure was during a summer internship he did in Silicon Valley at a company called Rapleaf, a data analytics platform. Ben shares, "This was my first exposure to the Silicon Valley-backed startup. The CEO there, Auren Hoffman, was an inspiring figure. Peter Thiel was on the board. I was there as an intern with thirteen people. It was an interesting place to move and build products in Silicon Valley." Ben went back to school at Yale, where he was a senior, energized, but he wanted a broader business background, so he took an associate position at the strategy consulting firm Bain following graduation.

After two years at Bain, he was ready to jump back into the entrepreneurial fray. While Ben was evaluating his options, he solicited the advice of Steve, a former Bain colleague two years ahead of him who was living in San Francisco. Steve had left Bain to join a private equity company and loved the startup culture in Silicon Valley. Ben acted on this advice to move back to San Francisco and work in venture capital so he could be close to the startup scene.

Ben and Steve went from casual acquaintances to roommates when the opportunity arose. Their friendship grew deeper and they came from similar backgrounds—both were from LA and raised by parents who owned small businesses. They loved working together and had complementary skill sets. Ben and Steve ended up being perfect cofounders for each other.

The key ingredient in their relationship was that they both loved to talk about business ideas. In their respective jobs, they were exposed to a significant range of businesses. Ben saw early-stage startups where the founders might only have the idea captured in a PowerPoint deck. Steve saw later-stage ventures that were looking for a boost of capital to facilitate a liquidity event such as an acquisition or an IPO. The couch conversations back at their apartment allowed them to pick out product and investment themes that they documented on a white board, which hung prominently in their living room.

But the conversation often went back to the character of the founders they met. How did they lead? How did they bring teams together? How did they work with their boards? Research showed the pet industry was a massive market ripe for disruption. They both owned dogs growing up. The pain point for Ben was that he had to say goodbye to his first dog, Bear, without any notice. One day Bear was healthy, the next he was writhing in pain from gastrointestinal issues. Bear was in so much pain, but so was Ben who had to lose his best friend.

Ben and Steve realized that data and personal experience were not enough to start a scalable business in the pet care market. They talked with owners and vets to form a more complete picture of the pet care business they imagined: an activity monitoring solution for pet owners to keep track of their beloved pets. There were other players in the market, but none were executing in the way that Ben and Steve envisioned. Their total conviction in creating a "Fitbit for the pet industry" allowed them to take the risk of quitting their jobs to pursue the idea full time.

Ben and Steve also brought on a third cofounder who could develop the product. During their search, Ben emerged from the basement of a bar in San Francisco and immediately called Steve letting him know about a potential prospect—Kevin, an engineer who specialized in wireless technology.

Kevin was difficult to persuade. He had a high-paying job at a publicly-traded, wireless technology company and had just gotten married. He made both Ben and Steve pitch his wife, an investment advisor and the CFO of the family, on the idea. If she approved, he was willing to join. Ben and Steve were all business. They brought their laptop and projected their deck onto Kevin's living room wall and reviewed their financials, strategic plan, and market opportunities. Kevin's wife asked tough questions that Ben and Steve fielded. She was sold, and Kevin was onboard.

Since 2012, Whistle, a GPS tracker and health monitor for dogs and cats, has grown from three to eight and now to over seventy-five people. Countless stories have flooded in that demonstrate the market need for Whistle, from the more serious, "I found cancer in my dog using Whistle so I was able to go to the vet immediately for treatment," to the more humorous, "My dog was chasing a porcupine, and he got quills stuck to him in a cave but we found him using Whistle."

In 2016, Whistle was acquired by Mars, Incorporated, the leading pet care company. Ben called his mom once the acquisition was solidified. She congratulated him like any proud parent would. But she also wanted to know how this might impact his day-to-day. Would he have to travel more? Who would be overseeing the executive team at Whistle now? Ben assured her that his life would be minimally impacted. Ben and Steve would still be the stewards executing Whistle's vision and building products to help pet owners stay connected to their pets.

Ben's mom wanted stability for her son. As a small-business owner, she never knew when the next paycheck might come. But she was able to weather the emotional highs and lows. The stability she didn't have was exactly what she wanted for her son.

Just as Ben wore a "Barbara Jacobs Events" t-shirt when he was a kid, he now proudly sports Whistle-branded clothing. His dog, Duke, roams around the office. The stability that matters to him is what his mom always had in her life: doing something that she absolutely loved. Ben's stability is grounded in Whistle's mission and in the people he works with who have become like family to him.

Ben now understands why his mother ran around like crazy. There was a thrill in making an idea—whether that be an event or a physical product—come to life. That thrill came with a lot of peril when sales were low or when employee morale was down. What Ben came to appreciate was how his mother handled the downtime when she decided not to work. Her time outside of work was a chance to recharge and reconnect with the things in life that truly matter: family. Watching his mother in this capacity gave Ben the opportunity to appreciate the journey he's been on that much more.

CHAPTER 9

I'VE GOT YOUR BACK, YOU'VE GOT MINE

RELISHING THE GRIND

Entrepreneur: Tom Coburn
Age: 26
Hometown: Hopkinton, Massachusetts
Company: Jebbit, the world's first declared data platform, giving enterprise brands the power to treat each customer as the individual they truly are through personalized marketing

Tom Coburn was furious when he realized he was locked out of his e-mail. As CEO, he wanted to get back to work. The company was in desperate need of financing, and Tom was responsible for venture capital fundraising. But Jonathan, his cofounder, had prevented him from doing so. He felt it would be best for the company, for Tom, and for their friendship if Tom took some time and space away from work so that he could grieve his father's death.

"I gave Jonny my passwords so he could access my emails while I was with my family immediately after my father's death," Tom remembers. "I was crying every day with my family, but it got overwhelming after a few days. I got antsy, and I called Jonny after I couldn't log on to the system. He wouldn't tell me the new passwords because he made a deal with our investors that I couldn't come back for at least three weeks. I was furious at the time. We were in the middle of fundraising, and we had three months of capital left. He blocked me from working those three weeks because my mother and sisters needed me to get through this difficult time."

Reflecting on that moment, Tom shares, "Jonny made it very clear that our friendship and my well-being were more important to him than the business. He could have easily said to come back given our fundraising crunch. But Jonny rallied the entire team where everyone picked up extra work to continue on as business as usual. This was what was best for me, and Jonny handled it."

Tom originally met Jonathan, an incoming freshman, when he interviewed him for the Shaw Leadership Program at Boston College. Tom was a junior who had recently won a business plan competition. He was looking for fresh recruits to help him build this marketing technology platform. His ears perked up when he heard that Jonathan had also won a high school business plan competition. After the interview, he asked Jonathan if he wanted to collaborate with him on his idea. Jonathan initially rebuffed his offer because he already had a business idea. Jonathan's attitude changed a few months into school when his cofounder left, and he started looking to invest his time in another venture.

Tom took a blitzkrieg approach to building his team. He signed up fifteen students to work on the venture and then he had all of them work with intense focus for a few days so that he could see who would last until the next task was assigned. There was natural attrition as some students petered out, while others, such as Jonathan, came back asking for more. This was how the foundation of Jonathan and Tom's friendship was built.

"I just assumed there would be rock stars, some good folks, and some students not a fit," Tom explains. "It was probably one of the best decisions I made to run it this way. Some faded out, a bunch of them did a solid job, like my buddy who was running accounts, and Jonny, he just outperformed all of them by 100x. He would email on Friday morning, and say, 'Instead of going out, let's lock ourselves in the library and get a bunch of work done.'

And I said, 'Fuck yeah, let's do it.' That was more than I could say about my two cofounders."

Tom, Jonny, and a few other students spent the entire academic year building the business. Summer came and decisions had to be made about who was going to stay on. Tom's cofounders decided to take summer internships in banking instead of working full time on the startup. While they promised to work on it nights and weekends, it was unrealistic to assume they would have any free time given the daily grind of banking. Tom wanted commitment. Jonny stepped up and approached to work on the business full time during the summer. Tom had no money to pay him, so they agreed on a commission structure and Jonathan would stay at Tom's apartment for free.

That summer was a grind. They held to the same routine every single day: wake up; do P90X, their fitness routine; head over to the Boston College campus and grab a room. The campus was completely empty and they seemed to be the only ones there as they sent out thousands of emails to potential marketing prospects. They sent out so many emails that both Google and Facebook suspended their accounts for suspicious online behavior. It wasn't glorious. It was all brute force as they tried to become a relevant marketing service.

"We celebrated two things," Tom remembers, "One was

getting a response. We stopped what we were doing whenever we got a response and gave each other a high five. Two was getting a call set up. When we got a call set up, it was a huge deal. We stood up, jumped, and then ran around the room. Once we progressed a few months into the summer, in August, I looked at the calendar, and we had calls lined up for the entire day. That was cool, and I was going to wake up, get in at 7 a.m., and at 9 a.m. our entire day was filled with calls. That summer was when Jonathan went from top employee to this is the guy that I want to run the company with."

Tom loved the intensity and the grind of that summer. Hard work led to real results. It reminded him of when he spent summers playing golf with friends in high school. Tom had turned to golf in fifth grade after he realized that he couldn't compete in basketball and football because of his size and height. Golf soon became an obsession for Tom and two of his best friends.

They spent every summer perfecting their game. They would hit the golf course at 6 a.m., play eighteen holes in the morning, have lunch, and then play another eighteen holes in the evening. One of their dads would be waiting at the last hole after dark and take them home. They would all sleep over at one friend's house and reflect on the day. The next day they repeated the cycle all over again. Nobody complained about the early wake-up time. They used each day to get better than the last.

"After our round, in the car we talked about who played well today, who played poorly today, and what we needed to work on," Tom recalls. "So for example, I would say, 'I drove the ball really well today but I could not putt. My irons were awesome today but I couldn't drive the ball.' That gave us the plan to direct us for the next day. We also had conversations about random interviews we watched from Tiger Woods or tips we learned from the Golf Channel."

Tom's goal was to make the varsity high school golf team, which was super competitive. Keegan Bradley, who later became a top golfing pro, had only been number three on the varsity team. The team was setting every record in the state by winning tournament after tournament. Practice paid off for Tom and his two friends as they made the cut as freshman and eventually became captains during their senior year.

Playing golf benefited Tom in several ways. First, it gave him mental toughness. He didn't have the most natural ability but he had the willpower to fight through a bad hole and come back strong in the next round. Second, it gave him a visible path to seeing how his hard work translated into tangible results, i.e. making the varsity team. Finally, it gave him a sense of what camaraderie looked like. He and his teammates were all pulling for each other to succeed. Tom's summer with Jonathan was the same way. They were in this venture together, building something bigger than themselves.

At the end of that summer, Tom and Jonathan had a difficult decision to make. They had created a ton of momentum setting up the company, which they didn't want to lose. During the fall semester, they kept working on the business and raised $250,000. Once the fall semester was over, they decided to quit school and focus full time on the business. It was a risky decision, but the right decision as they both believed that their company would succeed. They became even closer during the early years of the business. Tom's family adopted Jonathan as one of their own and invited him to join their holiday gatherings in Boston since Jonathan's family was in Ohio.

The most difficult period that tested their friendship and the business was the death of Tom's father. Jonathan still remembers, "I was in my hotel in New York City. I was with my girlfriend. It was Valentine's Day. We had gone to New York to celebrate. Tom called. It was that moment where everything came to a halt around me. We tried to pack, and I had a suitcase in my hand as we were moving to a different hotel. I was in shell shock."

After a few days, Jonathan collected himself. He had received a lot of advice from their board about how to handle such a difficult situation. The goal was to keep the team calm and focused while being completely transparent about what was happening. He wanted to use this opportunity for the team to come together by embracing what was going on instead of avoiding an uncomfortable situation. This approach was not forced. It was a natural outgrowth of how Tom and Jonathan had built the team—as a reflection of their friendship over the years.

In fact, everyone on the team attended the funeral. "After the funeral services, the entire team came back to my house," Tom remembers. "It was something that my dad really loved to have people just come over. There was three feet of snow already on the ground. We dug a fire pit that twenty people could sit comfortably around on benches. That was such an amazing balance between sorrow and outpouring of love and having fun and telling good stories and remembering good times. We kept it going for nine hours until about 11 p.m. That was an amazing experience. It was a day that I will remember for my entire life. It was a testament to Jonny who knew what I needed then and thereafter to make me feel whole again."

FINDING AN ENTREPRENEURIAL RHYTHM THROUGH JAZZ

Entrepreneur: Chris Altchek

Age: 29

Hometown: Westchester, New York

Company: Mic, the leading digital news company, reporting on the most important issues and diverse perspectives that challenge conventional thinking and give voice to the underrepresented

Jazz became an obsession for Chris Altchek in high school. At age ten, he learned to play the saxophone. It wasn't until he met Jake that he was pushed to really *play* the saxophone. He and Jake happened to be two of the best players in the high school jazz band. The teacher paired them together so that they would challenge each other to get better. It was competitive, but the competitive spirit drove them to realize their potential as individual performers as well as a team.

Chris remembers the intensity of their practice sessions: "We practiced up to six hours a day. Jake and I share the ability to grind that a lot of people don't have. Our teacher would give us four measures of a 6-minute Charlie Parker solo to learn. It was not a lot, but he expected them to be perfect. Through that, Jake and I appreciated the intensity and focus required to get something done. That cycle of intensity lasted four more years during high school. After that, Jake and I were on the same page. If I said I was going to do something or he was going to do something, there was never a doubt on what approach we were going to take. If we were going to get it done, we were going to get it done."

Jazz set the foundation for Chris and Jake's friendship. Their practice routine brought them together every day and music became another language for them to communicate in. They understood each other's musical styles and preferences so intimately that they didn't need sheet music to follow. They could improvise without losing each other.

Chris readily admits that Jake was the more talented musician. "I was not as good as Jake. Raw talent-wise, I wasn't there. I spent as much time on it as him, but he was far better than me." That realization did not dissuade Chris from continuing to practice and perform. The quality of their performances improved, and soon, they were booking local wedding gigs and bar mitzvahs. They even managed to book a regular Sunday-night performance at Cleopatra's Needle on the Upper West Side, a huge coup for a high school jazz combo.

Money started to flow in from these gigs. Chris oversaw the business side and sought out opportunities for them to gain exposure at bigger venues, while Jake drove the creative side of their performances. They complemented each other because, as Chris explains, "We both listened to each other's input. For our biggest gigs, he shared what songs we would be playing, which was ultimately his call. He would ask what I thought and I'd weigh in but he would decide. On the business issues, figuring how much we were going to get paid for this gig and who was going to get paid what, that was always my call. We trusted each other because we would look out for each other. As we have grown our relationship, we have been in very few run-ins where a disagreement lasted longer than a conversation."

By junior year, the high school band booked a gig at B.B. King Blues Club & Grill, a famous jazz venue in New York City. Armed with this confidence, Chris and Jake performed on larger stages at Prospect Park and Shea Stadium. Their friendship evolved outside of their music routine, often when they were in the car together driving to a performance. Music from the radio was often just the backdrop for the discussions they would have about current world and local events. Both were respectful of each other's opinions, and they could respectfully disagree on topics without holding a personal grudge.

Their relationship was tested when they fell on opposite sides of the debate around the invasion and war in Iraq. Chris explains, "Jake had a lot of conviction around it and organized a walkout from class the day before the war. I was on the opposite side. We would be driving from the Bronx to Newark for a show, and we would have an hour and a half, and we would be debating. We didn't have smartphones to scroll through Instagram for an hour. We would hash it out, and it was more high school kids trying to show who was smarter. Even though the stakes weren't very high, there was nothing to lose."

Chris continues, "It set the foundation for talking about things that we don't agree with without a lot of tension. There was very little tension in our relationship, which was very lucky. We can give each other feedback, and it is not intense. We can talk about tricky things that most founder relationships don't have because they don't have fifteen years of history together. Ultimately, Jake was right about the war, but never rubbed it in. It was always and continues to be a healthy discussion that didn't scar our friendship."

Starting a company never crossed Chris' mind growing up. He was surrounded by doctors, lawyers, and bankers who were extremely successful but had chosen structured career paths. At Harvard, Chris had classmates who became entrepreneurs, which planted the seed in his head that he could pursue a similar path. After graduation, he ended up getting an investment banking job at Goldman Sachs. He and Jake had remained friends throughout college and after graduation.

Their continued debates cemented their shared conviction

that the current state of news journalism didn't reflect how their generation consumed media. They decided to do something about it and launched an online news platform, *Mic*, to uncover meaningful stories that would resonate with a younger, millennial audience. The path to producing high-quality news journalism, however, has not been easy.

"When we first started, we were so resource constrained," Chris explains. "It was really about survival and just getting to the next leg. After we got to the next leg, we were able to fulfill our mission more and more, but we didn't fully know that it would happen from the outset. Building a trusted journalism operation that was fully resourced to go find and tell the truth and deal with the consequences was an expensive proposition. We had to build a business around it to support it. As the business has grown, we can invest more in truth-telling. We were lucky to stay true to what we wanted to do, and we continue to see the vision become more real. It could have taken a different turn, though, one way or another."

One of the biggest inflection points for *Mic* was landing an interview with President Obama in August of 2015. The presidential team selected *Mic* as the platform for the President to get his message out to the millennial community. They had five days to prepare for the interview. While Jake prepared for the actual interview, Chris helped organize all of the company resources to focus on this big moment.

His initial instinct was to get everything done in a cost-efficient manner. As Chris explains, "I sat down with one of our board advisors. He reviewed our plan and said it sucked. This was the moment for *Mic* where everyone should work twenty-four hours a day until it was published, where we would make sure this was the best thing *Mic* ever did. We could no longer check the boxes and spend as little resources as possible. We needed to make sure to have the proper people to in place—even if we had to hire someone—to make a ton of noise. That flipped the switch for me."

Their total focus on this experience paid off for *Mic*. "Jake was able to field questions from young people in Iran, which is really hard to do, given the political climate there," Chris shares. "We created an iPad experience for the President, and we showed up with six movie-studio cameras with additional wide-lens cameras to get the feel for the shoot. The White House said that they never saw anyone shoot with those kind of cameras, and the secret service had to do three to four checks on it. The graphics and the way we cut the interview turned out to be much better than *CNN*'s interview with the President later on in the day. Then we distributed it, and it was the highest-level work we've ever done at *Mic*. And that was a new benchmark for the kind of work we do."

Chris and Jake have built *Mic* into a powerhouse media company. Their paths rarely overlap. Jake is out traveling to uncover great news stories, while Chris is crisscrossing the country and building out the publication's operational infrastructure. Their friendship still remains steadfast, and when they do find time together, they will often default back to what started their friendship in the first place by enjoying a local jazz performance.

PLANTING THE SEEDS OF AN IDEA

Entrepreneur: Nikhil Arora
Age: 28
Hometown: Oakland, California
Company: Back to the Roots, a mission-based company that wants to redefine the future of food (a mission they call "Undo Food") by developing ready-to-grow indoor gardening kits and ready-to-eat organic cereals and snacks

During a lecture on sustainability at the University of California, Berkeley, the professor mentioned to his class of 150 students that mushrooms could be grown from coffee grounds. It was a throwaway fact. Nobody stopped the professor with any follow-up questions as he transitioned to covering other topics. But two students, Nikhil Arora and Alejandro Velez, couldn't get that fact out of their heads. They didn't know each other at the time, but they each emailed the professor separately to find out more about using coffee grounds to grow plants. Their shared curiosity eventually brought them together to start Back to the Roots, a business founded on their friendship and love for each other.

The professor didn't have additional information about mushroom farming from coffee grounds, so he connected his two students. Nikhil went over to the Beta Theta Pi fraternity house to meet with Alejandro, who also goes by Alex. They were both college seniors in their last semester and had jobs lined up after graduation. This was the first time their paths had ever crossed. Starting a company was not part of either of their plans. But they were both fascinated with the potential of growing mushrooms out of coffee grounds.

They went straight to YouTube to find videos on how to do it. After five hours of searching, they learned a lot about growing mushrooms but not how to do so out of coffee grounds. They became obsessed with making this idea a reality. After a few weeks, they were tired of researching. They were ready to get their hands dirty and see the results for themselves. Beta Theta Pi became their home base for the next three months.

"We turned his fraternity kitchen closet into this science experiment, and we planted mushrooms in ten paint buckets filled with coffee grounds we had gathered from local coffee shops like Peet's Coffee," Nikhil explains, "We planted them and then left for spring break. When Alex came back, he started screaming over the phone to me, 'You have to see this, you won't believe it!' It turned out that nine out of the ten were completely contaminated and had nothing growing. But there was one that had these beautiful mushrooms growing in it."

They were so proud of their accomplishment. It didn't matter that the other buckets were contaminated. They were blind to these failed attempts. They had the validation they needed to keep going. They were so exhilarated by this accomplishment that they walked around Berkeley with a bucket full of mushrooms—door-to-door mushroom sales. They didn't have an appointment anywhere.

Their first stop was Chez Panisse, the acclaimed organic restaurant opened by Alice Waters, where the chef agreed to sauté their mushrooms. The chef and Alice tasted them and said they were delicious. This gave them confidence to continue on to their next stop, Whole Foods. They explained their story to the first employee they saw near the product section, and soon had a small crowd of team members standing around, curious about their bucket. They connected them with Randy, the regional produce coordinator for Whole Foods in Northern California, and he loved what he saw. Their sustainable, locally-grown mushrooms fit with Whole Foods' greater mission of bringing healthy and delicious foods to their customers in a sustainable way. Randy was convinced that the national chain of Whole Foods, not just the NorCal stores, would get behind their concept if they could farm mushrooms on a predictable production schedule.

Nikhil and Alex applied for a small chancellor's grant from the university for $5,000. Once they were awarded the grant, they purchased a van for $1,000 and rented a warehouse on the outskirts of Oakland at a hundred dollars a month. Their commitment to working on this business idea was also a commitment to each other. They were in it together. "We had a lot of momentum those three months before graduation and were having a blast working together," remembers Nikhil. "And we turned to each other, and we decided we had to do this together."

Despite the recession in 2008, they notified their respective employers that they would be forgoing their offers and instead pursuing a food startup opportunity. At Nikhil's college graduation in May 2009, the chancellor told the class to embrace the future and then made a joke about two kids trying to grow mushrooms. "Alex and I looked at each other, and we gave each other the expression of what did we get ourselves into?" Nikhil recalls. They were about to find out as the next eight months tested their burgeoning friendship and commitment to becoming full-fledged mushroom farmers.

Having very little money, Nikhil moved in with his older brother, Arjun, cofounder of Retargeter, and slept on a broken futon, while Alex continued to live at his fraternity. Every morning, Nikhil and Alex awoke at 5 a.m. to head out for their early morning coffee grind runs. The process was physically taxing. The bags of grinds were often very heavy, so they parked as close as they could to the coffee house without blocking traffic. They rushed to retrieve these bags and throw them in the back of the van. Then they hopped back in and drove to their next destination.

The work was dirty and messy, particularly when they received bags that combined all organic waste. They had to manually separate the coffee grounds from half-eaten muffins and croissants. After separating the coffee grounds, they had to dry them through a specialized presser before planting them. It was an all-day affair that often ended at 1 a.m. after they finished cleaning the facility for the next cycle. It wasn't until four months in that they were able to grow a mushroom. All previous attempts failed.

"We were collecting thousands of pounds of coffee grinds between five to nine in the morning in these just dirty, heavy trash cans," Nikhil details, "We would come back and plant the entire day. You start to hope that things start growing with each batch, which is a three-week cycle. Batch after batch, there was no growth. Our biggest takeaway was that despite the grimy early mornings and the repeated failed batches, we still had a blast doing it together. We were just laughing and had such a fun time working together, blasting music. We got to know each other so damn well from all of that."

Nikhil and Alex didn't give up because they believed in each other and in their cause. Others believed in them as well. They had supporters across the community from that first chef at Chez Panisse to their cheerleader at Whole Foods, who kept inquiring about their progress because they wanted to share their mushrooms with their customers. "To them, it was a one-second task, but for us, it served as two months of motivation," remembers Nikhil. Their motivation was fueled by their first sale of 3.14 pounds of mushrooms for just over thirty dollars. Even though it was not much money, it validated their seed of a business, which grew like wildfire once they figured out how to successfully repeat the production process.

Back to the Roots' mushrooms has become a popular and sustainable source of food for local restaurants in the Berkeley area. Along the way, they also found a market for kits that kids and adults alike can take home and use to grow their own mushrooms from coffee grounds. Their business has become more than just mushrooms; it is about sparking a movement to get people excited about growing their own food and knowing where what they eat comes from. Building this business pushed them to learn about other food categories like stone-ground corn, which they developed into a cereal product, and aquaponics, which they used to develop their Water Garden.

While their business is about sustainable food, the core of their brand is about discovery. Back to the Roots has gone from selling their indoor gardening kits and organic cereals in a couple farmers markets and Whole Foods stores to nationwide outlets like The Home Depot, Target, and Amazon, as well as distribution at thousands of public schools. The team wants to help their customers connect back to the roots of where their food is coming from.

The journey of discovery is the experience that Nikhil and Alex want to share with their customers because they went through a similar kind of journey. Their friendship, formed through "pouring our heart into this one little thing," Nikhil says, is what keeps the business going. Nikhil refers to Alex as his soulmate. After spending time with Nikhil, I could tell his relationship with Alex went beyond just best friends or even family. They were destined to find each other and do something that nobody else had done before.

CHAPTER 10

LOVE LETTERS FROM ABROAD

THE LOAN COLLECTOR

Entrepreneur: James Beshara
Age: 31
Hometown: Dallas, Texas
Company: Tilt, a crowdfunding platform that allows groups and communities to collect, fundraise, or pool money online (acquired by Airbnb in February 2017)

Only six days after graduating from college, James Beshara headed to South Africa. He had studied developing economies and wanted to apply his textbook knowledge to the real world. So he lined up a job at a microfinance foundation that gave out loans to impoverished families. Originally, he was assigned to analyze reconciliation and repayment of loans. But soon, his tall stature became an asset to the foundation. They assigned him to collect loans out in the field. As one of his co-workers explained to James while laughing, "When they see someone white in the townships knocking on doors, they say, 'Oh fuck, this shit is serious.'"

As a loan collector, James had to knock on the doors of families who had defaulted on their loan payments. It wasn't exactly the role he had pictured taking on when he came to South Africa. He realized that reading about these slums was a lot different from actually being in them. The townships were some of the most dangerous neighborhoods in the world. He even had a body guard who accompanied him, but he was still the one knocking on doors and going into each home to speak with the delinquent customers.

As instructed, he brought along a video camera to document any collateral he noticed that the foundation could repossess if the family didn't pay back the loan. In reality, most homes didn't have anything worth taking that was anywhere near the amount of the loan owed. In fact, the video camera didn't even have batteries in it. Most of the houses were no bigger than 150 square-feet and looked like they had been built from matchbooks stacked up against each other. The walls were made of sheet metal while the ground was dirt. Having the camera present was just another psychological tactic that the foundation suggested to help improve loan repayment rates.

"I just knocked on the door, looked at the loan repayment sheet, saw how much they owed, and went into the house and pretended to take pictures," James remembers. "I asked for them to pay the amount they owed by a certain date. I would then ask why they hadn't yet paid. Everyone had a story. You get lied to so much that you didn't know what was true and what wasn't. I had to disconnect myself from caring too much about the stories because I needed to further the mission of the foundation. Repayment of a loan resulted in another ten families who the foundation could help."

The impetus to go to South Africa came from James' academic interest in the role that technology can play in developing economies. During his senior year, he wrote a business plan for a lending concept that could be applied in South Africa. He figured that landing a real job first could help him transition into life there and give him a cushion before starting up his venture idea. Several months as a loan collector quickly drained him, and he started to put his business plan into place.

Going to South Africa was a huge risk for James. But he had seen how his brother, twelve years his senior, slaved away as an investment banker. He worked 90 hours a week for a high-paying salary. As James explains, "Once you are on the train, you are on it for a while." But James didn't want to be his brother. If he was on a train, he thought that it might as well be something crazy. South Africa felt right.

The concept he came up with was a crowdfunding platform that channeled dollars to families and individuals looking for a personal loans, which he named Dvelo. It became one of the first crowdfunding platforms focused on personal loan exchanges in the developing world. The SEC had not yet set regulations on crowdfunding because the concept was so new. He was cognizant of this risk, but he wanted to test his thesis that crowdfunding could help impoverished families. He went through several potential cofounders until one of his friends from back home in Texas moved out to South Africa to help build the site. They worked on it for twenty straight months and started to gain traction just when the SEC put more restrictions in place for online lending.

James knew these regulations were coming, but he didn't know the form they would take. The regulations severely hampered the amount of capital that could flow through their platform. He had previously targeted transferring up to $100 million in loans, but the new regulations limited them to managing $1 million total. "We had adjusted emotionally for the change, but we didn't know just how much the regulation was going to change the business and the model," James says, "When it was announced and we read the new regulations, it was a kill shot to our approach and model. It took the wind out of the sails for the viability of what we were building."

James continues, "After twenty months of willing this startup off the ground, I was just exhausted. On top of the ground moving beneath me, the experience of starting this nonprofit was just wrong, from how I brought on a cofounder and friend who had very similar skills to me, to how I handed out equity, to how we were living close to the organizations we were working with but very, very far from the resources we needed to gather around us to build out our idea. I didn't maximize for financial returns. I wanted to do something that I loved. But in this case, the regulation was the final straw that really broke the model. At the time, it was pretty heartbreaking."

This experience overseas was a chance for James to get outside the bubble of college. He found out that things in the real world are a lot different than things in the class-room. James sums it up in a few words: "Holy crap, this was hard." The experience didn't deter him from starting up another company, though. In fact, South Africa was where he got his inspiration for his next venture, Tilt.

Despite relatively impoverished conditions, the majority of South African citizens have Android phones that they're tethered to twenty-four seven. This only hit James when he was waiting in line at a BBQ joint in South Africa in 2010 and noticed the person ahead of him looking something up on Google. "Here I was, a kid from Texas. But I had lived there long enough to decipher different socioeconomic classes. The person in front of me had very little in terms of Western possessions," he remembers. "But that didn't matter. He had the world at his fingertips because his cell phone was glued to his hand. It reminded me of this Einstein quote that the only thing that you need to know in life is where the local library is. Now, thanks to Google, there were 2 to 3 billion people who had this infinite library in the palm of their hands. This eighteen or nineteen year old ahead of me, with his Android phone, had more information in his pocket than the President of the United States had twenty years before. It was an incredible aha moment for me to recognize the power of technology in the context of international development."

Another pivotal moment for James was receiving advice from a local entrepreneur. "That entrepreneur said to me, trust and a network are the two most important things of significance," he recounts. "One is worthless without the other. You can have trust but it is pretty worthless if you have a network but nobody trusts you. And just as important, if you didn't have integrity or were not reliable, you might have a great network because you went to a fantastic school but it was equally as worthless."

The entrepreneur's words stuck with him because he was always looking for phrases that he could incorporate into his way of thinking. This was a trait he developed from his father who has a list of thirty-five principles that governed how he approached life. His father ingrained the practice of defining specific principles to live and work by into him from a very young age. For example, his father tested and rewarded him if he was able to recite the principles from memory.

"He would recite the first part of the principle, 'life is a cinch,' and I would finish it by saying 'by the inch.' He would say, 'Life's hard,' and I would say 'by the yard.' He would break things down into simple parts with the idea that these steps lead to accomplishing great things. It made it a game for us, and it was something to do. Looking back, it was so simple, and it was a game we'd play while driving in the car, while I was eight and nine years old. But like a compass, it's a really simple tool but makes all the difference in determining if you end up where you set out to travel or not. These principles had that effect on him, and looking back, the list of principles probably have had an outsized impact on me as well."

James continues, "Where I differ from him—his list is all about inputs with the output, with the result left ambiguous. Like a compass without a clear destination. My view on it is that it leaves you hanging. What are these inputs for? What is the outcome you are going to achieve? A leader starts from the future and works backwards. A manager starts from today and works forwards. For the leader, you have to understand what the outcome is and work backwards. For me, it's not about thirty-five inputs. It's more, how do I visualize what the outcome is that I want and work backwards from that? The compass plus the long-term destination. I'm sure I will try to impart wisdom in similar ways to my own children, and my hope will be that they similarly respond with something like, 'Well, that's a good foundation, but I'd like to improve it further in my own way too.'"

James lived in South Africa for two years. He started Dvelo but then closed it down. It was time for him to return back home. He didn't start his next venture until he decompressed and reflected on his journey abroad. The experience had planted the seed for Tilt, a mobile-based crowdfunding platform that was for-profit and for the entire world, not just nonprofits. Tilt was a chance to attack the world with eyes wide open and use what he had learned abroad to build a new platform with an improved plan on his own home turf. In 2017, James and his cofounder sold Tilt for over $50 million to Airbnb, and he is quick to say that, "It's hard, if not impossible, to embrace the heartbreak and failure while it's happening, but if I were to add a thirty-sixth principle, it would be that every path to success goes through failure."

Entrepreneur: Philip Cohen
Age: 34
Hometown: Levittown, Pennsylvania
Company: AudioCommon, a team of musicians and hackers redefining the way music is created, organized, and shared in today's connected world

Philip Cohen put down his weapon and removed his armor to greet the Afghan colonel. He hugged and kissed him as was Afghan custom. At twenty-four years old, Philip was a first lieutenant in the US military and in charge of a 300-person unit in the heart of Kabul, the capital of Afghanistan. His role was to appropriate, direct, and allocate resources to help build the country's military infrastructure. As a high-ranking official, he was a target. He was told to wear a flak vest wherever he went and keep his weapon at the ready.

The Afghan Ministry of Defense, where they were meeting, was considered a safe zone, but soldiers should never let their guard down. Philip made a conscious choice to disarm himself in order to build trust. He had to make himself vulnerable to get the colonel to see that he was serious about building an authentic relationship. Philip knew the colonel was the key to creating a successful partnership. He could garner resources on his side, but he couldn't tell the colonel what to do. His predecessors had tried and failed to broker a deal to get funding for a joint-military training program.

His approach paid significant dividends for both parties. The colonel went through his channels, while Philip went through his. They would meet somewhere in the middle when both parties agreed to the parameters of the training program. Philip and his Afghan counterpart built the trust necessary to bring a $63-million program to life when previous attempts had completely failed.

Their relationship extended beyond this official diplomatic mission. "The colonel was an amazing guy," Philip says, "He listened to me. He cared about me. We cried together. One of his guys got blown up in a suicide attack. I went to their ministry of defense and cried with all of their guys. It was a terrible moment, but it showed that we had a relationship that was deeply personal."

Philip's approach to coalition building was much different than his predecessors, who instead saw an obstinate Afghan coalition refusing to cooperate. What Philip saw was war-hardened veterans who had fought the Russians in the past and sensed that they didn't want to be told what to do by fresh-faced Western soldiers. What they wanted was empathy and understanding for their situation, their culture, and their lives. Philip was able to embrace their traditions in a way that signaled he could be trusted, and that trust was reciprocated.

As a first lieutenant, Philip's main role was to serve as a military diplomat to the Afghan government and help them set up their own training facilities. There was one time, however, that he was called on to lead a convoy of soldiers from Kabul to Bagram. After being on the road for over an hour, he received word that Bagram Airfield, the convoy's destination, was under attack. He had to make the decision about whether to continue toward Bagram or turn back completely to avoid the potential gunfire.

"The first thing I thought was holy shit—I was leading this convoy to Bagram," Philip recounts, "We were about twenty minutes out. I had to make a decision that would affect the lives of the people in the convoy. I got a lot of pressure from my colleagues in the convoy, and the operations centers at Bagram and Kabul, to turn around and head back to Kabul. I remember doing my best to think clearly about the situation, trying to analyze my options, as we were flying down the road, heading directly toward Bagram. If we stopped, we'd be targets. If we slowed down, we'd be vulnerable as well. If we turned around, the convoy's mission would have been a failure. If we kept heading toward Bagram, we might encounter the enemy forces who were behind the attack."

"I called the operations center and asked for an intelligence update. Parts of Bagram were on fire from the rockets that had hit the base. I saw the plumes of smoke in the distance, and told the convoy to chamber rounds and be on the lookout. I needed to make a very difficult decision very quickly; and I had no idea if I was right or wrong. I decided to press forward, and we made it to Bagram without incident. When we showed up at the base, the gates were literally shut. Our convoy was vulnerable, so a number of our drivers were honking their horns while I was calling into the operations center."

"A few MPs opened the gate, and immediately after we entered into the compound and the bunker, a higher-ranking officer confronted me as I was getting ready to join the rest of the crew in the bunker. He started yelling at me, saying that my decision to press forward to Bagram was irresponsible and could have gotten us killed. He was shaking as he yelled, and spit flew out of his mouth. A colonel, who outranked both of us, overheard my colleague's words, came out of the bunker, and said, 'Back up, Captain. The Lieutenant made the right decision.' Intense and pressurized experiences like these put everything into perspective."

Seven years of active duty was enough for Philip to know that he didn't want a military career forever. It also gave him a rich portfolio of leadership experiences that he could bring to the corporate world. After his second deployment, he had fulfilled his commitment to the military and came home with the goal of going to business school. "My Afghanistan deployment was such a transformational experience. It showed me how short life was," he explains, "It made me only want to focus on what I wanted to focus on, which was very important in my decision to become an entrepreneur."

Before starting business school at MIT Sloan School of Management, Philip messed around with some music he had written while he was overseas. Music had been a way for him to find release from his main focus, whether that be his military training or playing junior hockey growing up.

Right before he started business school, Philip went to a neighborhood block party. He met someone who turned out to be a drummer, and they rented studio time to cut an album. That drummer, Chris, eventually became his technical cofounder, who by day was a software engineer. The two of them both loved music, but they were frustrated by how complex it was to create their album.

There were multiple stems—the musical inputs that go into a song—that had to be mixed and mastered separately, and it was hard to piece everything out separately. That experience became the foundation for how they started their company, AudioCommon, which they began working on as Philip started and progressed through business school.

Part of building a music startup is building relationships with artists. Philip and his team didn't have any relationships in the industry when they first conceived of this idea. They would go to concerts as fans, but there was no plan to make connections with the acts they saw on stage. A few weeks after seeing The Killers perform, Philip's wife, Jessica, suggested a way for him to connect with their manager. AudioCommon's lawyer went to BYU as did The Killer's manager, Robert Reynolds. Within minutes, an email was fired off to The Killer's manager from their lawyer asking for an opportunity to introduce the band to their company.

The manager wrote back within the hour saying that they were not interested. Most might have given up at that point. Philip was determined to showcase how their technology would benefit the band, just like how his strategy with the Afghan colonel had been to showcase his vulnerability. With a band like The Killers, sheer determination wasn't enough. At that point, Philip was a nobody in the music world. He had to prove himself all over again. He realized that besides their manager, the band's studio engineer, Robert Root, was also a key influencer in their decision-making process.

"Most people will never see the sleepless nights at the

early phase of starting a company," Philip recalls. "On a number of occasions, I made the trip out to Vegas, without a meeting on the calendar, just to make myself available. I figured they couldn't refuse a meeting with me if I was in town. I committed to staying there until they met with me."

"I remember a time when I had a meeting on the calendar with both the manager and the studio engineer [of The Killers]. The day of the meeting, both of them said they were unavailable. I was scheduled to leave Vegas the next day. I called my wife to blow off some steam as I was really upset. When I spoke with Jess, she said something to me that really gave me a moment of clarity. She said, 'Enjoy the ride while it lasts.' Times like these were very tough; but, when I look back at these moments, I knew I was alive and in the game, and—in a way—that feels really good, even when things are a bit uncomfortable. The next day, the studio engineer ended up meeting with me before I left Vegas, which helped formalize our relationship with the band. Very few people ever really see the sacrifice and commitment needed to make something like this happen."

Philip has forged tremendous relationships now with bands like The Killers and Switchfoot, who endorse AudioCommon's technology. Their endorsement is not a passive endorsement, but one based on the value and trust that was built through their relationship with Philip. He's spent full days with The Killers, setting up a studio, having meals with their families, and listening to new music. His approach has been no different than the one he took with the Afghan colonel.

The structure of the military demands physical and mental discipline to prepare for life or death outcomes. There is a strict chain of command that officers and soldiers must obey. Making tough decisions in tense, hostile situations, however, is not always so clear cut, and often creative solutions must be devised. Philip shares, "In the military, many of the fast-burners, the people doing really well, were the creative types. They were the artists who think outside of the box. They were the entrepreneurs who were doing a great job leading people in times of peace and in the combat theater. Ultimately, I learned that I needed to show empathy and garner the respect of my peers and subordinates who were working with me. It's really no different than leading a company; just a different context."

Philip's overseas military experience shaped his leadership ability as a cofounder of a tech startup. In Afghanistan, the stakes were higher. At times, it was truly life or death. As a startup founder, the stakes are still high, but a poor decision won't result in people dying. Still, Philip doesn't relent. He takes his role very seriously as a leader who needs to be accountable to those who have decided to invest their lives in his vision.

Entrepreneur: Neil Parikh
Age: 28
Hometown: North Brunswick, New Jersey
Company: Casper, a company created to reimagine sleep from the ground up, beginning with an obsessively engineered, outrageously comfortable mattress

That first day in Dharavi, the largest slum in Mumbai, India, was emotionally jarring for Neil Parikh, cofounder of Casper. In college, Neil and his classmate Anshu read about how many rural villages within India lacked clean water. Cities were tackling this problem, but underdeveloped urban areas lacked the resources to deliver this basic human need to its citizens. Instead of just reading about it, they wanted to do something.

They applied for and received a $5,000 grant from Brown University, where they were rising juniors, to set up a clean water filtration program in Dharavi. On the plane ride over, they were giddy with excitement and grand visions that they were going to change the world. It turned out the world was going to change them.

The abject poverty of the beggars filling the streets in Dharavi was startling. Neil turned to Anshu and asked, "What are we doing here?" They were outsiders and they felt like outsiders. Neil was a little concerned, even scared, that he had made the wrong choice to go there. It felt good to declare to all his friends that he was on this clean water mission while he was at Brown. They expected the community to embrace them because they came with clean water filtration resources. The reality was that they were the ones who needed to prove they were worthy of helping.

Every morning, he and Anshu woke up at 6 a.m. and made a game plan for the day, which often required adjustments throughout the day. A great meeting might turn into a referral with an influential community leader who would agree to meet only that day. Or a meeting might not happen at all because they couldn't get to it in time because traffic was so congested. When they reconvened at dinner, they talked about what they had learned and what they were going to do the next day. They were trying to integrate themselves into a community by being a part of it, which was a continual learning process of getting to know the right people who had influence.

This community-driven approach was preceded by a more commercially-minded focus. Originally, they thought they could sell the clean water tablets that they purchased at cost on the street. That initial focus was met with resounding skepticism. Neil recounts, "People were saying that we were out of our minds and asked what the hell were we doing? It was one of those truth-defining moments when we realized we had no idea what we were doing, but as long as we had good intentions, we became a magnet for people wanting to help us out."

Even though this initial approach, and multiple other approaches, failed—including opening up a retail store to sell water filtration systems—their persistence is what got them noticed. Many other foreign volunteers had come and gone, but Neil and Anshu kept coming back. This caught the attention of a local community leader who owned a bustling stationery business in the center of town.

He had avoided Neil and Anshu for couple months after they first arrived at the beginning of summer. However, once they opened a retail shop, it showed the community leader how serious Neil and Anshu were about helping the community. Inviting them to his home was his way of showing them respect. Meeting with the local community leader gave them an unspoken blessing to work with the rest of the community. Dharavi needed help, but it needed help in a way that followed its own set of rules, not the rules of outsiders.

Before this expedition, Neil equated poverty with unhappiness. Families as large as six people subsisted on less than sixty dollars a month and cramped in rooms the size of a New York studio. What he came to realize was that being impoverished didn't necessarily mean that they were unhappy. In fact, he found the opposite to be true.

These neighborhoods were actually full of life. They had a bazaar-like feel with everyone trying to sell someone something whether it was spices or fruit or water filtration systems. Neil concluded that the people he interacted with in the community were some of the most happy people in the world because they could live with so little and yet give so much.

One day during monsoon season, Neil got caught in a torrential downpour when the dirt pathway he was walking on gave way and he fell into a trench filled with garbage. His entire leg slid down and was encased in sludge. He was already soaked and miserable, but this incident caused him a mild panic attack. Out of nowhere, a bunch of kids, no more than six years old, came out with white cloths and clean water to help wipe off the sludge. "They had limited resources and were probably saving that clean water for themselves," Neil remembers, "It was one of the moments when people who don't have a lot to give, they choose to give."

Travel experiences have the power to change the way we see the world and our own place in it. Neil's travel might have started out as self-serving, but eventually it became selfless. His time in India became about helping others who eventually recognized him as one of them. This was what allowed their venture, Waterwalla, which still has a sustainable presence in India to this day, to incubate and fund local entrepreneurs who want to tackle the clean water problem in rural villages and urban slums.

More importantly, this experience grounded Neil. It made him more humble and more realistic about how he could impact the world because he understood how the world worked a little bit better. "I think the problem with myself and a lot of young people is that we think we know everything because everything is a Google search away," Neil shares. "This gives you a superhuman feeling. When you go to an environment where you don't know everything, it humbles you and makes you appreciate what you have."

Upon returning to Brown, Neil met Luke, his cofounder at Casper, in an entrepreneurship class. Their friendship blossomed as they both had a passion for exchanging and testing ideas. Luke founded a company that drove customers to restaurants during non-peak hours by offering discounts. Neil disliked the idea from the outset, but was proven wrong when Luke generated $20,000 from this venture, a large sum of money for a college student.

Even after Neil enrolled in medical school, he and Luke would still exchange ideas about potential startups. The summer in between his first and second year of medical school, Neil decided that he wanted to invest time into bringing a product to market. They homed in on creating a crowdfunding platform where ordinary investors would have access to startup capital. The JOBS Act had just passed in 2012, and they felt they could capitalize on a new wave of regulations that created more liquid capital markets.

A few weeks into building the product, they encountered too many strategic, technical, and regulatory roadblocks, which forced them to abandon the effort. The next idea they had was to build a backend social commerce platform to enable creators to open their own digital stores to sell products without having to worry about order-processing infrastructure. Neil decided to postpone medical school to work on this idea with Luke for close to a year and a half.

"My parents thought that I was crazy. My dad, in particular, didn't think this was the best idea. But I felt like I needed to pursue it. I didn't know if it was the right idea or not. What I did know was that I liked who I was working with and I felt like we were onto something big. I didn't want to look back and hate myself for doing this."

While the idea gained some market traction, the product didn't scale and their seed funding dried up. Neil was despondent. He considered returning to medical school. But an encounter with Philip, who also later became a cofounder at Casper, at a coworking space changed Neil's mind and persuaded him to try yet another idea.

Philip was known as the mattress king. He had been selling mattresses online since college. Neil learned from him that the industry was ripe for disruption as the product quality was poor, the sales practices lacked transparency, and the overall customer experience was confusing. Collectively, they felt they could reinvent the entire experience of purchasing a mattress online. Neil enlisted his friends Jeff, who had design experience, and Gabe, who had a technical background, to round out the team.

The team originally positioned their offering as mattresses for the millennial generation. As they evolved the concept, they saw that they could build a brand that aspires to be the world's foremost authority on sleep. It was a grandiose vision but one that was instilled with more purpose and meaning. It motivated the founding team while also attracting employees to join them.

"We refer to the Casper culture as a community," Neil says. "It's just like a village where you spend more time working than any other activity except sleep. We are very much a tribe where there are informal and formal leaders, where sometimes informal leaders are more powerful than formal leaders. Our community will continue to grow if we actively manage it and allow those to lead while having people come to their own conclusions."

"What we are trying to build here is a sense of community

where there is a shared sense of purpose. When you build a company, the role of the founders is to get people to row at the same time in the same direction on the same boat," Neil explains. "But we are not trying to mandate how to row and when to row. We want to build a community where the people here support each other emotionally, motivate each other, and are the ones that guide us to the north stars to where we are all going."

When Neil first started Casper, he put himself back in the frame of mind of that first day in Dharavi. Everything was new. He had to learn the local economy, iterate on the business model, and connect with the right influencers. This was the same approach he used when launching Casper, yet it was applied to a completely different industry.

"When we started Casper, I thought a lot about my India experience where I went in and thought that I knew everything, but I found out how little I really knew about the world," Neil concludes. "While the industry is different, the psychology of getting to a desired outcome is not so different. What do people fundamentally want and how do I deliver that to them? It has helped me be more confident in approaching this new industry because I was able to use the psychology of what I learned in India and apply it to this venture."

CHAPTER 11

COMING TO AMERICA

STICK-TO-IT-TIVENESS

Entrepreneur: Nelly Garcia
Age: 29
Hometown: Monterrey, Mexico
Company: Rocheli Patisserie, a bakery that specializes in novelty cakes, wedding cakes, and international pastries

On the plane ride from Austin to Miami, Nelly Garcia looked around and saw that all the other ladies had their *Cosmo* magazines out. She had brought a business book, *The Richest Man in Babylon*. She and eighteen other women, all Latinas except one, were headed to South Beach for a weekend bachelorette celebration in April 2015. There was palpable excitement in the air on the plane ride over, but Nelly kept to herself, content to read her book.

After checking into the hotel, the group of women convened to decide their party plan for the weekend. Mimosas were served and makeup was applied. A big night was ahead of them. Instead of getting ready, Nelly scooted over to the restaurant under construction next door. She wanted to see how it was laid out from the kitchen to the front of the house. Even though Nelly's body was in Miami, her mind was still on business.

That night she went out to the club with the ladies, but she was distant. She tried to relax and party, but she was thinking about her bakery business back in Austin, Texas. She was back at the hotel by 1 a.m. At 6 a.m. the next morning she got up to have breakfast according to her normal routine. Her day was just getting started when she saw her friends stumbling back to the hotel. She wanted to check out how other shops were set up in Miami and apply what she observed to her own business.

On this trip, Nelly realized that she had little in common with her friends anymore. Her priorities had changed when she started her business. She wanted to celebrate this happy occasion with friends, but her new set of priorities made it difficult to focus. Her friends tried to rope her into the weekend festivities but she resisted. She didn't identify with them anymore. "I was kind of sad," recalls Nelly. "I wasn't sure if I recognized them. And I am not sure if they recognized me. Are they wrong or am I wrong?

It was then I realized we had nothing else in common."
When they returned to Austin, Nelly said goodbye at the
airport—not realizing that that goodbye meant possibly
forever. She hasn't seen most of those women since.

Nelly was born and raised in Monterrey, Mexico. Her
father was a doctor but fashioned himself as an entrepreneur. He started his own business in the car resale market.
What started as a promising venture soured in the end.
He was unable to access capital to purchase more inventory, so the business collapsed. He tried to start another
business and risked the family's house as collateral. That
business failed as well, and the family was left homeless.
Food was hard to come by and many nights Nelly went
to bed hungry. The family had to make a change.

Nelly's family decided to move to the United States. They
already had visas, so they packed up their belongings and
moved to Austin in December 2003. Nelly waitressed for
seven months so she could contribute to her family. It
wasn't until August 2004, when Nelly was fifteen years
old, that she was able to enroll in high school.

She was excited about the first day even though she didn't
know anyone. She had seen movies that glamorized the
high school experience in America. She wanted a taste
of it herself. Her biggest takeaway that first day was that
everything was free: books, cafeteria food, classes, and

transportation. In Mexico, Nelly had to pay for everything herself. Here in Austin she had all of these resources at her disposal. She wasn't going to let it go to waste. For instance, she signed up for French class even though she had passed out of her foreign language requirement.

On weekends and after school, Nelly's father took her to the local Barnes & Noble. She and her dad would sit for hours flipping through magazines over cups of coffee. Her father steered her away from the novellas to business magazines. She sat and read the articles in *Forbes*, *Entrepreneur*, and *Inc.* for hours. One particular issue of *Entrepreneur* had a woman on the cover wearing a suit. Nelly didn't know who she was, but she wanted to be on a cover like that inspiring millions of women one day. She didn't realize that her father was preparing her to become an entrepreneur.

At Barnes & Noble, Nelly's father confided in her. "You can do anything you want," Nelly remembers him telling her, "You are a really smart girl and you aced school. But I want you to know something. I can't afford college for you. You have to pave your own way. You have to work at it if you really want it. You have to get good grades to get a scholarship. You just aren't going to have the economic support that others might have from their parents." Nelly was already a hard worker. She went to school from 7 a.m. to 4 p.m. After school she worked at a restaurant from 5 p.m. to 12 p.m. in order to support herself and her family. She did homework whenever she could in between school and her waitressing job. She was relentless in her path to achieve success.

Nelly explains, "I call it 'stick-to-it-tiveness.' It's not so much drive or ambition. When failures come, and things that don't go right, I've had a lot of those—you still believe in it and you still believe in yourself. If I fail 1,000 times, I still have the mindset that I will not accept failure because on the 1,001st time, it works. It didn't work, do it again. Just stick to it when things start to go bad."

Her resilience and persistence initially paid off. Nelly got straight A's and was in the top ten of her class despite the fact that English was her second language. She got into prestigious schools like Harvard but received no financial aid or scholarship offers. Nelly was devastated. She felt like the system had failed her, but she remembered that her life was much better in the United States than it had been in Mexico. She wasn't going to let this experience defeat her. "I was disappointed in the system, not in the effort that I had invested," explains Nelly. "I went to plan B, which was to enroll in community college for two years." After Nelly's student visa expired, she had to return back to Mexico where she looked for a job.

She found a job as an executive assistant at a company that

imported marble for kitchen countertops and floors but left after three months for a job that paid significantly less but had more opportunities to learn. Nelly worked directly with the owner, who took her under his wing and taught her the ins and outs of the import-export consumer goods business. She was able to travel with him and his team, and during a trade show in Chicago, he gave Nelly a piece of advice that she would never forget: "Most people talk about the beautiful parts of entrepreneurship. They don't tell you the hard parts. Some days, your family is going to be mad at you if you are not there. I just want to tell you this to prepare you for it because it can be very lonely."

After two years in Mexico, Nelly returned to the States because her father learned that he had cancer. To help pay for his chemotherapy treatment, Nelly got a front desk job at a local hotel. She worked while also spending time with her father at the hospital. Despite his deteriorating health, Nelly's father was still extremely spirited. "He was always asking how my day was," she recalls. "Whenever I had any doubts about my abilities, he would always pick me up. He was my biggest cheerleader." After a four-year battle with cancer, her father passed away.

Nelly was devastated, but she knew she needed to pursue her own dreams, as that was what her father would have wanted. She enrolled in community college to finish her degree. In her spare time, she started baking and posted her creations on Facebook. Friends started to ask her to bake cakes for their birthdays. At first she only charged for the cost of ingredients. As more inquiries came in, though, she started to charge more. She was doing cakes for all sorts of occasions, including weddings, birthdays, and anniversaries. Cakes symbolized key moments in people's lives.

"I baked a cake for a kid who never celebrated his birthday before because he had cancer since he was nine months old," recalls Nelly. "He never was able to celebrate his birthday. He was told for his sixth birthday that he was cancer free. His parents wanted to throw a huge birthday party for their child but they didn't have enough money for the cake. They asked me to provide them with the cake for free. I put a lot of effort into it. By the time I delivered it, the kid started crying. He thought it was such an amazing cake. There was so much emotion in his eyes. This was a moment that made me realize the effect of what I could do for people with my baking."

The business, Rocheli Patisserie, grew organically, and soon she was making more money than she made at the front desk of the hotel. Eventually she was able to focus on her cake business full time.

Her family initially embraced her new business. Everyone said they wanted the best for Nelly. Most of them, if not all of them, changed their attitude towards her once she received public attention and was on local television. "I would go to a dinner for someone's birthday, and someone might make the quip that they didn't think I had the time to come anymore because I was too famous," Nelly says. "They stopped asking me how the business was going or how the cakes were. They just stopped caring."

The resentment was particularly acute among Hispanic females because Nelly was going against the cultural norm of raising a family as her first priority. She understood where their mistrust came from, which made her sad because she knew this was the path she needed to follow. The advice her mentor had shared years before really sunk in during these moments of reflection.

Nelly uses a sports analogy to illustrate her point: "I thought that when somebody plays football and does what he dreams of and he scores the winning touchdown in a huge football game, everyone would be happy for him. That was what I thought would happen for me. But people did not like it. I had to go into hiding it and I didn't feel comfortable sharing my accomplishments on Facebook. When something good happens, I would rather just keep it to myself or share it with a limited number of people."

Despite these headwinds, she knew she was on the right path when she made it on the cover of *Entrepreneur*. It felt amazing to realize a childhood dream, but what was even better was seeing how her story inspired others she had never met pursue their own dreams. She got letters from all over the world, one in particular stuck out. "A woman from Africa sent me an email after she read my article," recounts Nelly. "She always loved to bake but didn't know that she could turn it into a business. After reading the article about me, she decided to start a cupcake shop."

Nelly continues to serve as an inspiration to others. "I speak at local high schools to encourage kids to go to college, be entrepreneurs, and don't give in to adversity. I have received so many letters from students who said their lives have changed from listening to my story and knowing that there is always hope at the end of the tunnel. I cherish those letters so much!"

Nelly wishes that her father was alive today so that he could see how far she has made it since the days when they were at Barnes & Noble browsing through business magazines. He was Nelly's number one supporter. "Whenever I had self-doubt of any kind, he would pick me up," she explains. "When I looked at other people who had more things like a new car or got married at a young age, I would question why those things were not happening to me. But he made me compare what I had with what they had. He always reminded me that I was doing something real with my life." And Nelly is doing something real. She is planning to open her first retail storefront in Austin in early 2018, an accomplishment that both she and her father can be proud of.

CRAMPED, COZY SPACES

Entrepreneur: Nadya Nguyen
Age: 24
Hometown: Moscow, Russia
Company: Hidrate, a smart water bottle that helps manage and track hydration goals

Quitting her job at Deloitte Consulting six months after graduating from the University of Minnesota left Nadya Nguyen with minimal savings. She had to live frugally in order to get by. She and her cofounders moved into the attic of a house in Kansas City so they could attend the Techstars accelerator program. Their business concept was a smart water bottle and app called Hidrate that measures and monitors water intake. The attic apartment had been vacant for a long time because the ceilings were low and sloped. One could easily bump their head if not careful. But they took the apartment because it was cheap and fit their budget.

There were two rooms, one with windows and one without that was actually a closet. They were improvising. Nadya pushed a mattress into the hallway every night and erected a cardboard box around her for privacy. She was used to small spaces because she had grown up in a tiny apartment in Russia with her grandmother, mother, and brother.

Nadya's parents immigrated from Vietnam to Russia when she was a baby. Similarly, they only had two rooms in their apartment, one for cooking and one for everything else. During the day the couches were pulled out for Nadya and her brother to do homework and for her mother and grandmother to relax. At night, one big mattress came out for the entire family to sleep on, except for her grandmother who had the most privacy in the kitchen. It was normal in Russia for families to be in such close living quarters with each other. Nadya rarely got flustered. It was just a natural way to live with her family.

Her father brought the family to Russia to start an import business. He sensed a market opportunity in Russia when it opened up its economy to the rest of the world, and he wanted to import domestic domestic goods to supply a market that lacked its own production capabilities. What Nadya's father didn't anticipate was the legal and political infrastructure that made it difficult for him to import goods. Ultimately, he made some poor business decisions that led to bankruptcy, so he fled the country without his family in 1998 because of the physical danger he was in due to outstanding debts.

Eventually, collectors started to show up at their apartment. Her mother turned off the lights, shut the curtains, and asked Nadya and her brother to hide. She had nothing to give the collectors. She offered them her car, but it was a no frills, run-of-the-mill Russian-branded LADA model. Rusty parts dropped to the ground like breadcrumbs when they drove it. The collectors refused the car as payment. That was the only time Nadya really ever noticed that her father was in trouble.

She didn't see her father for six years. Once he sent her a postcard from Hawaii. She knew her dad lived near the coast of China, and she asked him if his surroundings looked like the tropical coasts in the picture. She missed her father and wanted to find a way to relate to him.

When she opened up an email account in early 2000, Nadya was able to communicate with her dad more frequently. She asked when he was coming back home. He would usually say in a few months. Then a few months passed, and she asked the same question again. Her father gave the same response. The cycle continued until Nadya realized that he wasn't coming back any time soon. He wanted to come back but he lacked the resources to travel and if he did come back, he had to answer to his debt-collectors. He was putting all of his money into starting another business venture in China.

Meanwhile, Nadya's mother held the family nucleus

together. She worked multiple jobs to support the family. When she came home, she wanted to help Nadya with her homework but was too exhausted. As a compromise, Nadya and her mother would lie down on the couch together to do homework. Her mom was able to rest while helping her daughter learn.

Nadya finally did get a chance to see her father in 2004. They traveled from Moscow to a tiny town on the border of China. From there they flew to Shanghai to meet her father who greeted the family with flowers and tears. No words could express how Nadya felt in those first few minutes. She hadn't seen her father for six years. A mixture of emotions— elation, admiration, resentment—cycled through her. They went to dinner at 3 a.m., but it felt like 7 p.m. because the restaurant was packed. It was incredibly comforting for Nadya to reunite with her father in person instead of trying to build a relationship through email and postcards.

Her parents had always dreamed of living and working in the United States. Nadya's mom told her that Russia had limited career opportunities for her, especially as a minority woman. She didn't want Nadya to get stymied by a system that did not reward her hard work. Nadya was a superb student in school and was accepted to the University of Minnesota as an incoming freshman in 2008.

The campus was huge. In Vietnam and Russia, universities

had very few buildings that were designed only for classes. Nobody lived on campus. Nadya embraced her new life and made friends even though her English wasn't perfect. She signed up for different clubs like the Asian American student group and the TEDx campus chapter. She was a foreign student but she never felt foreign. The experience felt natural to her and she was excited to be there to take advantage of all the opportunities presented to her.

"I was never nervous. I was excited," recalls Nadya. "There were so many people on campus. I was not too shy making friends. English was a barrier but it wasn't that big of a barrier. I had trouble saying things, but all in all, I could understand what was going on. There were certain words that I didn't know. In one case, I went out to the laundry room and I forgot my detergent, and I tried to ask the girl for some of hers without knowing what the word was. It was funny—I just pointed at it and asked if I could have some of it?"

Nadya caught the startup bug while recruiting prominent speakers for TEDx. The first speaker she booked was a local entrepreneur who had passed up a corporate marketing job at Target to start his own company. This was when Nadya realized that she too could start a business. She sought out a summer internship in Silicon Valley and gained the confidence to start her own company, a virtual idea box where users could rank the quality of submissions. It never gained any market traction, so instead of pursuing it full time, she took a job at Deloitte Consulting after graduation.

But the startup bug continued to gnaw at Nadya. Her cofounders from the virtual idea box startup were disenchanted with entrepreneurship after they failed to get the venture off the ground. They had safe corporate jobs, but Nadya was determined to recruit them to start another venture together. She had an idea for a smart water bottle during the summer of 2014. She was so dehydrated that she almost passed out on the bus ride home. She looked at the landscape of smart water bottles and felt she could build a better product experience. Her former cofounders wouldn't quit their jobs to pursue another idea full time, but Nadya persuaded them to join her for a weekend startup competition. It was a risk-free way for them to work on an idea together without having to jeopardize the safety of their corporate jobs.

The weekend of the startup competition they built a Frankenstein-like prototype with a circuit board strapped to a Nalgene bottle. A hair tie pulled it all together. People came up to Nadya after the competition was over and told her they would buy the product. She gained confidence that she had a viable business idea and iterated on the idea on nights and weekends until she made enough progress to get accepted to the Techstars Boulder Accelerator. Then she gave her notice at Deloitte Consulting, the company that sponsored her visa. She believed in her concept enough to risk being deported.

What scared Nadya the most was sharing the news with her mom. She couldn't stop crying whenever she thought about breaking the news, but she knew at some point she had to tell her mom she had left her job. "My mother's only dream was for me to live and work in the United States," Nadya says. "Now that dream could disappear at any moment." She kept putting off sharing the news, but her mother was coming stateside soon for her younger brother's college graduation. She needed Nadya's employer's address for her visa application process. She kept asking until Nadya finally had to tell her that she was no longer at Deloitte.

Her mom was shocked. In that moment of silence, Nadya feared that her mom had a heart attack. But after composing herself, her mom asked a lot of questions. She listened and understood why Nadya took this path. It was her dream and also part of her heritage to risk everything that she worked for to achieve a bigger dream. Her mother saw this same entrepreneurial spirit in Nadya's father, who risked everything to create a better life for his family, even though it ultimately resulted in exile. That experience didn't deter him from starting new ventures. He started six different businesses after fleeing Russia, including his most recent business, an import construction concern in Vietnam. Out of anyone, Nadya's mother was the one who could understand that exile was part of the entrepreneur's gamble.

Nadya and her teammates released their product for sale in February 2016 after cycling through two accelerator programs, launching a successful Kickstarter campaign, and living in a cardboard box. She recognizes how far she has come but appreciates how far she still needs to go. What remains the same is her appreciation of what being here in the United States has allowed her to do, pursue, and accomplish. "All in all, I am extremely thankful for being able to be in America in the first place," exclaims Nadya. "No matter what the ups and downs are when running a startup, at least I am in America doing it." She is living out her parents' dream of pursuing a life in America and continuing to further her family's entrepreneurial heritage.

FINDING A NEEDLE IN A HAYSTACK

Entrepreneur: Idan Tendler
Age: 35
Hometown: Rishon LeZion, Israel
Company: RSA, the security arm of Dell, acquired Fortscale to become its security analytics platform

Finding a needle in a haystack. That was Idan Tendler's

specialty when he led a team in the elite military intelligence unit, 8200, in the Israel Defense Forces. He and his team sifted through mounds of data from various sources to find actionable pieces of intelligence. They were just twenty-year-olds when they entered into mandatory service. Youth was on their side because they thought anything was possible even if the odds were bleak. They complemented the tried-and-true techniques of field work intelligence gathering with new data-mining technologies that could, for instance, isolate a voicemail message at a particular time and location. They didn't have a choice but to succeed as it was a matter of national security to protect themselves from a pending threat.

When Idan first arrived at base camp, he was in shock just like the other recruits. The camp was in the middle of a forest. Above ground, things were peaceful. Below ground, the bunker was buzzing like a newsroom. Everyone was walking around with a purpose. There was a process in place for generating and acting upon intelligence, and technology was at the core of improving the quality of the intelligence. Idan's job was to report their findings to his superiors who could make actionable decisions in the field based on the intelligence.

Idan had joined this unit after he graduated at the top of his class. School was easy for him and he had been head of the student counsel. He liked it when he could organize the student body to block new construction proposed by his school's administration. He felt like he could lead, which is a skill he continued to hone in the military.

At a young age, he was put in charge of his unit's most important team. But there were no formal lines of authority. His role was similar to a director in a movie. He had to coordinate the actions of everyone around him through his own ability to persuade with insight and empathy. He improved the quality of intelligence gathering by improving the process of collecting the intelligence. His superiors noticed and granted him more responsibility and resources through a promotion. Leadership was something that came naturally to Idan. He was able to maintain a calm disposition in the face of potential crisis and chaos.

"We were brave enough to do stupid things," explains Idan. "We were not afraid to make mistakes. I had friends who missed important pieces of intelligence, and the result was people died from suicide bombs. It was their mistake. After such mistakes, we debriefed and understood what we did wrong and how we could improve it for next time. That's it. The tolerance for mistakes is extremely high. It is part of the job. It is part of Israeli culture. Part of the journey is making mistakes. Making mistakes forces learning. Learning forces us to get better and continue to experiment."

When Idan re-entered Israeli civilian life after his military service was complete, he decided to join the defense contract company Elbit Systems. The ex-commander of his unit was now a top executive and wanted Idan to lead a cybersecurity startup within Elbit. He thought Idan was well qualified to build a product from scratch in a growing market because he saw Idan lead in times of crisis. There was no doubt in this ex-commander's mind that Idan would find a way to get the job done, but this time in a corporate setting.

Idan was essentially given a blank canvas with which to create a new business within a bigger, pre-existing one. Three advisors, all twenty-five years older than him, came on board to help him understand the market.

In two years, he had seventy people working for him and the unit was generating millions of dollars of revenue. Despite this apparent success, he didn't feel as successful as he thought he should. In fact, he felt frustrated most of the time. The approval process was extremely slow in a corporate environment. He also didn't feel a sense of accountability for any of his actions. If the unit lost millions of dollars, it was a small blip on the corporate balance sheet that could be covered up. Idan wanted to really *feel* accountable in his own actions. The only way that he could do that was to start his own venture.

One night Idan came home visibility frustrated. His wife

embraced him and knew exactly what to say. She told him to quit and try something on his own. Though he had already been thinking about it, it took this moment to make him realize that he had to quit. He needed that push. "I was ready to make a decision that I wasn't aware of it," explains Idan. He went in the next day and handed in his letter of resignation. Now he was free to find an idea that he could own. And that ownership would give him the accountability that he so desperately craved.

Idan recounts, "It was scary but I loved it. I was connected to myself and to what I loved to do. What I loved to do is to initiate and create things. I wanted to form teams and build product. I Once I understood this, it was an easy decision to make to quit."

One of the advisors who Idan bonded with at Elbit was Yona Hollander. He was a serial technology entrepreneur. On more than one occasion, Yona came into Idan's office, closed the door, and told him that he could be CEO of his own company. Idan thought Yona was paying him a nice compliment, but at the time didn't take it seriously because he had been so focused on growing his business unit. After Idan left Elbit, Yona reached out to him once again. This time, the circumstances were different. Idan was ready to discuss startup ideas. It took several meetings at Yona's house to figure out the direction they wanted to take in the cybersecurity space. When they landed on an idea that had potential, they both went to Silicon Valley to see what prospective customers might think.

Idan had traveled to many places before this trip to San Francisco, but he was nervous about this particular trip. His English wasn't perfect and he didn't know the cultural norms. He was unsure about how to present himself and felt vulnerable for the first time about pitching his idea. He didn't have the backing of the Israeli army or a major defense company. It was just Idan. He was the business lead and would do most of the talking, while Yona, the technical cofounder, would only chime in when necessary. It was an unsettling experience for him being outside his comfort zone, but he was able to compose himself and gathered enough feedback in California to feel confident that the startup idea around insider threat detection was worth pursuing. They named their company Fortscale.

But they needed to raise venture capital to fund the idea. He went to one investor with five slides who invested $2 million partially because of the idea, but mainly because of what he saw in Idan. The investor placed a bet on Idan's ability to build a successful business. He saw his passion, reliability, and vision. The investment would also hold Idan accountable for his work, which is exactly what he craved. Success or failure rested on his shoulders, and he wanted to embrace that responsibility as his own.

Since raising that initial capital, Idan says, "It is like riding a roller coaster. First of all, I take everything personally if I lose a deal, if I lose an employee, or if our product isn't perfect. Taking it all in perspective, I know three years ago, we had nothing. Now we have contracts worth millions of dollars. We created a category with the biggest accounts of the world. We help them to find bad guys. All of the time, I want us to get better because it is mine. There is nobody to blame. At my old company, I might say that I hate my boss or my CFO. At a startup, there is nobody to hate. That is real. I love it. It makes me passionate."

In building Fortscale, Idan moved his wife and daughter from Israel to San Francisco. In Israel, family was at the center of Idan's life. Every Friday he went to Shabbat dinner. On weekends he spent time with his parents and his wife's parents. Friends cycled through their apartment for dinners. They had a routine for being together and proximity facilitated that routine. Leaving Israel broke that routine, but a new one has formed in its place. "It created a bonding experience with them. They are in this with me. We became stronger as a couple, as a unit."

His parents and in-laws now come over to San Francisco to visit his three-year-old daughter. They get a chance to see Idan's new life. It is not a better life, just a different one. It manifests in subtle ways from the way that he drives to the way his home is set up. What it does signal is his growth as an entrepreneur. Before, his confidence came from familiarity. Now, as an entrepreneur, he draws his confidence from the unknown because he knows that he'll be able to take on the challenge of uncertain situations, just like successfully raising $23 million from prominent venture capitalists Intel Capital and Blumberg Capital. He feels at home in America as an entrepreneur who is tacking a new market and a new country.

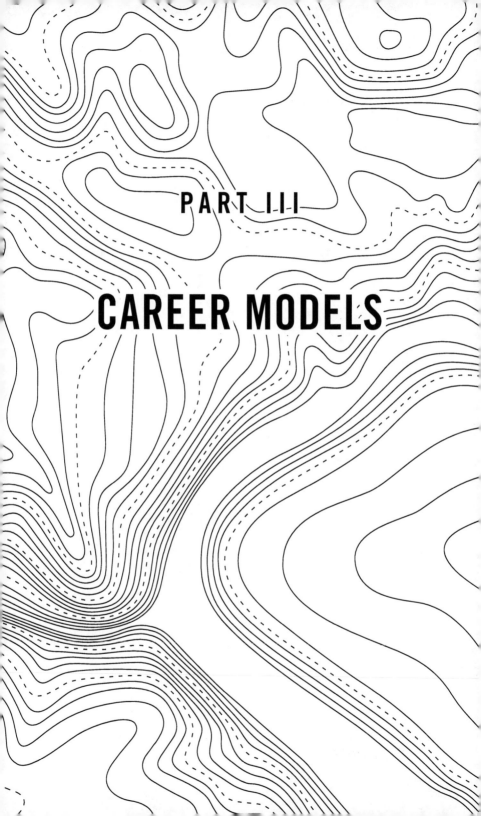

PART III

CAREER MODELS

CHAPTER 12

ACCELERATING YOUR CAREER THROUGH ENTREPRENEURSHIP

DON'T WAIT TO CREATE YOUR FUTURE

Entrepreneur: Chris Lyons
Age: 29
Hometown: Duluth, Georgia
Company: a leading venture capital firm

Chris Lyons was the top grossing server out of all The Cheesecake Factory restaurants in Atlanta, Georgia. He didn't get to the top by pushing what he liked; instead, he relied on customer feedback. "I didn't really eat the dishes myself but was getting feedback from other guests about their experience," Chris explains. "I used those descriptions when guests asked what to order. They trusted me because I wasn't so pushy, so they always ordered more. I could always sell dessert."

Chris also knew that people ate with their eyes. Pictures are worth a thousand words. The Cheesecake Factory had a menu with an overwhelming number of pictures of its dishes. Chris used the layout of the menu to direct guests to dishes he thought they might like after hearing what they were interested in. He'd then accompany that with a description of what other guests had said about that particular dish. He had never even tried most of the food on the menu.

Working as a waiter at The Cheesecake Factory allowed Chris to support himself while he was in college at Full Sail University in Atlanta. It also served as inspiration for a new business idea. As a server, he noticed that all of his guests were playing with their new smartphones. The picture menu didn't have to exist only in a physical format. It could also exist in a digital form that guests could access from their phones at any restaurant, not just The Cheesecake Factory.

Chris did some market research on the idea with the guests he served. He would ask them, "Hey, wouldn't this menu be easier if you could read it from your phone?" or "How would you like to view these pictures?"

"I acted like I didn't know what I was doing," Chris says. "I wanted to get real-time customer feedback and understand the industry. It was very purposeful to get that feedback. I would run back and take notes during my breaks. That was how I started to build the product. I had to be in the mix to be in the game."

Gaining this insight was the breakthrough Chris needed to form his product concept. But executing the idea was a different matter. He didn't know how to code or have a lot of money. But what he did have was his own willpower. He moved back home to the basement of his parent's house.

"There was a naiveté. I didn't know how hard it was going to be to build an application or build a restaurant tech concept in general," he remembers. "It didn't matter to me. I would worry about the problems later. But I just wanted to focus on the best that it could be to make it happen."

Whenever Chris got tired of focusing his startup, he turned his attention to mixing and mastering new music. Chris wasn't just a music fan. He knew the fundamentals of sound engineering. He got turned on to the more technical aspect of music, strangely enough, when he mowed lawns as a teenager. Because it was such tedious work, Chris listened to music to drown out the drone of the lawn mower.

"I listened to the music differently. I started to deconstruct the music into its components: beats per minute, drum patterns, and average tempo. I then recognized a producer style, for instance, like The Neptunes, who had a unique sound. I knew the vibe, the groove, the drums, the chords, and the overall orchestration. When I listened to music, I couldn't just listen to it. I needed to analyze how it was created. Where is the song going, I can predict how it will go. Is there going to be a bridge? This habit all came from listening to so much music while I was cutting the grass."

In total, Chris mowed close to 500 lawns as a teenager, so he listened to a lot of music during each 90-minute job. Cutting grass was an invaluable learning experience. "The reason why I loved grass and what it taught me is that there is no short cut. It is art," Chris explains, "I had to have art in everything that I had to do. Cutting grass had to be perfect. The edge had to be completely lined up. The trim had to perfect. I took a lot of pride in it. It was a lovely business, but it provided cash for my other interests like music."

Chris reinvested the money that he made from mowing lawns into purchasing the latest tech gadgets. Eventually, he had saved enough money to buy studio equipment. This allowed him to experiment with producing music and add to his credibility when he sought and secured an internship at Artist Factory, a music studio. His aunt knew the owner, Hiriam Hicks, a former label executive at Island Def Jam Music Group. Only sixteen years old at the time, Chris soaked up everything as Hiriam took him under his wing.

"I loved the recording studio. I was there every single night," Chris explains. "I got a chance to see what the music industry was like when artists came through the door, watch the choreography, listen to live music, and see how business was handled. It all helped me take my understanding of the music industry to the next level. If someone asked me to do something I didn't know how to do, like auto-tune a song, I would Google it and figure it out. I got to see artists like Lloyd, Rock City, and Bow Wow as an intern, and it showed me the blueprint of what I wanted to do, which was with each opportunity, I could take things to the next level."

Through hanging out at the studio, he was able to gain the trust of the famous music producer Jermaine Dupri, who agreed to take Chris on as an intern. Jermaine had his own creative process for making music and working with artists, which Chris was able to observe. He certainly respected Jermaine and his accomplishments, but he was there to learn, not to admire. Chris shares, "The biggest thing I realized was that I would never be bigger than Jermaine if I was under Jermaine. I never saw anyone who he was working with who had the ability to really come to or surpass his level. He gave me an experience and memories and feeling of what success looked like. I just had to make my own moves to size my own opportunities."

The opportunity was right in front of him when he developed the prototype for his open sourcem picture-based menu concept while working as a waiter at The Cheesecake Factory. While producing music was in his blood, what really moved Chris was creating a technology product that gave him a chance to be the star. A San Francisco-based incubator called New Media accepted Chris into their program. He bought a one-way ticket to San Francisco from Atlanta to start this new adventure, but things were rocky at first. "I felt out of place. I was nervous. But I didn't have a choice. It was either do it or not do it. There was no in the middle. I can rock with this. I was still comfortable within myself and had to believe in myself."

The incubator experience created a strong foundation for Chris in product development and connected him to key individuals in the Silicon Valley network. His defining moment was when his app, Picture Menu, was released in the Apple App Store. It became real when people downloaded the app and wrote reviews. He had worked hard to build the product and line up pilot projects with restaurants like The Cheesecake Factory.

In the midst of developing Picture Menu, Chris got

approached for a role at a prominent venture capital firm. He decided to accept their offer to join the company and stop development of Picture Menu. As Chris explains, "The reason why I did it was that I wanted to be around the best of the best. I want to learn. I want to be a master at my craft. I had to go down a little bit. I didn't go to school for any of this. I just read books and magazines. I went off intuition. I had the chance to get real conversation and expertise and background and develop my chops in a great environment."

Chris' journey from mowing lawns to producing music to serving food to developing a technology product wasn't linear. The common thread was Chris' ability to learn and strive to be the best in whatever field interested him at that moment. While he wasn't always able to predict his next steps, he took what he learned and figured out how to apply it in future contexts.

"Picture Menu was an opening for me to get out into this world and establish myself on a positive career track," Chris explains. "If I didn't have that, I would never be here today. That wasn't the end. That was its purpose. I realize that I loved Picture Menu, and what I want to contribute to this world is so much more than a restaurant menu. That was a vehicle to get me into a situation of learning about the real world to turn into something bigger. For example, most people saw serving at The Cheesecake Factory as something less than it was. The biggest thing that I saw serving was an opportunity to change my entire life."

MY DIGITAL EDGE

Entrepreneur: Ryan Bonifacino
Age: 34
Hometown: Wilmington, Delaware
Company: ALEX AND ANI, an American retailer and producer of jewelry that creates meaningful, eco-friendly jewelry and accessories to positively empower and connect humanity

Ryan Bonifacino was overwhelmed by the feeling of FOMO. All his buddies were out drinking across the bay in Newport, Rhode Island, while Ryan was stuck in Jamestown. A huge storm was coming in that had forced state officials to shut down the bridge back to the mainland. Ryan was marooned for the night with a business acquaintance, Carolyn, whom he had met several months earlier through friends.

Carolyn had one jewelry store at the time. She had been in business for a few years and had ambitions to expand distribution with more stores and develop a digital presence. Digital strategy and marketing was Ryan's specialty, and his agency helped clients, mainly investment funds and tech companies, build brands online. Ryan wasn't looking to bring Carolyn on as a client, but instead to become a strategic investor in her business. What he didn't predict was that he would end up giving up his agency to work for Carolyn full time and help scale the Alex and Ani brand.

"Carolyn was looking to find the right people and partners to bring her business to the next level," Ryan remembers. "I crunched a few data points for her like sales per square feet, e-commerce penetration rate and repeat purchase rate. I also showed her how to use Twitter and why Magento, an e-commerce platform, was so powerful. She shared what inspired her, like her Byzantine art collection and her philosophy on personal relationships. We stayed up until three or four in the morning engrossed in conversation. When I got up the next morning, that was when I decided to help her in a big way, not just make a few introductions."

The business of selling jewelry wasn't inherently interesting to Ryan. He had spent his career building digital solutions for various kinds of businesses, ranging from building websites for super yacht manufacturers to even photography to hedge fund marketing. However, he was in charge when he worked for those businesses. Everyone answered to him. With Carolyn, Ryan felt comfortable supporting her vision as CEO and founder because he felt connected to the story of why she decided to go into the jewelry business in the first place. There was more meaning in being part of something bigger than being the leader of a smaller business that didn't have as much impact.

"I cared about her story. I wanted to take that passion and make it mean something to me and then communicate that to the world," Ryan explains. "I knew the backstory, but as I dug into it, I started to understand how special it was as her family had a factory in Cranston, Rhode Island, which used to be the world's capital for jewelry manufacturing. She was steeped in this rich history that she was trying to make relevant for today's times."

Ryan continues, "I found more purpose in working for her. When I committed, the company was small. But what she did was create an environment that allowed subject matter experts to thrive at what they did. She wanted to have intrapreneurs to work for entrepreneurs. She wanted to create a workplace where people could do what they did best. She understood that I had expertise in digital marketing and let me be responsible for my own decisions and let it work until it didn't. That was the level of trust she had in me even as her own money, reputation, and brand was on the line."

Ryan was a free spirit when he was a kid growing up in Wilmington, Delaware. When he was twelve, he hopped on an Amtrak train to New York City by himself. He wanted to experience the city personally instead of through the movies. Because he didn't have a ticket, Ryan locked himself in the bathroom with a video game magazine and waited until the train stopped in New York to exit. A few people knocked on the door, but Ryan laughs, "I was pretending to take a number two. I disguised my voice in a very muffled and deep tone and explained to anyone who knocked I had too much coffee so it was going to be a while."

Stepping out of Penn Station, young Ryan was met by a flurry of people whisking by. While some kids might have felt overwhelmed, that was not the case with him. "I wasn't nervous. It was more excitement," Ryan shares. "I was a boy scout who was great with a compass and navigation. It was like playing Super Nintendo where I had topographic maps of New York I carried around in my JanSport backpack. I remember just sitting on St. Marks Place and just watching people pass by for an hour before I walked back to the train station."

Ryan's sense of adventure endeared him to the older members at the golf club he grew up playing at. He became quite good at golf to the point where many of the members placed bets on how well he would perform on certain holes. The pressure didn't intimidate Ryan. It helped him form relationships with club members who wanted to take him under their wing and give him life advice in his early teens.

There was one particular member, Mickey, who had a huge impact on Ryan's outlook. "Mickey absolutely killed himself work wise," Ryan explains. "He went to an investment bank where he worked 100 hours a week. His bank paid for his MBA and then he climbed the corporate ladder back at his firm. He had a place in the Hamptons. Materially successful but personally unhappy. But he loved the current version of his life. If he had to do it all over again, the only way to get to where he was at the time, was to follow the rules. Following the system. He said to do the opposite. That stuck with me because that is exactly what I did."

In fact, Ryan had the chance to follow a similar path and went into investment banking. When he was a freshman at University of Delaware, he did most of his school work in a quiet room next to the dean's office. One day he struck up a conversation with a man who was waiting to see the dean. "He was wearing a ripped-up plaid shirt and a Timex watch when I met him. He looked like the janitor," Ryan says. That man peppered him with questions about all aspects of the school from curriculum to student life and alumni fundraising. Ryan answered candidly and honestly, not knowing who he was talking to, and used the same conversational tone he struck up with older members at the golf club.

A few weeks later, the dean called Ryan into his office

and said that someone wanted to meet with Ryan. It was the man he had talked to, who turned out to be John Weinberg, Vice Chairman of Goldman Sachs, one of the most prestigious investment banks in the world. John was meeting with the dean to establish the Weinberg Center for Corporate Governance, a forum for business leaders to interact, collaborate, and improve the field of corporate governance and capital markets. John was impressed with Ryan's maturity and poise and wanted to have lunch with him. Just like when he went to New York City or had a few thousand dollars riding on a golf putt, Ryan wasn't nervous. All he had to do was be himself.

At lunch they talked about not only whether Ryan was qualified to work at Goldman, but also about what Ryan was seeing happening around him. John was interested in hearing honest and direct feedback from someone who didn't have anything to lose. Ryan shares, "My big thing was combining two things, two disciplines, and two industries. Taking marketing skills and applying them to financial services. I was talking to John about this inter-section and ways to digitize his business to make even more money."

Ryan gained a lot of his digital insights from a business called Party Pics that he started when he was a college junior. The concept was simple, straightforward, and lucrative. He could hire a photographer to go to a party, take pictures, and upload them to the Party Pics website that night. The next day anyone could purchase the pictures for $20 each, even though they only cost about 20 cents to print. Within six months, Ryan secured the rights to shoot at parties at fourteen campuses and then sold the business to a partner who ran a photo lab. While not a huge exit, Ryan gleams, "It gave me some drinking money for the next few years."

Soon thereafter, he conjured up an idea to start up an agency called Hedge Interactive that had an expertise in digital production and marketing. He had worked with a bunch of freelancers through his Party Pics business, and he thought he could get clients to pay his agency for their digital expertise. Through his family and golf connections, he had a deep rolodex of connections at law firms. He locked in one client, a global intellectual property firm, to build a directory of lawyers and launch a new website. Ryan was able to charge rates that were half the cost of a New York ad agency but provide equal or better quality. The partners of this law firm were impressed with what they saw and started to refer Ryan to their venture capital clients out in Silicon Valley.

Ryan's agency expanded its digital capabilities beyond building websites to search engine optimization. Running Hedge Interactive was a grind for six straight years. He first started working with folks in the startup space and did everything from optimizing their Google ranking to helping founders recruit new engineers through fun, buzzworthy social events. Ryan then pivoted the company to fully focus on helping emerging hedge funds build a digital presence since most of them didn't have any sense of how to brand themselves online.

"In 2008, after Bear Stearns and Lehman shut down, these people who were managing billions of dollars on a desk, were now on their own," Ryan explains. "They couldn't get away from the computer because their money was tied up. They had no idea what to call themselves and how to get themselves out there. I was so focused on helping them because I knew I had the ability to do something that nobody else was able to do on the Street. I was able to brand them."

Since starting his agency in 2003, Ryan maintains that, "My edge came from working seven days a week. On my team, none of us, including myself, had lives. We did have a life but it was all embedded within the work." He loved what he was doing—seeing what nobody else saw and using his growing range of skills to help founders realize their vision. He was a founder himself helping other founders. He had always worked *with* other founders, but never *for* founders until he met Carolyn.

Because of her passion, Ryan spent five years helping

build the Alex and Ani business as one of the first digitally-native chief marketing officers, exiting in early 2016 after a private equity liquidity event valued the company at over $1 billion. He did work for Carolyn, not as an outside advisor, but as an employee who understood the emotional and financial volatility of what she was experiencing as a founder. He knew that it was her company with her roots, and his responsibility was communicating that story to the world through a digital platform. His role evolved from focusing on digital marketing to overseeing all of marketing, a shift that signaled the growing trust Carolyn had in Ryan's abilities. He protected the founder by being a founder's employee—someone who is more than just a salaried worker, someone who wants to go the extra mile because that is what he would want as a founder himself.

After leaving Alex and Ani, Ryan established an investment firm called Mount Cuba Capital, where he provides both strategic and financial capital to startups. This new business allows him to focus on a few different ventures but with the same principle of helping founders realize their visions. He wants to be the voice that protects their interests because he is as skilled at talking about digital marketing as he is about conducting complex financial transactions. His broad-based skill set allows him to truly be a founder's advisor because of his experience as a founder's employee.

CHAPTER 13

HACKING YOUR WAY TO HAPPINESS

THE PERFECT BALANCE

Entrepreneur: Anton Cobb
Age: 35
Hometown: Chicago, Illinois
Company: hOURLUNCH, a movement to invest lunch money to fight child hunger

Hour Lunch. HOURlunch. HourLunch. hOURLUNCH. Anton Cobb played around with different configurations and formats until the name looked right. Anton loved words. As an English lit major at the University of Illinois, he had set out to become a writer. He had a writer's vibe: scruffy hair, an unkempt beard, and a nose ring. That vibe did not pay the rent when he moved to Chicago.

He cleaned up his look to apply to be a waiter at a local hotel pub.

When a position opened up for sales manager at the hotel, he applied for the job. For the interview, he put on a suit and made the best first impression he could. He got the job, which gave him the financial stability he wanted. The corporate world, however, did not allow him to express his full creativity. Anton was searching for more, and because he had lived all of his life in and around Chicago, he thought a change in scenery might energize him more creatively. Because he performed well in his role, he was able to transfer to the office in Portland, Oregon. There was something about the city's energy that appealed to his creative soul.

In this new environment, Anton felt the writer's vibe come back to him. Ideas started to flow, and he shared them with his then girlfriend (now wife). One particular idea stuck. What if people could volunteer and ask for donations for worthy causes during their lunch break? It was just a seed of an idea, but something about it stuck for him. He started to put together the visuals of what it could look like: the name, the sign, the tablecloth, the flower, and the donation box. His creativity was coming to life. This time, instead of words, it was a concept that would transform his life.

Anton sent his design to Kinko's to get the sign produced,

which cost about $300. It was an expensive commitment for an idea that he had yet to fully flesh out. At the time, his girlfriend was reading the book *The $100 Startup*. She realized that this small investment was his startup idea. Anton had never intended to become an entrepreneur. He came from a middle-class family. But his gut told him to go for it. He picked up the sign and purchased the rest of the materials for his concept. It was up to him to go out and execute his vision.

Anton decided that he was going to be the one to solicit donations and that he was going to do it wearing his work suit, on a Wednesday during lunchtime in the park next to his office. He would donate the money to an organization that fought child hunger. He brought all of the materials to his office, but Wednesday came and passed. The next Wednesday came and passed. His excuses varied. *The weather wasn't warm enough. I had too much work. This was just not a great idea.* He was convincing himself not to do it until one perfectly sunny day in May when he ran out of excuses.

He grabbed the materials from his office and walked out without anybody noticing. Over at the park, he set up everything just like he had pictured, and then he waited. He was completely exposed to the world and didn't know if anyone would even care. A few people came up to him thinking that he got stood up for a date. One wanted to understand what his cause was about. Anton stumbled through his explanation because he hadn't practiced his pitch for the concept. It didn't matter. That person understood. She handed him $5 because she wanted to give up her lunch for that day to feed a needy child. Anton made $15 that day for Oregon Food Bank. He was hooked. He finally had validation for his idea.

"When I walked out, I got a little excited and manic about this idea. I had planned for several weeks to do it, and here I was, latching on and seeing through the creation of this idea," Anton remembers. "Most people find themselves powerless to do something about a cause they care about, but I've come up with a way to have an impact on an issue that means a lot to me."

The one thing that Anton had forgotten to bring that first day was a flower, so he just picked one from the flower bed next to where he set up his table. The parks director saw this, came over to him, and cited this transgression. She also let Anton know that he needed a permit if he was going to continue collecting money in the park. That didn't dissuade him from showing up the next week and the following week after that. He had tapped into an idea that he was going to see through because it fulfilled him in a way he had never experienced before.

The local TV station KGW got wind of the story of a guy

in a suit asking for donations. The reporter interviewed Anton and broadcasted it. He had never been interviewed before, much less for TV. He hadn't expected this kind of publicity.

That local TV interview did two things. First, the parks department reviewed the footage and granted Anton a special permit to pursue this endeavor. Its credo of "healthy city, healthy parks, healthy children" aligned with what Anton was trying to do, which was fighting child hunger. Second, the piece was noticed by a producer for the *Rachael Ray Show* and she was interested in learning more about Anton's story.

The *Rachael Ray Show* was kicking off its ninth season and partnering with Feeding America to donate $9 million in meals. The producers wanted to invite people who had contributed to fighting hunger. Anton was one of them. They flew him out to New York for the taping. Anton was nervous. A few outlets had previously picked up his story, but they were only local news. The *Rachael Ray Show* had a national audience. He practiced his story in front of the producers. They told him he came off flat. He had to pick up his game.

This was his one chance to make an impression as the show only did one take. Anton sat in the audience and waited for his cue to come on stage. The lights went down. A video reel highlighted what Anton had accomplished with hOURLUNCH. The lights went back on. Anton stood up. At six foot seven, he was hard to miss. He walked down from the audience, and even though he was nervous, he refocused his internal energy to project outward confidence. His voice boomed as he explained what he had accomplished. He hugged Rachael and handed the money he collected for this particular drive to her. The crowd cooed and applauded. It was a moment of validation for Anton and showed how far his idea had come.

Initially, Anton was fearful of telling his colleagues and managers at the hotel about his appearance on the *Rachael Ray Show*. He kept his two lives separate, his corporate life and personal life outside of work. In Anton's mind, taking an hour off for lunch was an unwritten no-no. But Anton was surprised and delighted when he found out how much his company wanted to support him. In fact, the CEO awarded him their highest team member recognition. He flew back to Chicago to receive the award in front of all the top executives.

And even after appearing on the *Rachael Ray Show*, being featured in a Ford car commercial, and giving a TEDx Talk, Anton continues to go out every Wednesday at the same time to solicit donations to fight children's hunger. He gets a kind of fulfillment from raising money for this cause that he doesn't get from his job. And his job fulfills him in a way that he can't get from hOURLUNCH. Anton likes sales. And he also likes using creativity to express what he is passionate about. They live in balance with one another, and they feed on each other to give him a more complete life.

"I felt less skittish about the way that I was living my life," Anton shares. "There were a lot of things that I wanted to do and that I thought I was going to do, but I was biding my time to find what that opportunity was. When this came about, it scratched every itch that I had. I got to mess around with words. I got to write a TEDx Talk. I got to write copy for a website. I got to help people. Before, I was very scattered. Now, I can invest all my energy into this."

Before Anton started hOURLUNCH, he expected his job to give him something that it couldn't—fuel for his creative soul. He expected too much, which led to frustration. What hOURLUNCH gave him was an outlet to express his creativity. "I had to make something. And this is what I made. By making it and seeing it through and growing it and changing it and really investing myself in it, all of a sudden, I couldn't love my job more. The job didn't change. I changed. I was asking too much from my job. I wanted it to be creative and do all of these things. Now I love it, and I am more successful than I have ever been, and I am happier because of it."

Entrepreneur: Carey Bentley
Age: 26
Hometown: Ann Arbor, Michigan
Company: Lifehack Bootcamp, the definitive experience to achieve productivity mastery that transforms the way you work and frees up time to make the impact you want in your family, community, and the world

Ding—an email notification popped up on Carey Bentley's iPhone. She had finally pried herself away from her job at PopChips, where she served as marketing manager, and was on a ski vacation with her boyfriend in Colorado. She had handed off her work to her team and given them detailed instructions, but here they were, pulling her back in. Carey picked up her phone and started to type away. She could feel the stress seeping back into her shoulders.

Her boyfriend at the time, Demir, now husband, was incredulous. He wanted Carey to keep her work and personal life separate. Carey shot back, "This is my job! I have to do it." Demir was hurt because he was on her side; he was defending her vacation time. The situation quickly turned into a huge fight, one of the worst they'd ever had. But it was one of the most important days of Carey's life because it became the day that Carey decided to leave PopChips. The fight made her realize that work was only going to get worse. The more she worked, the more responsibility she held, and the more stress she accumulated. The stress wore down on her and the auto-immune disorder, ulcerative colitis, she suffers from. The cycle had to stop, which is exactly what happened when she left the company six months later.

Ulcerative colitis is a disease of the digestive tract where white blood cells attack the lining of the intestine. Carey has battled this disease ever since she was a kid. It is hard to digest anything and difficult to absorb nutrients. Lack of nutrition results in low energy and overall irritability. High stress situations exacerbate the disease. When Carey turned eighteen, doctors were finally able to diagnose her condition. But for ten years she lived with the disorder, knowing something was wrong but not knowing what it was.

Suffering from ulcerative colitis has been formative in shaping Carey's entrepreneurial drive. Even though she knew something was wrong, she did not let that hinder her. There were things that she had to avoid like playing sports or sleeping over at friend's houses for fear that her illness would flare up. She focused on studying, making good grades, and getting accepted at a top college. After college, she joined Kraft and became the youngest brand manager on the billion-dollar Oscar Mayer bologna business. PopChips recruited her and gave her even more responsibility as marketing manager. Her ambition from a young age was to be the best at whatever she put her mind to.

Carey was homeschooled, which put her at ease and allowed her to learn in a stress-free environment. There were no more trips to the nurse's office, and she was able to take an active role in directing her learning based on specific interests. For example, Carey developed an interest in salamanders through her involvement with a local nature group. Salamanders can only spotted during certain times of the year for a couple of hours at a time. Carey put on her headlamp, went out late at night, tracked their movement, and reported the data back to the larger group. She was part of a larger mission. This exploration exhilarated her and the sense of belonging fulfilled her.

During her senior year in high school, her brother committed suicide. He was only a year older. It was a very sad, tragic moment for Carey and her family. "Life was unfair. It was completely unbiased. There was nothing I could do about it. I couldn't fix or solve it. It just sucked." Instead of letting that defeat her, Carey used that event as fuel to live life to the fullest. "It lit a fire under me. I didn't have a lot of time. I could go at any moment. I started to think about what legacy I would leave and what would people think of my life. How could I maximize my chance at life?"

That ski trip in Colorado helped refocus Carey's life priorities. At PopChips, her career defined the way she lived. She was tethered to work and a simple email could pull Carey back into the fray from anywhere. She accepted her illness as a constraint and decided to design a lifestyle that fit her life, instead of a career that dictated her lifestyle. It wasn't until she left PopChips that she gained leverage over her situation. That was the beginning of Lifehack Bootcamp.

"Was I working to get somewhere and be happy, or did I want to be happy now and then be happy in my own life?" Carey remembers asking herself. "My whole life then was about fulfilling my purpose instead of trying to fulfill a goal. At my corporate job, I felt like I was shaving years off of my life. I was decreasing the amount of time that I had. Time was a non-renewable asset. I didn't get it back. I could make money in numerous different ways. Money was renewable. That was the point where I wanted to live my life instead of live for my career. The first thing that went was the job."

Friends and family watched with amazement at how she restructured her life. Former colleagues asked her for productivity tips because PopChips had to backfill her role with not one, but two people after she left. Productivity also extended into her personal life. Carey explains, "At home, I was Relax Captain. I was in charge of scheduling downtime. Electric devices were not on. Candles only.

Massages to help us wind down. Demir was the social captain where he was in charge of scheduling dinner dates and all of the fun stuff." These defined roles helped them create structured time where they could truly be in the moment. What they practiced in their careers at work and at home ultimately became the template for a business around productivity.

As Carey wound down her job at PopChips, she and her boyfriend decided to host a weekend brunch at their house with fifteen friends so that they could share their hacks on how they ran their lives. They asked their friends to pay $40 each to attend the event. Carey set up the session in her living room and everyone sat around a big round table with Carey and her boyfriend leading the session. They videotaped the session to capture the content and sell what they taught online. What happened in the room was completely transformative.

The impact of what they taught was immediate. For example, a friend never found the time to tuck her kid into bed because she was a wedding planner. She was always running around in service of her clients. After she left that weekend, she changed the way she worked and implemented what she learned. She was then with her son every evening without compromising the quality of service she delivered to her clients.

Carey and Demir started to host more and more boot-camps. More people were impacted by what they learned. But they couldn't sustain the business on just word-of-mouth referrals. So they went to work on building a sales pipeline that would supply a more reliable flow of students who signed up for their Lifehack Bootcamp. New clients eager for their advice signed up for their sessions as stories of transformation continued to flood into their Facebook page.

They now had a business that was in service of their life-style instead of a business that they were tethered to at all hours. If, for example, they wanted to be on a sailboat in the middle of the Mediterranean Sea for three months, they built the flexibility to pick up and leave because both their business and personal ties supported them taking this step. For example, renting out their house on Airbnb kept their housing costs at a minimum or eating gourmet meals at home with friends reduced their restaurant expenses. The most extreme example of designing their lifestyle was when they hacked together their wedding in thirty days.

For Carey, the most important objective was getting married to the love of her life. Nothing else mattered. She didn't want to deal with the drama of wedding planning and the expense of putting on such a huge event. They had nothing planned, so Carey's friends took charge. One found a wedding venue. Another got the wine donated. Another helped make the flower bouquets. Everyone wanted to pitch in and participate in the experience of putting on a wedding.

Carey shares, "[At most weddings] it's all about the bride and groom. It is clear the guest doesn't matter. In our case, everyone had a role and purpose for being there. That made it more fun and engaging. The community helped us plan the wedding. Because we had only thirty days, it simplified the decision-making process. It was an opportunity to throw out some crazy ideas and execute on them. It wasn't about having the perfect day. It was more about the guests and family and creating this amazing memory. It was a crowdsourced wedding. There was very little that we did ourselves. It was rough around the edges, it wasn't perfect, but it was what I wanted."

Entrepreneurship has given Carey more control over her life. Even though she is in charge of a business, she is way less stressed because the energy she puts into it has a direct correlation to the results she gets out of it. She can work from home in her pajamas, which allows her to minimize her distractions. Her autoimmune disease rarely flares up anymore, and she has a lifestyle where her business supports her to be on a sailboat in the Mediterranean. She is no longer fighting with life. She is embracing what it has to offer though her Lifehack Bootcamp business.

In the two years since starting Lifehack Bootcamp, Demir and Carey have traveled to eighteen different countries. They've grown their business from a small startup in Los Angeles to an online business serving hundreds of clients a year in dozens of countries. They speak internationally and have become true leaders in the online course industry, consulting with other coaches to share how they get such tremendous results with their clients. They shot a TV pilot about their unique lifestyle. And yes, at one point they managed their business from a sailboat off the coast of Croatia.

"In hindsight, my condition was something I was annoyed at. It was the few things in life that I couldn't change it," Carey concludes. "It was this brick wall and I had to get through it but it was hard to break through. It was a big factor making me realize to build my lifestyle and not a career. Lifestyle design is what I am most interested in. I am passionate about my business, but it is in service of my lifestyle design."

THE CULINARY CONNECTOR

Entrepreneur: Leiti Hsu
Age: 31
Hometown: Los Angeles, California
Company: Journy, a modern-day travel concierge service that pairs you with a personal concierge to design your perfect trip

I'd never had Taiwanese beef noodle soup before, much less been invited to a gathering of New York food lovers. When I got to Khe-Yo on a Monday in Tribeca, the place was buzzing. There wasn't even room to move. People were clamoring for the food. And this was no ordinary group of foodies, as I came to realize. They were top chefs, restaurant owners, food critics, TV producers, and social media influencers who had built their careers around food.

It was an eclectic crowd, and everyone I spoke with had such an impressive culinary pedigree. I met Erica (aka @ eggcanvas on Instagram), who had more than 350,000 followers. She was the digital marketing director at Barneys New York, but outside of work she was a storyteller who photographed her upscale lifestyle around fashion, art, and food. I met Jenna, a producer who worked on shows for the Food Network and with celebrity chefs like Guy Fieri and Bobby Flay. I met Matt, a journalist who'd also penned several cookbooks. Each of them had come to Khe-Yo for the food, but also because they knew it was a great opportunity to network and potentially meet someone who had the influence to help them grow their business.

Leiti Hsu, cofounder at Journy (gojourny.com), took a circuitous route to becoming a culinary connector. As a child, she went to Chinese language school every Saturday morning. Afterwards, she went with her family to eat Taiwanese food, which was Leiti's consolation prize for missing out on Saturday morning cartoons.

They feasted on pig feet, scallion pancakes, and mapo tofu. This became their ritual after Chinese school. Eating out was considered a luxury, something to strive for. Leiti's family usually ate at home while she was growing up because it was more economical. At one point when she was very young, even McDonald's was considered an indulgence. Over the years, however, they began eating out more frequently as her parents grew to have more disposable income. That was the American Dream; while Leiti appreciated a delicious meal plain and simple, food ultimately signified economic mobility.

Both the promise of a reliable financial reward and the challenge of competing with the best of her peers drove her to gun for a summer internship at one of the biggest investment banks while she was in college. She thought nothing of it when she emailed the president and CEO of one of the top five largest investment banks in the world for a coffee meeting. As a student journalist, she was used to interviewing interesting, often powerful, people such as the prime minister of New Zealand or a Ringling Bros. clown. This was no different. The CEO responded from his BlackBerry within thirty minutes to set up a discussion over coffee.

Leiti wasn't jockeying to get ahead. She genuinely wanted to get to know the CEO. She thought she should get to know how he got to where he was over a 15-minute coffee should he feel like sparing the time. After all, the man must be busy! She went in expecting to ask all the questions, like all of her interviews as a journalist; instead, he took her by surprise—he was the one asking the questions, gaining valuable intel on the summer intern experience. But the fallout that occurred from that meeting was something she had not expected.

Her fellow interns found out that she had had a meeting with the CEO and were in disbelief. This was not proper protocol. The HR director found out and pulled Leiti aside to chastise her for this behavior. Leiti felt blindsided. After all, the CEO had been willing to meet. What started as a positive connection turned into something else when the HR director made her feel silly and stupid.

Leiti was not defeated, though. After graduating from UCLA, she secured a full-time job at a top management consulting firm in New York City. She loved the company's spirit of team culture, hard work, and camaraderie, but soon began to realize that she wasn't suited to the work. For instance, she was placed on a project and asked to validate the Canadian economic capital financial model for a major credit card company. Wasn't this something better suited to a math or physics Ph.D., not an undergraduate economics major? Everything she'd worked for to be that overachiever climbing the corporate ranks was just not working out. She'd followed the rules and offended nobody getting perfect grades as a student, but it was clear that her forte in life was not spreadsheets and slide decks. So now what?

As a twentysomething career-shifter, she had no savings after living in Manhattan, one of the most expensive cities in the world. She was terrified by the thought of not being able to pay rent and by not having that continuity from one job to another. What would her peers and potential new employers think? What she didn't realize was the skill she heaps of: the ability to connect people. This eventually became her calling card.

Bringing people together was a skill that came naturally to Leiti. She relished seeing two people, who might not otherwise meet, connect through her. The joy of introducing people was enough, even if nothing came out of it for her. However, in the long run, what goes around comes around. Opportunities began to come to her when she least expected it.

For example, for her twenty-third birthday party, she didn't want the experience to focus solely on celebrating her. Instead, she wanted to celebrate the wonderful people in her circles and encourage them to meet each other. Every year, her birthday celebrations got bigger and more ambitious because of her drive to connect more people together. This was a way for her to deepen existing friendships and make new ones.

"I am the most introverted extrovert you'll meet," Leiti reflect. "To be on and engaging and to ask good questions is hard. Watching two people connect and start a friendship, a business relationship, or a romance even... that's so satisfying."

After management consulting, Leiti found a role at a dream startup where she was the tenth employee—it had to do with wine and e-commerce, both sexy businesses, it seemed (at the time, e-commerce was a booming industry). But while she gained valuable experience as the first operations team member who made sure all the wine shipped out on time, her responsibilities were relegated purely to operations. She'd been doing the same shipping spreadsheet every day now for a year. The customer service team relied on her for answers when, say, a package went missing, because processes were built in a hurry. The company had raised $50 million and grown too big too fast. Though she raised her hand to help with partnerships, content, and social media in her spare time, management said no to her.

The only thing left to do was quit. Her freelance business

blossomed from what she loved and knew best: connecting people around a shared interest, which was increasingly becoming about food. Her clients were paying her for what she loved to do anyway, and she was able to begin to make a living by making these connections.

One particular founder noticed how skilled she was at making connections with restaurant owners. His company, Cover, was the first to enable top-notch restaurants to let diners pay without waiting for the check. He gave her a task to close thirty restaurants in thirty days. This request was difficult, if not impossible, to fulfill given the typically long sales process to get a restaurant to adopt and implement a completely new technology. But Leiti didn't back down. After all, she loved to talk to chefs and restaurateurs.

She started by developing a process to kick off, build, and grow relationships. Every time she dined out, she tagged the restaurant on social media as way to say "hey" and "thank you." She was offered the opportunity to host and produce her radio show *Word of Mouth with Leiti Hsu* on Heritage Radio Network to interview chefs, which introduced many of them to a national audience. Food gatherings like the Taiwanese beef noodle soup party was her way of bringing her network together. Leiti was at the center of this community, but by no means the center of attention. The food always took center stage and people discovered what she already knew—food brings people closer and allows them to forge relationships.

Before working for Cover, she had been an outsider in the culinary world. Now, by putting in the hours of going to one, two, three—sometimes four!—drinks, dinners, and events per evening, she found this small world shrinking fast. Soon she was emceeing events and hosting red carpet interviews at the James Beard Foundation Awards, the Oscars of the food world. She had made it into the inner circles of the culinary elite. Networking was more than just a job for Leiti, it was a lifestyle.

In 2014, Leiti's mom got sick and was diagnosed with stage IV lung cancer. Leiti was beside herself as she booked a one-way ticket back home. Before she left New York, she hung out with one of her best friends, Susan, and shared a cab ride home. Leiti and Susan had met while they were dancing on speakers in a Shanghai club a decade ago. "I looked up and noticed this other girl dancing," Leiti recounts, "...and well! We got to talking, and after the night wound down, I asked her where we could find some good Taiwanese food. This Shanghainese native showed a Taiwanese girl where to get the good stuff in her city. Our friendship began because of food and exploration."

Leiti kept in touch with Susan throughout the years and even connected Susan to a high-profile job at Fab, where she ended up running operations. In Leiti's moment of despair over her mother's cancer, she opened up to Susan.

"I was devastated because I didn't know what was going on with my mom. I didn't know just how long she had, and I didn't know how to balance that with handling my clients who were counting on me to deliver results."

Susan tried to comfort Leiti. As the ultimate problem-solver, her way of comforting Leiti was to declare that she was starting a travel startup and wanted Leiti to be her cofounder. She'd have all the flexibility to go to LA and be there for her mom and her family. It was an awkward time for Susan to bring up such an opportunity, but she wanted to signal that even in the darkest moments, she would be there for Leiti, in a way that was different than any other friend could. "Susan respected and embraced my difference," Leiti recalls, "She was totally about building a billion-dollar travel business, but let me do my thing, which was connecting people and getting us that unlikely, outsized access to chefs, experts, influencers, and partners."

Leiti went back to Los Angeles on a monthly basis to tend to her mom. Being home was also a chance for her to reevaluate her life. She had stable paying clients, a growing savings, a radio show (which eventually turned into wordofmouth.fm and a newsletter with half a million readers), and connects to nearly every chef in the world. She was getting somewhere, and not by doing a desk job. But there was something about Susan's proposal to start a company from scratch that resonated with her. Susan wanted to work with Leiti for who she was and build something they owned together. The startup concept for Journy was to create a travel agency for the modern traveler, "not your grandma's travel agency." Leiti's role was to help tap into that local expertise through her deep connections with the global community of food and travel pros.

While her mom's health had its peaks and valleys, Leiti decided that time was too short not to travel more and create her own destiny. She joined Susan at Journy as cofounder. She had realized that her ambition as a connector could be scaled through technology because of Susan's strategy and operations genius. The travel industry was in dire need of innovation, and she and Susan were the ones to do it. She could create personalized experiences for others through her existing connections without her having to be there. Connecting became more than just a lifestyle for Leiti. It has become a way of life where limitless doors open for her and for others each time she creates a connection. "I can't believe I get to make a living doing what I'm meant to do in this life. I am connecting people at a much greater scale than I ever possibly imagined."

CHAPTER 14

FEELING GOOD BY DOING GOOD

A SENSE OF DUTY

Entrepreneur: Jerelyn Rodriguez
Age: 28
Hometown: South Bronx, New York
Company: The Knowledge House, a nonprofit that empowers and sustains a talent pipeline of technologists, entrepreneurs, and digital leaders who uplift their communities out of poverty

Jerelyn Rodriguez was at a complete loss for words when her best friend told her she was dropping out of college. As childhood friends who had grown up together in the Bronx, Jerelyn and her best friend were always at the top of their class at the charter school they attended. They were both bright, talented students whose families didn't have much but were able to enroll in top colleges. Yet her best friend struggled to adjust to college life, which resulted in poor grades.

Before this incident, Jerelyn had been studying film. As she describes, "I always had a passion for digital storytelling and using digital media as an outlet to create a platform for muted voices. Originally, I was thinking of how to tell the stories of black and brown people." Seeing her friend struggle forced Jerelyn to rethink and refocus her academic efforts. She pivoted her attention to education, specifically the role that local education plays in shaping college and professional outcomes. She had been interested in this topic since high school, when she had the opportunity to attend a conference on it.

"I went to a conference at Yale, and I was able to attend this talk about the topic of the achievement gap. At that time, I realized that only 10 percent of low-income people persist through college," she remembers. "Growing up in a poor neighborhood, I didn't know about this statistic. This was a statistic that stayed with me, and when I heard about my friend dropping out of school, this was when I decided I really needed to fix this achievement gap."

In fact, she had seen this gap first hand even before she reached college. Many of her peers weren't persisting through high school. These kids weren't even on the college track, so they fell through the cracks at an even earlier stage. The skills and opportunity gaps are what Jerelyn decided to tackle. The Bronx, her hometown, seemed like the perfect place to start and try to solve the problem.

Her reasoning was, "Being from the Bronx and having a low-income background, I have an authentic perspective and can find more innovative ways to solve this issue." After college, she initially worked at a nonprofit startup that focused on youth leadership. Even though it was a startup, Jerelyn remembers, "As an employee, I felt powerless. If I were leading this organization, I would do things differently."

Before taking the startup job, Jerelyn had worked as a field director to organize support for Reshma Saujani, who ran for political office in 2013 for New York City Public Advocate. On the campaign trail, Jerelyn was looking office space when she discovered a tech incubator, the BXL Business Incubator in the Bronx. At the time, the local technology scene was just another pathway to meeting potential voters. It was only later that Jerelyn realized she could use technology to drive career outcomes for low-income teenagers. BXL was where she met her eventual cofounder, Joe Carrano, who managed the incubator.

The role that technology could play in her community

didn't dawn on Jerelyn until she attended a Bronx Tech Meetup event. "The conversation was led by white Columbia students who were doing a project to increase tech education for kids without the buy-in of local educators," she remembers, "My concern with their approach was how teacher unions were going to react. They might feel threatened to adopt technology because it threatened their jobs. Leaving that event inspired me to dig deeper into finding a place for myself in the tech community."

When Jerelyn met Miguel Sanchez, a self-taught coder from the Bronx and the CEO of Mass Ideation, a technology agency, she saw the huge role technology could play in catalyzing career growth. Miguel's story inspired her and made her want to help discover and nurture other students like Miguel from her local community. This led her to build a ten-week curriculum in collaboration with Joe that would give students a foundation in digital coding skills. They called it The Knowledge House.

To kick off the program, Jerelyn and Joe held an information session at a local community organization and forty young people showed up. Because these kids didn't know what a technology career was, they decided to show them through demonstrations. One of their friends, a drone specialist, did a demo on how to fly a drone. "I saw their eyes light up," Jerelyn exclaims, "and one of them asked, 'How can I make drones as a job?' This was what I wanted to do, to bring everyone together and expose them to technology to improve career outcomes."

The capstone of the ten-week program was a demo day. This was very fulfilling for Jerelyn who saw her students create technology to tackle problems within the community, such as: an anti-school bullying marketing campaign; a blog that spotlighted stop-and-frisk violations by the police; and an app that encouraged pet adoption. These were ideas that could make a true difference in the community. What was missing was a way to transition from the program to full-time employment. The curriculum was geared heavily toward technical skills, but didn't spend sufficient time on the soft skills. Jerelyn shares, "We tried to get a lot of them jobs, but even though they knew how to code, they were not resourceful enough to research, interview, and secure an internship, much less a full-time job."

That insight led the team to create a job-training program that combined both soft and hard skill acquisition. They scaled back some of the more technical skills and incorporated more workplace skills that employers value. The new curriculum tracked well with their local community. They also got calls from other boroughs who wanted to replicate the training program in their own tech communities. Within a year, they had served 150 students who, before coming into the program, made only minimum wage.

After graduating from the program, many were making $25 an hour in jobs that had true growth opportunities.

Jerelyn points to Sergio, a student who never had the opportunity to go to college and went through The Knowledge House program. He was a talented gamer who discovered his coding ability there and was able to find a job by building his expertise in it. His story represents everything wrong with how society marginalizes students from poor zip codes, yet everything right with Jerelyn's strategy of finding talent locally in the community. Sergio's story now serves as inspiration for the next kid who enters into the program and shows that career growth and success is attainable. Everyone just has to do their part.

"When I was growing up, in my schools, I knew I was poor but my teachers never talked about it," Jerelyn explains. "Whereas my approach with my students is to let them know why The Knowledge House exists. We are all in this together. Joe and I are going to help you get a job, so you can have a family-sustaining wage. And you have to do your part because we are going to prove the world wrong. Everyone has these negative thoughts or pictures about the Bronx. All of our students understand that our mission is to uplift our community and to develop ourselves as leaders."

Her sense of duty and loyalty to her community was

cultivated by her mother, Reina, whose name means "queen" in Spanish. Even though she didn't have a lot of money, Reina still welcomed family members who were less fortunate than her into her home. Jerelyn, her sister, and her mother all squeezed into one room while other family members stayed in the other bedroom. Her mother's perspective was that you should always take care of yourself and take care of your own.

Jerelyn feels the exact same way about the Bronx, a community she wants to see grow and thrive. As she explains, "Even today, very few low-income people make it through high school. I look at myself, who grew up in the Bronx and made it through college. I have a sense of duty. It's not a surprise that I am taking that ownership role. If I don't do it, who else will?"

SAFE ANYWHERE

Entrepreneur: Jacqueline Ros
Age: 26
Hometown: Miami, Florida
Company: Revolar, an app-enabled personal safety device made for everyday use

In her classroom of thirty sixth-graders, Jacqueline Ros sat silently at her desk as her kids took a math test. She had moved out to Colorado for the Teach for America program after graduating from the University of Florida. The previous night, she had just read a statistic that one in four women were sexually assaulted before they graduated from high school. At her desk, she started counting in her head each of her students—one, two, three, four—safe. Then again—one, two, three, four—safe.

The sobering reality was that several of the kids in her classroom were going to be sexually assaulted by the time they reached college. A few months later, Jacqueline witnessed this firsthand when she found out that one of her students had been raped by an eighth-grader. The fact also hit home because her younger sister had been the victim of a sexual attack when she was a freshman in high school. Jacqueline felt compelled to find a solution to address sexual assault out of a concern to protect the young women in her life.

What happened to her younger sister was inexcusable. Jacqueline wouldn't and couldn't let it go. At first, she didn't want to believe what had happened to her sister. After a few months had passed, everything seemed to return to normal. But while others might have moved on with their lives, Jacqueline's sister was only starting her healing process.

On a family trip to Argentina, Jacqueline remembers, "We were going to a bathroom in a restaurant, and we were laughing on our way to the bathroom, and by the time I came out of the bathroom, she was hysterically sobbing and had broken down crying. And I was like, 'What happened? We were just laughing?'"

Jacqueline continues, "She barely could get the words out. And she said that, 'I thought I saw one of them.' And it just hit me all at once, right before I left for college, that this had really happened to her. This was not something I could ignore that she was dealing with. She was going to deal with this alone or she was going to have me."

In college, Jacqueline's instinct was to be there for her sister as much as she could. For instance, she came home every weekend to spend time with her sister. She wanted to do everything within her power to prevent this from happening again. But the challenge was that she couldn't realistically be with her sister all the time. She still had to live her life as well. When her sister was sexually attacked again, Jacqueline was devastated. She was tired of being afraid for her sister and also for herself.

During her senior year of college, Jacqueline took an entrepreneurship 101 class. The professor pushed the class to think about problems in their own lives and see what kinds of technology solutions they could devise to address those problems. This was when the idea for Revolar, a personal safety device, was born: a discrete device that could send for help at the push of a button. Jacqueline was not a technologist and she wasn't interested in entrepreneurship. She just wanted to stop feeling afraid that she and her sister had no control over their own lives.

The next weekend she went home to see her sister, the two of them sat at the kitchen table and Jacqueline drew her idea on a napkin and explained what the device did. "My sister just started crying. She was so moved that I cared enough to try to find a solution," Jacqueline remembers. "She had thought she was alone in this fight. She said that this device would have made a difference, and she would have not been so alone. She would have been able to talk to me a lot sooner."

The power of her sister's emotional reaction to the idea gripped Jacqueline. She couldn't stop developing the idea. What she lacked in experience, she made up for in tenacity. She researched what she didn't know and found answers that helped move this concept to reality. The more that she worked on the idea, the healthier and stronger her sister became.

Jacqueline spent the entire summer after she graduated on this project. The daily process of developing the product was a grind. Jacqueline didn't have an engineering background to build the product. Afraid that someone would steal her idea, she asked everyone she met with to sign non-disclosure agreements. Nobody would agree to the NDA. Since she had just graduated from school, she was comfortable disclosing her idea with professors, who she felt had a high degree of academic and moral integrity. Her professors recommended a few different students to connect with, and after sorting through many candidates, Jacqueline found an engineer who specialized in Bluetooth technology who agreed to sign her NDA and build a prototype.

Jacqueline was tenacious. For two years, she worked on developing the concept during nights and weekends while she was assigned to teach at a school through Teach for America. It was clear, though, that she needed to focus on Revolar full time. There was market demand for the product as it had performed well on Kickstarter, where she was able to raise enough funds to start manufacturing the product. What kept her going was the outpouring of responses that she received whenever she talked about Revolar in public. Jacqueline recounts several of these stories:

When I was fifteen, I was raped. I don't want my fifteen year old to get raped. I don't want what happened to me to happen to her. How quickly can I buy one?

My husband and I are going through a divorce, and he has threatened to kidnap the kids. I am scared. Do you have one on you now?

My sister is afraid she has a stalker and she is trying to tell people at work but nobody listens. She doesn't know what to do. Can I get one now?

In late 2015, Jacqueline raised $3 million from Foundry Group, a prominent venture capital firm in Colorado. This was a huge milestone for Revolar, which had been only a concept on a napkin a few years back. "This journey has been very emotional. I have cried plenty of times because it kills me," Jacqueline shares. "It kills me that these people that I knew would have never spoken up if I never spoke up. If nothing else, we are starting conversations around a subject that is so taboo and filled with shame that there is not enough positive conversation around survivors. I wanted to let them know, what you have gone through, it isn't fair."

Jacqueline continues, "Hopefully, they can get the support they need and also have the data to prove that something happened so that they can stand up to their attacker. They won't be re-victimized because the data will completely prove what would have happened."

Looking back at her journey, Jacqueline draws strength by remembering what her father taught her. He passed away when she was sixteen, but she still remembers: "He always told me to have a mind of my own. Throughout my entire life, he said that there are double standards that are not fair to me. He always told me that I could be better than that if I moved past it."

"If he could see me now, I think he would be proud to see me think for myself, make my own decisions, and be independent," Jacqueline says. "I am getting to do exactly what I want to do and I get to do it surrounded by people who I have nothing but the utmost respect for. This is the first time in my life where I can be who I am."

IMPACTING THE WORLD ONE HOUSE AT A TIME

Entrepreneur: Alexandria Lafci
Age: 28
Hometown: Long Island, New York
Company: New Story Charity, a pioneer in providing solutions that address global homelessness and work toward a world where no human lives in survival mode

Alexandria Lafci and her mom were well traveled, but not in the traditional sense. Every Friday, they went to the library and selected a PBS VHS tape that exposed them to the culture, history, and food of another country. This is how they traveled virtually to places around the world like Peru, Thailand, and Japan. "People probably thought we were well traveled," Alexandria laughs, "because we knew so much about so many different countries." The closest they actually got to visiting any country was eating at local ethnic restaurants. They simply did not have the financial means to travel there in person.

When Alexandria was fifteen, she committed to a volunteer trip to Peru to work in local health clinics. However, she registered for the trip without having the $5,000 needed to get there. Her mother told Alexandria she could go but that she would have to raise the money herself. Alexandria was determined to find a way to get to Peru.

"I lived on the south side of Bethlehem, Pennsylvania, which was not very affluent," she says. "On the other side of town, there were many beautiful homes, so I figured they might be willing to support me on my journey. I wrote close to forty letters on who I was and why I wanted to go to Peru, and I stuffed them into the mailboxes of the nicest houses. I hoped for the best. A few months go by, I received no responses but I was convinced that I was going on this trip. Three weeks before the trip, I got a call from a woman who said she read my letter and wanted to give me the opportunity to travel. She had the means to do so even though she was too unhealthy to travel herself. I found out later she was the heir to a Fortune 500 company, and she supported me academically and professionally for a very long time thereafter."

After touching down in Peru, Alexandria was assigned to work in a local medical clinic. "I wanted to join Doctor's

Without Borders. There was one woman who worked at a cocoa leaf farm where a dog had bitten a huge chunk of flesh out of her calf. She couldn't get to the clinic for a long time, and a bowl of maggots nested in that area. They wanted me to clean it out and sanitize it. I didn't have the stomach to do so. I started and then I felt like I was about to faint, so I went outside to get some air. I had these fainting spells, and I realized then that I was not cut out for medicine."

Instead of heading home defeated, Alexandria knew she still wanted to make an impact even if it was not in the way that she had originally envisioned. She stayed in Peru and was assigned to lead a community center in that same neighborhood that entertained kids whose parents were unable to tend to them because they were working. The clinic was in shambles. The toilet was broken and filled with feces. The games were missing pieces. Books had torn pages. Nobody came to the center because it was in such disrepair.

Alexandria mobilized resources to turn it into a place that kids wanted to congregate. She got a plumber to fix the bathroom and hired local help to remove the lead paint from the walls. Alexandria's friends from back home donated coloring books, toys, and puzzles. The center was completely transformed and now offered a space that invited kids to come in and enjoy playing there.

By the end of Alexandria's three months, she felt proud of all she had accomplished, but she also worried about how the center would run after she and the other volunteers left. "What happened if the toilet broke down again? Who would replace the puzzles if pieces were missing? The health of the organization was dependent on volunteers instead of indigenous talent," she explains. "I didn't have a word for it at the time, but it wasn't sustainable. From that moment, I knew the kind of work I was going to do in the future. If I was going to leave something behind, it had to survive and thrive without me. It set me on my path to study international development in college, where I learned about sustainability and what the implications were when building something."

After graduating from Boston University, Alexandria enrolled in the Teach for America program in Washington, D.C. She wanted to make a difference, but she noticed that many of the leaders in the social impact space had private sector experience. She finished the teaching program, and instead of continuing on in the education field, she accepted an offer from a logistics and supply chain company in Atlanta to gain corporate experience. Two weeks into the job, she knew the role wasn't right for her. "It was a yes-man culture with no creativity," Alexandria says, "and it was very top-down and authoritarian. I felt like a cog."

Despite the paralyzing culture, Alexandria took advantage

of this opportunity. First, she was able to gain logistics experience that she had never been exposed to in her nonprofit work. Second, the job offered her stability when her mother passed away. Third, she had the financial means to help take care of her then thirteen-year-old sister while also building up a sizable nest egg for the future. Ultimately, the job gave her the flexibility to explore ideas for a social impact business because she had a set, nine-to-five schedule.

The call for social entrepreneurship continued to tug at her. Although Atlanta didn't have a thriving social impact community, Alexandria was still able to find others whose interests intersected with hers. At one social impact meeting, she met her two future cofounders, Matthew and Brett. Brett had recently come back from Haiti, and he described the rampant homelessness that shaped their community. That story resonated with Alexandria on many different levels. She reflected on her experience in Peru at the community center. Many of the children she taught while she was in D.C. lived in shelters. Her mother had been a product of the foster care system and had told Alexandria about that time in her life.

"My mother was very open about her upbringing," Alexandria remembers. "Although my mother grew up in a decent household, her mother kicked her out of the house at eleven. On the streets, with nobody to turn to, my mother would go to restaurants, order food, and then run out without paying the check because she had no other option. She eventually entered into the foster home system. Even though my mother was able to claw out of that system and become a registered nurse, many of her peers were not as fortunate. Some were incarcerated, while others succumbed to drug addiction. She was able to survive despite not having any housing stability."

Alexandria, Matthew, and Brett met in October 2014, and by November they had built a minimum viable product for New Story Charity, a nonprofit dedicated to building homes in third world countries. They found themselves in Haiti in March of the following year, building their first home. Alexandria vividly remembers this experience: "Haiti is very hot in the mid to high 90s. During the daytime, nobody is lounging around in their makeshift homes as the heat gets trapped inside as there is no ventilation. The smell is terrible as there is no sewage system. I've been around the world and slept on floors, in the jungle even, but this was one of the worst things I have ever seen in terms of human living conditions."

Building their first home was a memorable experience. The night before the first family was to move in, a heavy downpour flooded the area. Alexandria was overcome with emotion when she imagined the floors turning into mud from the rainfall, rising up and forcing the family to huddle on the single bed that was the only piece of furniture elevated from the ground. It underlined for Alexandria why she had embarked on this initiative to build homes for people in the first place.

New Story Charity collected the stories and photos of each family, and Alexandria carefully reviewed each piece of material. It was heart-wrenching. All of them had been displaced after an earthquake in 2010, and they were living in makeshift shelters until Alexandria and her team came in. When she met Anita, who was moving into the first home, she was overcome with emotion again, but this time, it was joy instead of pain. Now, she and her cofounders were part of a new story, one where these families could restart their lives again.

On the plane ride from Haiti back to the US, Alexandria felt that this trip had been different than her trip to Peru. "A home has a lasting impact and continues for generations. Families own a home that they sit on. It allows a family to move from survival to stability. It has a direct impact on both safety and educational outcomes," Alexandria shares. "In reflecting back on that plane ride, I was much more satisfied with the short-term deliverables while also being hopeful that we are making a long-term, sustainable, generational impact."

CHAPTER 15

SELF-MADE

BE A HOMIE, THEN MAKE THE ASK

Entrepreneur: Shaun Neff
Age: 35
Hometown: Los Angeles, California
Company: Neff, an active, youth headwear and apparel brand supported by some of the globe's best athletes, musicians, and personalities

Out until 3 a.m. Wake up for class at 9 a.m. Get through the day. Prepare for another night out until the wee hours of the morning. Rinse, wash, repeat. This was a typical week for Shaun Neff as a college student at Brigham Young University. He wasn't partying with fellow classmates. He was hanging out and raging with pro snowboarders who had descended on Salt Lake City from Europe to train during the winter months. Because of all the time he spent hanging out with them, they built a genuine relationship based on trust.

That eventually translated into his friends-slash-snowboarder-influencers wanting to support Shaun and his interest in building a lifestyle clothing business. They wore his clothes because they liked him, not just because he paid them a huge endorsement fee. Shaun understood that these snowboarders were influencers who could move product. He bonded with them not because he had to, but because he wanted to. He was forging authentic relationships and became a part of their posse.

"Some of these dudes are nuts," Shaun remembers vividly, "There was one particularly gnarly snowboarder who I needed to get into my program. I had to chill with him, take him out to dinner, and do the whole thing. We were all hanging in and around my car really late at night, and everyone was mad hammered. And all of a sudden, I saw this guy in my rearview window—who had way too much to drink—come flying out from the back and kick a big dent in my car. Here I was, trying to chill with this dude so that maybe he wanted to wear my beanies. And he literally went up, kicked a dent in the back of my car."

Shaun continues, "After that, we started to drive to continue on our night. As I was driving, I saw a cop to the right. Everyone was raging in my car. I thought to myself that I was going to jail. There was a 10 percent chance that he would look over, pull us to the side, and discover what we had in the car. Luckily, that didn't happen, but I still had to face my parents. When I got home, my mother lit me up, screaming, 'What are you doing with your life?' She drilled home the point that there were a lot of people who start businesses, but hanging out until 4 a.m. was not the way that you started a business."

Reflecting on that moment, Shaun says, "I had this ponderous moment where I asked myself, 'What am I doing?' I answered that with, 'Yes, I have drive. I have passion, and I am going to make sure I am successful.' To get into this game, I had to be credible and to be respected. I was young at the time. I didn't have three to four million dollars to pay these kids. The guy who kicked the dent in my car and I ended up wrangling, I would have to pay them that kind of money. If I was going to do this business, this was the game I needed to play for the next ten years. I felt this mad peaceful calm. This was what I supposed to do. If I was going to be in the fashion and youth culture space, I had to hang out with these wild characters in the morning to make sure they knew I was down with them. That was the biggest moment between my parents and me."

Growing up, Shaun was always the ringleader among his friends. Hanging out with pro snowboarders was no different. It just happened that these snowboarders exerted a huge cultural influence with what they wore, the lifestyle they led, and the friends they associated with. Shaun understood their power to shape culture, and he understood how a brand could be built through their influence with clear messaging and consistent imagery.

"My gig was always branding," he explains. "My pet peeve to this day is a dude that is driving a truck wearing Oakley sunglasses and has a Ray-Ban sticker. There is this ridiculous brand confusion. Or kids wearing this sporting gear, where they have Under Armour shoes, Nike shorts, and Adidas shorts. I can't even look at them. If you are going to be a Nike cat, be it. Don't swap brands. It's just brand confusion, and it freaks me out, and it is like nails on the chalkboard."

In high school, Shaun was obsessed with the idea of having a brand. He didn't know what a company was. He wanted a brand, which he thought of as a "magic cloud that sits in the universe that pumps out cool stuff."

"When I wore a shirt the first day of school, it was dope because it was telling something about me. I had my vibe," Shaun says. "The kids who would mix sports and action sports, it was a no-no. People who would be wearing the Quiksilver hat and then a football jersey or a team thing. That would freak me out. That was my dream growing up to create a brand that I want to rock because that was the lifestyle that I wanted to live and showcase to others."

Shaun was a sophomore in college when he started Neff, his activewear brand. He tried to register at least fifteen different names, but all of them were trademark protected. Finally, he decided to just use his last name, Neff. "It was short, it was simple, and it would look good on the tag. Let's go." The brand represented Shaun. His business happened to be apparel, but what he was doing was selling a lifestyle—his lifestyle.

Shaun recalls, "By the time I was a senior, I was doing $3.5 million off my cell phone. I had five or six homies helping me with all of the inventory that we housed in an office of a different business. We would use all of their shipping and logistics capabilities. They gave me a container where I would put all my hats and beanies. And when they shut down at 7 p.m., we would come in and use all of their stuff and pack all of our orders. And then we would have it sitting there when the company employee came back in the morning to ship everything out. It was a mad hustle."

He continues, "Starting this brand in college was prime time to roll the dice. I was young. I didn't know what it took to run a business or to manage it or to grow a company. I had no idea. If I had known then what I know now, I would have been like that was too gnarly, I can't do that. It was this naive belief and dream that took over me. I started as a clothing company. I got the cool DJ, the cool dudes in an uncool college town, Provo, Utah. I got everyone who was cool rocking this stuff."

His instinct was to scale his business beyond Provo. To do so, he had to enlist his influencer friends to help him get more eyeballs outside of town. He tried to get them to wear his t-shirts, but they couldn't because it violated the terms of their current endorsement deals. Still determined, Shaun asked his snowboarding friends for their contracts so that he could examine them for any loopholes. As he poured through the documents, he discovered there wasn't a clause about hats or beanies. That was the night when he decided Neff was going to be a headwear company. The problem was that he didn't know how to make hats or beanies.

But he didn't want to wait. In fact, he didn't have time to because that weekend there was a snowboarding event in Park City, Utah, that was going to be televised on a major network. "I went to a 99 cent store. I bought 99-cent ghetto headbands and beanies. I wrote my last name on it with a sharpie," he recalls. "I went mad ghetto hustle, and I sold them the dream that this was going to be dope. Only the rad guys were going to support this. This was how it started. It was this crazy ambition and being nimble in my mindset. If I was going to have a brand in the space and the only way it was going to get notoriety and expand, it was if these guys were going to wear it."

Even after that advantageous event, Shaun struggled for the next year to figure out how to produce headbands and beanies at scale. "I was purchasing beanies off the Internet at a wholesale discount rate, acting like I had a store. And literally, I was ripping their labels off and sewing Neff labels back on them." It was a lot of trial and error until he found the right manufacturer in China that could produce the quality of what he was looking for at the right price point. But what was most important that year, even as he was fighting through his production challenges, was preserving the relationships he had forged with his snowboarding friends.

He was only able to ask his snowboarding friends to wear his makeshift headbands after he had invested in a personal relationship with them. Brands threw money at them and asked for favors all the time.

"The key is doing it in a moment where they have gained your trust," Shaun says. "When I was first in the game, it took two, three, or four months until I was like, yo, we were homies. There was no way that they would have given me their endorsement contract to look at. Gain the trust, be a homie, and then make the ask in an authentic way."

Despite brisk sales, Shaun had to put all of the revenue he made back into making more product. He still didn't have any money to invest in endorsements. To expand distribution, he attended trade shows so that other retailers could discover his brand. Having a booth at the biggest industry trade show was cost prohibitive. But what Shaun lacked in financial capital, he made up for by flexing his network of relationships.

Shaun shares, "I would call up the director of the trade show and let them know that I had the biggest roster with thirty of the dopest dudes. They are going to sit in my booth. That was what you needed at the show. I want to be right next to Burton, the biggest snowboarding company. The dude came back and got me that perfect location because he knew he needed energy for this event."

Even though Shaun got the space, he still needed to create a booth where he could house all of his riders. Burton spent millions designing and building its booth. Shaun spent less than $500.

"It was a day or two after Halloween, and I drove past a haunted house," he explains. "They were taking it down, and I saw that they had the right materials—wood and pipes—that I could take to build my trade show booth. There were spiders and skulls still on the wood. It stood out like a sore thumb, mad ghetto, but I had the biggest dudes in the building chillin' at my booth. I made a mad statement."

Since these early times, Shaun has grown his business

by creating deep personal relationships with influencers in entertainment and sports. He has followed the same formula he used when he was just starting out with pro snowboarders. It only hit him how big he had become when he was about six years into his business. He was listening to the radio in his car. He realized that he had locked up deals with the artists who had the top three songs in pop culture at that moment: Snoop Dogg, Kid Cudi, and LilWayne. Neff had finally broken out of its niche as a surf and skate brand to a general lifestyle platform.

"When I started, I was so intrigued from the first kid who wore a Neff t-shirt. It was a trip. He was wearing my last name on his chest. I thought that was crazy," Shaun concludes. "Then it got picked up in these magazines. I saw this little brand with my name on it in these magazines that I read in the past ten years. It was never about how rich I could get. I wanted to have an influence out there in the culture. I wanted to put my little Shaun Neff impression on this world, and now, I want to see other ideas that I can create and turn a thought into an action. I want to make a dent in the world with these other projects that I am advising such as investing in Sun Bum, an upstart sunscreen protection brand, to helping that business explode. Another one is to think through the brand strategy of how to redesign Target's kids private label apparel business. I want what I do to become something that is meaningful. That has always been the big driver."

Entrepreneur: Jen Mozenter
Age: 29
Hometown: Miami, Florida
Company: The Jane Doze, New York-based DJ and production duo in the electronic dance music industry

Sitting down in Washington Square Park on a cold February afternoon in New York, Jen Mozenter was contemplating her future with her business partner Claire Schlissel. They were the musical talent behind The Jane Doze, a DJ dance duo, who had broken on to the music scene in 2010. Four years later, shortly before that park bench meeting, they let their support team go in an effort to reduce expenses and regain financial security.

"We just weren't sure if it was worth moving forward," Jen explains. "As we were having this conversation, some girl walked over and said, 'So sorry to bother you. Are you The Jane Doze?' That was our 'holy shit' moment. This thing is working. People had heard the music. We had chills, and right when we considered quitting, she was sent at that exact moment." This chance encounter was the inspiration Jen and Claire needed to keep pursuing their musical career.

Both of them had jobs in the music industry before they formed The Jane Doze. Making music was a fun hobby that allowed them to mash up popular songs and share them with friends. It started with friends requesting them to play at parties. Their first paid offer came in from a fraternity at Syracuse University that asked them to play at a Halloween party in 2011.

"I remember we were sitting on a plane together, and we were looking at each other in insane bewilderment that we were getting flown out and paid to play at a college Halloween party," Jen recalls. "The party was in the fraternity basement, and everyone was in costumes. It was wild. I knew I wanted that feeling all the time. After the show ended, it was blizzarding in Manhattan, so we were unable to get back. We ended up staying in the frat house and hanging out with the guys. To us, it didn't feel strange. It felt like it was part of the experience."

Fueled by this experience, Jen started to consider a music career more seriously, where instead of supporting other artists, she would actually become an artist herself. She kept her day job at Columbia Records while she played gigs at night.

Jen and Claire wanted to break into the industry based on the quality of their music and talent and build a platform to help other women stand up for things that they felt strongly about. Their vision was to build a community based on collaboration instead of exclusion.

What Jen loves about music is its ability to bring people together. "Music—no matter the color of your skin, your sexual orientation, or your religious background, it is one of the few things that brings people together," Jen explains. "If you stand at a concert, and you look around—you'll see so many different kinds of people. It reminds me that music is this universal language, which is a powerful thing. It can heal or be part of the healing process. Music brings people together, and being a part of that is very powerful and special to me."

The Jane Doze affectionately called their fan base and community of followers "the herd." "It came from this concept of a female deer—doe—who act as a unit, a herd," she explains. "They moved together, spoke their minds, and supported one another. The number one thing was about acceptance, diversity, and embracing the differences in people. The community we built was authentic and organic, and our herd was there because they wanted to be."

Navigating a male-dominated industry was incredibly challenging for the duo. Jen recalls an incident when Spinnin' Records, a popular dance label, uploaded an image of a Pioneer CDJ turntable photoshopped onto a stove burner with the caption "Finally Pioneer Invited a CDJ for Women."

"My blood was boiling," Jen says. "Our responsibility to

ourselves and to our herd was not to let something like that fly. If that meant that we would be outspoken about it and risk losing the opportunity to sign with them or not be able to work with some of their artists, so be it."

She continues, "We wrote a very honest blog post about what that meant to us, and tweeted at the founder of the record label to ask, 'Why would you do that?' to which he responded that it was only a joke. We partnered with *Buzzfeed* to write an entire editorial piece exposing what was wrong with this post. He poked fun at how we felt women were being portrayed in the space, and we thought it was our responsibility to stand up against this using the platform we built."

Music was the fuel that brought Jen and Claire together, and ultimately, their herd. Fans rallied around them after that incident. They deepened their relationship with their herd by connecting with some of them one on one. For example, Kirby, a fan who had stage III breast cancer and was a cycling instructor, always liked to play The Jane Doze during her classes. "Somebody let us know that it would make her day if the Jane Doze tweeted at her," Jen says, "and of course we agreed."

Jen continues, "We immediately started a conversation over Twitter, and we started to build a genuine relationship. It was so evident how important music was to her, not just in her spin classes, but in her recovery process as she just started chemotherapy. We wanted to do more to help Kirby through some of her darkest times."

During that time period, Jen and Claire were working on a track called "Lights Go Down." They wanted to do a music video but none of the treatments they saw captured the true meaning of the song. "Curtains, the featured singer on the track, brought this concept to us where even when the lights have gone down, and you are at your lowest of lows, you can still break through to the other side. You find things that inspire you to get to the other side," Jen says. "We thought, 'Holy shit, this is the perfect place to tell [Kirby's] story.' We looked at the song over and over again, and we tried to figure out what it meant. We had all of these dark times, and we didn't see the light at the end of the tunnel. Then it came to us. It was Kirby's story who personified what this story meant. We made her the main storyline in the music video."

The duo planned a show in Dallas to announce the news to Kirby that she was going to be the main storyline in their music video. They coordinated in advance with Kirby's mom and the cycling studio owner to make the surprise visit. Kirby was floored when she saw Jen and Claire bust through the double doors and dropped to the ground crying. Jen recalls, "I have never experienced anything like that in my life, seeing someone who has a reaction to this experience and it was so powerful."

Later that night, Kirby came up on stage with The Jane Doze. It was an incredible experience for Kirby, but it was just the beginning of her friendship with Jen and Claire. In fact, Jen continued to be a part of Kirby's journey by sending playlists to help her power through chemotherapy. Eventually, Kirby received the news that she was in remission. To celebrate, Jen and Claire sent Kirby to a program called First Descents, which takes people who are battling through cancer on a week-long adventure of kayaking, hiking, and rock climbing. It's a chance for cancer survivors to feel normal again after being sapped of their energy for so long.

Jen points out that, "We are still close to her. We could have put it out at any time and showed our fans, 'Hey, look at the cool thing that we did with a fan.' But we made it so that it had the most meaning. We were thoughtful about the best way to tell her story. I'm grateful we had a small platform to raise awareness for what she went through. Everyone has had their own dark moments and what defines us is how we pick ourselves up to let the light shine through."

THE JUGGLER

Entrepreneur: Olga Kay

Age: 32

Hometown: Crimea, Russia

Company: MooshWalks, a lifestyle brand that has turned socks into a fashion statement, giving young girls and boys the ability to stand out, make friends, and start a conversation

Olga Kay never wanted to juggle. Her dream was to be an aerial artist whose body dangled and danced from a ring trapeze 100 feet above the ground. This dream was never realized. As Olga explains, "At fourteen, I was too old and my hips were too wide. My womanly heavy bottom would prevent me from lifting up my legs to do all of the acrobatics in the air." Olga had to settle for juggling. It was at least better than cleaning up animal poop.

She had joined the Russian circus as a teenager to escape the tiny peninsula of Crimea. "We lived in very poor conditions," Olga remembers, "We didn't have candles so my dad would teach me how to make candles out of olive oil and gauze. We needed the candles because our village only had electricity two hours during the day and two hours in the evening."

Her family had very little money so they had to be resourceful and creative with what they did have. "I asked my mom to buy me shoes when it was winter but we could not afford them. Instead, my dad would either patch up my old shoes or I would borrow my mom's boots and stuff extra paper in the back of the shoe so they would fit. I would then go out and play with friends. We all didn't have anything so it didn't make a difference that we wore the same thing every day."

Over time, conditions in the village worsened. There was often no electricity for days, a sign that they should leave. Olga had an aunt who was in the circus and she encouraged them to join because staying in their village was not an option. They packed up their house, took what belongings they could carry, and left to join the circus.

Cleaning animal poop was the only job available to Olga, which was not the kind of job that she wanted. She wanted to be performing in the circus. The only performance option available to her was to juggle. Her uncle, who was in the circus as a juggler, was able and willing to teach her this skill. Olga shares, "It was one of the skills that I hated, as I felt like it was very masculine. But that was the only thing I could get good at, and if I put eight hours a day into it I could probably do it. I started juggling with three objects over the bed in my hotel room. I was able to do it in the first twenty minutes very poorly. Maybe I would be able to achieve something if I practiced, and I tried more complicated combinations while increasing the number of objects. My eye-hand coordination improved, and I was getting better every day."

The circus initially tasked Olga with warming up the crowd with her juggling act before the main acts came on. Her practice prepared her for this, but performing in front of a live audience was intimidating. She practiced to the point where she had the confidence and skills to partake in the main act, but every time she went on to perform, she still had butterflies in her stomach.

Olga recalls, "We performed our juggling act on free-standing ladders, which we had to balance while juggling. It was awesome. Two young chicks on ladders. Nobody else did it. People were screaming for us, and I couldn't wait to do it again as soon as we would finish our act. But every time I had to wait an hour or two between the shows, my stage fright would creep up on me and I was forever stuck inside the never-ending circle of emotions. The next day came, and I am about to perform, and I had that nauseating feeling over again."

When Olga was sixteen years old, she was invited to join Ringling Bros. Circus. She left her mom, dad and brother, and she immigrated to the USA. Olga thought she would come back home in two years once her contract was up, but in fact, she never returned. Olga remembers "I didn't speak English when I first arrived in America. My high school diploma wasn't translated into English so the government did not recognize this accreditation. American law required minors to be in school, and because I spoke no English and my degree was not recognized, I was placed in the second grade." It was a humbling experience, but it helped her learn the language. Only after nine months of studying was she finally able to escape her nine-year-old classmates.

After her contract with Ringling Bros. Circus finished, Olga did not want to return to Russia. "I loved America. I was making money, had a bank account, and learned how to drive," she exclaims. So she signed up with another family circus for only a few months. "I realized that family-owned circuses were so different from the corporate circuses. I remember I was doing my act, then running to help with a horse act, then assisting an aerial act and then selling cotton candy during the intermission. I don't mind working hard but that was working hard on steroids."

Olga quit her circus career at nineteen and moved to Los Angeles to pursue other entertainment avenues. She landed a job on a cruise ship. "I was told that if I were to incorporate comedy into my show, I could earn more per show, so my English was terrible and there I was, trying to be funny working as a cruise ship performer. That didn't last long enough to gain any kind of experience," she says. It was only when Olga decided to focus her juggling skills on a more lucrative market—television commercials—that she started to achieve success.

At first, she was pigeonholed as a circus juggler. Her agent booked her gigs overseas to juggle inside theme parks, which Olga gladly took to pay the bills. She was also able to do work on movie sets and TV shows as an extra to fill out the scene. Even though she wasn't hired to juggle, she juggled anyway whenever there was downtime on a shoot. "The extras and I sat in a holding area for hours and then they would come and get us for twenty minutes for a scene, and then all of us would go back and sit some more," Olga recalls. "They told us to bring books. Instead, I would juggle and make friends. All of the casting agents and production associates knew me as the juggler."

After six months of persistence, Olga's agent finally watched her demo reel. Her agent had previously never bothered to watch it because all of her clients claimed something similar, so she was skeptical when Olga made this request. Her agent, though, was impressed, "You know, every girl says that she's a good juggler and all they do is just, like, twirl some sticks. But when I watched it, I was like 'Oh, wow, you're actually talented.'" That was when her agent started to commit more time and effort to booking gigs for Olga. As Olga became more visible to booking agents and casting directors, she started to land roles in television commercials.

She did her first commercial for Burger King. The concept was that people in an office were each juggling something, but the hero of the story was Olga, who was juggling burritos, a product that Burger King had just introduced into the marketplace. "It was the first time I juggled food. I was always against it even though people requested it. It was my pride because I wanted to be taken seriously. But this was different as I wanted the execution to be perfect as I had to juggle food and walk simultaneously while making sure I didn't hit the camera."

This first commercial kicked off a string of bookings with other big brands like Smirnoff and Dirt Devil. Every time she went into an audition for a juggling role, it felt as if "all of the other girls that auditioned were like 'Fuck this chick! She's here again.' I remember that I thought I was getting somewhere."

At around the same time, Olga discovered YouTube in 2006. She figured it was another avenue to promote her juggling capabilities to casting agents. In reality, the channel turned out to be a platform for her to showcase her other creative talents beyond juggling. "I remember watching all these people who were posting. I didn't understand why it was so fascinating to see somebody talk to the camera except that it was so fascinating," Olga shares. "I saw all these personalities and I knew that I had a fun personality and I should put myself on camera, so I decided to start my own videos. I didn't have a camera, and I didn't know how to edit, but I just kind of learned as I went. It helped me overcome my stage fight because I could perform but just edit what I wanted the audience to see versus having one take to do it right. "

This passing interest turned into an obsession for Olga who learned how to shoot, edit, and distribute her content. There were no manuals for YouTube back then, which had just launched in 2005. "My friends, when they saw me spend twelve hours a day trying to build up my channel, they really didn't get it. They thought it was ridiculous. Some were even embarrassed when I posted these videos of being silly and showcasing my personality. They just didn't get it. And I wasn't sure why I was doing them but I knew it was gonna pay off. It was like this internal feeling that something good was gonna come from it. I didn't know when or what."

Soon, Olga was amassing a following. It started with a few hundred followers. Then thousands. They gave her a chance to find her own voice. In studying her audience, she found that her personality resonated the most with a young female audience between the ages of thirteen and twenty-five. She thought to herself, "What does a teenage girl want to see? What does a teenage girl go through? They hate everything. They are complaining about their parents, they hate everything, they're very emo."

She decided to create an emo character, Razor Blade, who

carried around a stuffed animal decorated with bones all over its body. People fell in love with the character because they could see themselves in her. Olga also played herself in addition to Razor Blade. She posted weekly episodes that kept her audience engaged in how the plot was going to evolve. This is how Olga built her audience.

Even though she had more than a few hundred thousand subscribers, she was not very business savvy. Several brands approached her to integrate their product into her YouTube show. But she didn't know how to charge them. She went to a friend who was also making videos and asked, "If I were to give you this kind of video, how much should I charge with my kind of numbers?" Olga remembers, "His response was something that changed my mind for the rest of time. He said, 'If you don't know how much you should be charging for your services, then you have no business being in this business.' That's all he said. And I was just like, 'Wait, what?' So I realized that I had to learn every aspect of my career."

As a result of that conversation, she started to ask herself key questions like: Who am I as a business? What kind of business am I providing? How do I brand myself? "I didn't even know what branding was," Olga explains, "And my branding happened by accident. I had a cat Mushka and her nickname was Moosh, so when I was looking for a special word, my fans and I can use, we landed on

Moosh. My fans started to gravitate to this word, and soon, this word took on a life of its own where it started to represent me as a brand. My audience started calling themselves the Moosh Army and refer to me as their Moosh Mommy. We even replaced bad words with Moosh. Moosh was everything"

Instead of relying only on sponsorship dollars, Olga moved into merchandising her brand under the Moosh trademark. She had an audience who was willing to buy her products if she could get them to tell her what they wanted. So she asked her audience what kinds of things they wanted, from shoes to t-shirts and trinkets. She obliged all of their requests.

Olga remembers, "I was making t-shits with Moosh on it for $20.00 to my viewer and people didn't seem to care that much. Then I teamed up with a shoe company where I was able to create a custom shoes with my viewers' help, we had zippers, dog tags, clips, and picture pockets on them. By the end of the creative process the shoe was $75.00 to the customer and I thought to myself, *No one would every pay that much!* My shoes were selling WAY better than t-shirts and that's when I realized that if I can create something unique and special, people would pay."

At one point, Olga started questioning her YouTube career. She realized that she didn't want to be known just as a

YouTube star because she felt that she had more value to give to the next generation of women who looked up to her. She thought that a fashion business built around her unique sense of style and personality offered the best avenue to achieve this vision. Her inspiration was Betsey Johnson, a famous fashion designer, and Olga looked at her as a model to build something very similar where her sense of fashion made her followers feel like they were setting trends." This was how MooshWalks, Olga's socks business, was born.

Olga continues, "MooshWalks it's 110 percent my personality. It's my inspiration. It speaks in my voice. I cried for a week writing my brand story, which brought me back to my village where I came from nothing. I didn't own my first pair of jeans until I was seventeen. I could never follow the coolest trends. I just wasn't able to do so. I could never be a teenage girl. Now, I have a business where I can create my own trend for the new generation to be the coolest teenagers in their schools. This was my whole drive, my whole purpose, to give young girls a loud expression."

Olga always had an entrepreneurial fire lit inside of her. Now, she has found a path that offers her an opportunity to scale her business and brand to touch millions of people. She shares, "When I was a circus performer, I was scared. When I was acting in Hollywood I became insecure. When I became a YouTube Star, I've learned how to be competitive but once I became an entrepreneur—I am unstoppable."

CHAPTER 16

THE NEW MOM AND POP

THAT GOTCHA MOMENT

Entrepreneur: Hunter Pond
Age: 29
Hometown: Dallas, Texas
Company: East Hampton Sandwich Co., a Texas-based, gourmet sandwich shop, specializing in house-made proteins and sauces

"Pond, this meat is fucking legit," Hunter's friends exclaimed. This made Hunter Pond smile. The food was so simple, yet so good. Sometimes it was smoked pork butt served with a dollop of whole grain mustard on a Hawaiian roll. Other times, it was a marinated chicken breast smothered in homemade BBQ sauce served on a toasted hamburger bun. Hunter lived for these moments where he could serve his friends food on Saturdays at Texas Tech before the game. It took nine hours to prepare the food, from buying the meat from Sam's club to smoking it. But it only took nine minutes to enjoy it. The time he spent making delicious sandwiches just to see his friends smile was worth the effort. This was what gave Hunter true joy.

As a kid, Hunter recalls, "Our fridge was always packed to the brim. It was never with one chicken breast, one vegetable, one starch, and a gallon of milk. It was packed with sauces and spices, all of the ingredients really. When my mother went to the store, she would bring back the protein, the veg, and the starch. We pretty much had a laboratory within our fridge and pantry to play with. The best way to describe cooking with my mom was to get creative and put random ingredients together. Sometimes it worked. Sometimes it didn't. But that is what made it so fun. It got me intrigued in food at an early age."

Hunter was in awe of his mother's cooking prowess. She never followed a recipe. She was always experimenting with different spice blends and sauce combinations from all over the world. She made amazing dishes using these extra ingredients. It wasn't just Stouffer's macaroni and cheese, a piece of grilled chicken, and a vegetable. Hunter's mom made macaroni and cheese from scratch with a hint of paprika and cayenne pepper for flavor.

There was magic in the way that she put together a meal

that tasted just as good as it looked. Every Sunday was an occasion with a different meal on the table. One week it was fettuccine alfredo. The next week it was a Ritz-cracker chicken. The aroma was always different week to week. Hunter developed his palate by experimenting with so many different flavors through his mom's cooking. His culinary-inspired upbringing was what carried Hunter through his school years.

He had a lot of free time at Texas Tech. When he got bored, he went to the grocery store and experimented with different kinds of foods. One time, he ended up purchasing a whole octopus. He brought it back to the house, butchered it, and made octopus soup. His roommates were aghast when they saw the octopus carcass all over their kitchen counter. The soup did not turn out to be as delicious as he thought it might, but it didn't matter to Hunter. He chalked it up to a learning experience.

Entering the food industry wasn't on Hunter's radar screen during college. He felt the pressure to get a job, but in 2009, the employment market was terrible. He headed to law school to wait out the recession and get a valuable degree in the meantime. In his first semester classes, though, he became easily distracted. Instead of taking class notes, he was doing research on how to open a restaurant. It was just what he gravitated to until one day, it actually hit him that he needed to enter into the restaurant business.

Once he had had this realization, he didn't hesitate. At the end of first semester, Hunter left in a dramatic fashion. His professor handed out the tort exam. Hunter glanced over the questions, closed the booklet, and handed the test in without answering anything. He immediately went to the registrar's office and dropped out. That same day, he rented a U-Haul, packed up his belongings, and headed home to Dallas. "Fuck this, I'm just going to jump off into the deep end."

Hunter's parents were pissed. They admonished him for being so hasty with his decision. He understood his parent's position, but was resolute. He wanted to pursue a career in the food industry. He ended up getting a job at a local pizza place. He started out washing dishes. He then rotated to managing the salad bar. After four months, Hunter learned enough to feel confident he could start his own restaurant concept. The most important lesson he took away from that experience was treating staff with respect and appreciation. He saw one of the owners micromanage the staff, and Hunter vowed to take a more hands-off approach when he opened his first restaurant.

During those four months, Hunter hatched his food concept. He didn't want to play in the fine dining space because it required culinary skills that he didn't possess. He didn't want to be in the fast food segment because he didn't think he could compete on price. He focused on fast casual, specifically the sandwich market. His concept was simple yet powerful. Most sandwich shops focused on the quality of the bun. But nobody focused on the quality of the meat. Most of the deli meat was injected with fillers and chemicals to preserve its freshness and flavoring. This process wasn't natural.

Hunter flipped the sandwich model on its head. He felt like he could elevate the quality of sandwich offerings by focusing on the meat. He organized his business model around this insight. Unlike other sandwich chains that dedicated most of their square footage to baking bread, Hunter did the opposite. He outsourced the bread to a high quality European bakery and purchased the necessary equipment for grilling and baking different kinds of protein, from steaks to chicken to ham. Nobody else was doing that. Now he just had to find a great name.

He drafted up a business plan and raised money from friends and family. He broke ground on the first East Hampton Sandwich Co. location in summer 2012. Hunter recalls, "I say this tongue in cheek, but I didn't really know what I was doing. I wish I had known the daily operational systems to thwart theft and waste. I had zero experience. It took me two years to learn how to run this as efficiently as possible. I left so much money on the table because I didn't know the systems."

Word got out on their opening week that Hunter's sandwiches were amazing. By the second week, he had a huge line out the door. They were grossing $10,000 a day, but it was taking over twenty minutes just to get one sandwich out. Success didn't come easy. Hunter had to make tough choices along the way to maintain that level of success.

One of Hunter's employees who was overseeing operations for the restaurant had gotten into a car accident a few miles away. He broke his ribs and couldn't see because his glasses had shattered. He had no money and no cell phone. He ended up walking 3 miles to the restaurant nearly blind with his broken rib. He wanted to work but couldn't. Hunter called his parents, and they sprung into action. Hunter's dad took the broken glasses to Target to get his prescription. His mom took his employee to a doc-in-a-box to place a bandage on his body to set his ribs. Hunter stayed at the restaurant to get the hourly staff ready. The employee made it back by 11:30 a.m., hopped on the line, and crushed it that day. He was a star in Hunter's eye as this employee ate, bled, and sweat for the company that first year.

As much as that employee earned his keep, he also ended up causing Hunter a lot of headaches by showing up to work on other occasions with his breath still smelling of alcohol. He got arrested and thrown into jail for a DUI. Hunter received a call from his employee's mom at 3 a.m.

one night imploring him to bail out her son. She didn't have the cash to post his bail. It was up to Hunter to do something. He didn't have to bail him out. His initial instincts told him not to involve himself. He'd been burned before when he lent money out to an employee who never paid him back. This was different, though. Hunter felt a loyalty to him and a calling to do the right thing. He got out of bed, drove to the station, and posted his bail. As much as Hunter saved his ass, this employee had also saved Hunter's in the early years.

Since the first East Hampton Sandwich Co. location, Hunter has opened three more stores. He sold 500,000 sandwiches in 2015. East Hampton Sandwich Co. won "Best Sandwich Shop" in *D* magazine, a Dallas-based publication, three years in a row—an unheard of feat as the award typically goes to a newcomer or an old standby, not a chain. The quality of the product has improved even in expansion. Typically the opposite happens. The emphasis on quality remained the same whether Hunter sold a half million sandwiches or served seventy-five people in his backyard.

When Hunter sits at the bar at his sandwich shop, he surveys the customers in the restaurant. He looks around and watches his customers take that first bite of one of his sandwiches. They look up at their friends and point to their sandwich while they are chewing. They don't manage to say anything, but the look in their face is a look that Hunter remembers well from his college days. They are relishing every moment of the food that he has had a hand in creating. That is the gotcha moment that Hunter lives for: knowing he made a difference in someone else's life.

THE COMMUNITY CHOCOLATE SHOP

Entrepreneur: Alexandra Clark
Age: 29
Hometown: Hamtramck, Michigan
Company: Bon Bon Bon, a chocolate shop with internationally-trained confiseurs who use classic French technique in conjunction with a little Detroit ingenuity to create a wide variety of flavors for their bon bon bons

Hamtramck is a gritty enclave just inside Detroit, Michigan. Modest houses are lined up right next to each other. To get a feel for the neighborhood, I rented a room through Airbnb. I walked the streets and ate at local restaurants. Hamtramck also happened to be the neighborhood where upstart chocolate shop Bon Bon Bon was based. When Bon Bon Bon first opened, lines ran out the door. But the store did not put the town on the map or transform the neighborhood. Instead, Bon Bon Bon reflects the character of the town, which is what Alexandra Clark, the proprietor, wanted because she ultimately reflected the hard-working, blue-collar ethic of the people who are proud to call Hamtramck their home.

Alexandra explains, "You have this rough-and-tumble chocolate shop from this rough-and-tumble town. If you want to go to Godiva, you can drive a few miles on Interstate 75 to go to the fancy mall. If you want our chocolate, you have to be part of our community. There is nothing I could be more proud of than representing a community that I love. The community takes such good care of us."

Before Bon Bon Bon opened, neighbors would stop by as late as 10 p.m. to drop off food, whether it was Swedish meatballs or leftover macaroni and cheese. Some even volunteered their time to help package chocolates for wholesale. They wanted to be a part of Alexandra's business because her success was the neighborhood's success too. These small gestures had a huge impact on Alexandra and helped her understand the weight of her responsibility in representing the community well.

The journey to opening Bon Bon Bon took eight years. Alexandra concentrated on studying food science and the business side of hospitality in the hospitality business program at Michigan State University. At nineteen, she decided to travel to Norway, inspired by her Norwegian roots and because a visa was easy to procure. Through mutual friends, she ended up meeting a family who manufactured candy for a living. They produced a very specialized piece of candy that was placed on a certain kind of cookie and eaten only once a year. This gummy candy business had sustained a family for generations.

"I realized this family was doing okay with this weird, bizarre, candy company," Alexandra shares, "and this was my aha moment when I thought this could be an option for me too, such as opening up my own bakery or sweets shop."

While still in college, Alexandra went to Europe to travel. She had very little money, but her one indulgence was treating herself to one piece of chocolate per city. This ritual was luxurious yet affordable and forced her to wander through towns in search of their local chocolate shop. In Amsterdam, she went to a chocolate shop called Puccini Bomboni, which solidified her desire to focus on opening a chocolate shop of her own.

"At the time, it was the best chocolate I ever had," remembers Alexandra. "I went in and it was the first time that I ever had chocolate in a way that I wanted to do chocolate. I went back in line and got in another piece, which was unusual to have two. I bumped into a friend, and I told him that I just figured out the rest of my life. It was not a bakery or sweets shop. It was a chocolate shop."

That visit prompted Alexandra to handwrite letters to hundreds of chocolate makers around the world to see if she could serve as their apprentice. She wanted to learn the right way to make chocolates by honoring the traditions of the profession. Most didn't respond, and the ones that did didn't want to take her on as an understudy. But there was one chocolatier willing to take a chance on her: Mimi Wheeler. She ran a chocolate shop called Grocer's Daughter Chocolate based in Northern Michigan. She agreed to teach Alexandra about the chocolate craft and steered her on how to hone in on her own chocolate concept.

"She was so welcoming and so forceful," Alexandra says. "Mimi would see what I was good at and I would listen to her. She told me I had to make bon bons. I gave her all of this attitude: 'Okay, Mimi, I will make bon bons. But what do you want me to call it?' She told me I had to figure it out."

"I went home back to my apartment, which was someone's garage, and I wrote down every single idea on a sketch pad for making a bon bon, from flavoring to packaging. All of the flavors that you want to come up with. I went to bed that night, and I woke up at 3 a.m. like I normally did to commute back to school for my morning classes. That particular morning was when I said Bon Bon Bon. That was the name. I Googled it. The domain name was available. It was expensive but I bought it fearful that somebody might take that name if I didn't do it immediately. This was the beginning of Bon Bon Bon."

With the name down and a concept focused on a specific kind of chocolate, Alexandra was ready to start looking for real estate to open her own chocolate shop. Mimi told her to slow down and encouraged her to work for a bigger chocolate manufacturer to gain managerial experience first. So Alexandra found a management role at a global chocolate shop where she oversaw budgeting, training, and scheduling for a store in Boston. The experience was invaluable because it allowed her to see the inner workings of a huge multinational company.

"If this company was this big and was this dysfunctional," Alexandra realized, "I can open the tiniest chocolate shop and be okay. We will at least be as organized as this."

Alexandra looked for real estate in Detroit for three and a half years, sometimes flying from Boston back home just to scout locations. She knew what she wanted to accomplish but was getting impatient with how much time had passed. She started to question herself.

"I wanted to open the chocolate shop so bad. It was so hard. I was impatient. Why do I have to do these different things? When you don't know where the end is and don't know if it will work, you start to look around and compare yourself to where your friends are, who were buying expensive homes. I was making $7.58 an hour trying to learn about chocolate factories on the line overnight and sleeping for two to three hours before the next shift started. These were the experiences that made me more dedicated to the concept. This has to work or else what? What am I doing?"

Making quality chocolate was incredibly important to Alexandra. She wanted to source the best ingredients, and as a result, contacted cocoa bean producers in Sierra Leone, Central and South America, and Southeast Asia. Making these connections also helped her model out the cost structure for these ingredients. More important, Alexandra was able to define what quality chocolate means beyond just taste. She exhaustively researched sourcing practices, distribution channels, and certification standards to shape how she wanted to build her chocolate brand. Through this process, she realized that what the chocolate tasted like was just as important as the inputs that went into making that chocolate.

Alexandra wanted to put what she learned from her research into practice. Opening a chocolate shop was more than just selling great tasting chocolate. It was important for Alexandra to build a brand that had true purpose. "The name Bon Bon Bon, translated from French to English, means good good good," Alexandra explains. "Our motto from the outset has always been that good people deserve sincerely good chocolate that provides good jobs, using good ingredients that are sourced through good relationships."

For her first location, Alexandra was naturally drawn to Hamtramck because her family grew up in the area as well as a few of her college roommates. She had $32,000 that she was awarded from a taxi accident and used that money to fund the opening of her store and buy equipment like custom molds and packaging. By the time she opened the store, only $7 remained. Alexandra had to borrow two hundred dollars from her mom for the cash register. The entire community rallied behind her as there was a huge line out the door when they opened. After that first day, she was able to pay back the loan and the first year's rent.

Alexandra has fond childhood memories of teaming up with her sister to sell whatever little crafts they made, like painted rocks. Whenever their parents went over to their friends' houses for dinner, they tagged along and set up a shop there. Dinner parties were perfect because they had a captive audience. No detail was left untouched, from pricing to the branding and logos. It wasn't the money that motivated them, but the idea that something they had made was valuable enough for somebody to give them money for it.

The feeling she gets at Bon Bon Bon every day is no different than what she felt as a kid. And what is more, the community she belongs to whole-heartedly supports her business. Alexandra concludes, "I can't be more thankful that we are here. We don't belong anywhere else. We belong here."

THE NEW MAD MEN

Entrepreneur: Keenan Beasley
Age: 34
Hometown: Los Angeles, California
Company: BLKBOX, a data-driven, brand growth accelerator focused on creating value by closing the gap between people and brands

"Isolated. That's how I feel," Keenan Beasley told me as we strolled down Fifth Avenue in the Flatiron District of New York City on our way to grab lunch on a blustery November day in 2017. On that walk, he explained that he was always meeting with someone. An investor. A customer. A staff member. His cofounder. It didn't matter who it was. He was always selling the vision of BLKBOX, what he saw as the marketing agency of the future—one that was tapped into the culture by leveraging the power of both creativity and analytics. And it was run by an African American.

Starting an agency was hard. Keenan was always hustling for clients. But he didn't want to be an agency that simply serviced clients. He also wanted to connect clients to the culture using data analytics to back up their creative approach. That formula appealed to big brand clients like Lysol, Samsung, and Tide. It was an isolating and lonely path because Keenan knew how much focus he had to exert in order to get where he wanted to be. He saw the opportunity. Now, he had to close the gap between the present and the future. It was on his shoulders to drive the agency forward and make that future a reality.

When I first met Keenan in January 2015 at Armani Ristorante in Midtown New York, he exuded confidence. He had just accepted a job as head of marketing for the hair care behemoth, Garnier, a brand active in the music space. I wanted our first meeting to be casual, but there was nothing casual in the way that I had prepared. I had my data ready and music samples ready to hand him. I wanted to build a relationship with him that might eventually translate into business for us—event sponsorships, video integrations, and music licensing.

Keenan walked in and sat down beside me at the cafe. He was a handsome, youthful black man. It didn't surprise me that he had ascended to a top marketing job at such a young age or that he was managing a beauty business that targeted women. He had an amazing pedigree. He was a West Point graduate with a Procter & Gamble marketing background. What surprised me was that only a few weeks into the job, he decided to give notice. Most people, even those ten years his senior, never earn the vice president stripe, and when they did, they clung on to that role. Instead, after Keenan got the title, he decided to leave and start all over again.

His father instilled a sense of determination in him so that Keenan never backed down from a challenge. Every Saturday morning when Keenan was six years old, his father asked him to read a newspaper article out loud and talk about it with the family. Keenan's father wanted him to be able to talk about adult topics, not just kid drivel.

At an early age, Keenan felt extremely comfortable talking about and sharing his opinion. His father often challenged him. Once in sixth grade, Keenan shared what he had learned about the bathing habits of a North African tribe from his teacher. As he reported his findings, Keenan's dad stopped him, asked how he know they were true, and fired off a series of questions. "Was the teacher from that region? What was his perspective? How did he teach the concept?" He wanted Keenan to verify everything he learned. Keenan went to his Encyclopedia Britannica for another perspective. The underlying lesson was that his dad didn't want him to take anything at face value. He wanted Keenan to form his own opinion based on a variety of inputs instead of just one perspective.

Whether that be intellectually or athletically, Keenan didn't back down. His father was a great basketball player who tried out for the Los Angeles Lakers back in the day. Keenan didn't want to live in the shadow of his father. He wanted to carve out his own legacy and pursued football instead. He didn't make varsity his sophomore year, but he was still growing and getting stronger. He made the team his junior year and was invited to the Nike combine camp. He competed against the likes of DJ Williams and Sean Coty, two guys who are now professional players. But Keenan held more than his own. Scouts recognized his talent, and the scholarship offers flooded in, including high profile football programs such as USC, Michigan State, and Wisconsin.

Keenan loved football, but he was also academically motivated. His chances of making it to the pros were small, and he wanted a backup plan. All of the schools courting him had amazing academic programs. But one stood out— West Point. The football coach from West Point visited Keenan and his parents at their home. He sat down at their kitchen table and laid out the Book of Rings, a list of prominent CEOs, generals, and state leaders who were all West Point graduates. Keenan was sold. He felt that he could secure his future and his family's by enrolling at such a prestigious school.

Keenan suffered several injuries that ended his football

playing career at West Point. He had two shoulder surgeries and also learned that his breathing capacity was only at 54 percent of a normal person's because he has asthma. He had been preparing himself for active duty in April 2005, but he was ultimately medically discharged after graduation. Keenan graduated without a job and needed an income. He went to a job fair that May and fumbled through the interviews. He was in over his head but managed to land a job as a systems engineer at Raytheon.

His path to becoming an entrepreneur was obvious in some ways and not so obvious in others. After he acclimated to civilian life, he developed a game plan and targeted P&G for his next job because of its reputation as a top marketing company. He was hired first in purchasing. Once inside, he developed a relationship with the CEO, a former West Point graduate, who helped coach him into the marketing department.

Tide, the biggest brand in the P&G portfolio, was Keenan's first marketing assignment. He launched a Febreze sport variant of detergent that turned into a $60-million business in its first year, despite consumer testing that said it was going to fail. After his P&G stint, Keenan went to Reckitt Benckiser to run the billion-dollar Lysol business. He grew the business by double digits with new messaging that focused on promoting a healthy lifestyle instead of killing germs. This caught the attention of the recruiters at L'Oréal, the parent company of Garnier. He was on a trajectory towards bigger marketing jobs, but he left at the very moment his career started to hyper accelerate.

Keenan had always showed entrepreneurial tendencies in his marketing roles. He shot homemade videos of guys working out at gyms to prove that there was a market for a Febreze sport line extension. He trusted his gut despite what the testing said. Nobody believed him, but he secured a three-month test at Target that turned into the number one performing variant upon launch. His entrepreneurial instincts were there.

Almost every other Sunday for a year, Keenan sat out on his porch with a friend who brought over several 40s to stoke his creativity. His friend was a Carnegie Mellon business graduate who was good at writing business plans. Keenan had a lot of ideas. Together, they had a productive working session. Keenan came up with ideas while his friend asked questions to refine the ideas and capture them in his laptop. By the time they finished up, they had at least twenty ideas fully fleshed out. It was only a matter of time before they launched one.

Almost ready to leave and start his own thing, Keenan paused for a moment when he met his girlfriend's parents for the first time at their lake house in 2010. His girlfriend's mom had started a chain of salons. What stuck with Keenan was that she admitted she didn't know how to do hair or nails. What she knew best was how to run a business. Most of her competition were experts on hair or nails, but the owners couldn't run a profitable business. She understood how everything came together. With this in his mind on route back to Cincinnati, Keenan typed out his business plan for a marketing agency run by millennials that would help brands target millennials better.

One month after leaving Garnier, Keenan set up shop for The Strategy Collective, which has now evolved to BLKBOX. He took on several clients from the outset who wanted to tap his creative and strategic talents given his previous successes. He found office space in the hip Flatiron area and invited his creative friends to redesign the space. The office is a creative sanctuary with quotes on the wall that scream things like, "This is your LIFE. Do what you love, and do it often." The decor is as much a reflection of Keenan as it is a reflection of the kind of consumer he helps find for his clients.

Keenan fashions himself a new kind of Madison Avenue man. The face of advertising has changed. Suits have been replaced by jeans. Television has been supplanted by digital. Keenan understands that seismic shifts in the industry are taking place. He is doing his part to lead this change by being visible on social media platforms like Instagram and Facebook. He's not holding back his look.

He shows off his tattoos. He rocks his throwback Nikes. He sports his Rag & Bone jeans. He is a living, breathing image of the new millennial, and he needs to be seen as such so that clients and potential clients know that he lives and breathes this multicultural generation. That is the insight that they are paying for.

Although the business started out extremely well, more recently, Keenan confided that the company has been embroiled in a legal battle that forced him to use his personal savings to help bridge the company through its cash flow issues. Keenan, though, just as his father taught him, is taking inputs from everyone—his cofounder, his staff, his employees—to help him be a better founder and grow the agency. He is the new face of advertising and marketing not just because of the color of his skin or the experiences he has accumulated, but because he embraces his own diversity along with the diversity around him.

BOHEMIAN STREET INSPIRATION

Entrepreneur: Shaun Lee
Age: 29
Hometown: Johannesburg, South Africa
Company: Bohemian Guitars, oil-can guitars inspired by South African street musicians

Shaun Lee turned his bedroom and his parent's basement

into a workshop. He moved out the furniture, laid down tarp, and retrieved his dad's toolbox from the garage. He used a ping-pong table as his work bench and sat there to work with his key components: a vintage Castrol oil can; a used Fender neck; a block of wood. He spent three weeks configuring these parts into a makeshift guitar. Shaun had become obsessed with this idea since he saw a street musician perform using a guitar made out of a vintage oil can in South Africa. He felt compelled to replicate this model and wasn't going to stop until he had a guitar that worked.

He finished his first prototype on the day that his mother was hosting a Shabbat dinner. Shaun wanted to show off what he had been working on for three straight weeks, so he plugged his makeshift guitar into the amp. The sound was off key but it didn't matter. What mattered was that Shaun had made progress. He saw that the bridge was out of place and causing the atonality, so he started over again to make a second model. Shaun was hooked.

With each iteration, he learned something new that he applied to the next version. He eventually made eight guitars that passed his personal quality standards. He knew what a guitar should sound like from playing one in the past. His friends wanted to buy some of the guitars, so he decided to start selling them. One Saturday he went to the local arts fair in Piedmont Park in Atlanta close to his home. He set up shop and sold all of them that day. That was Shaun's "holy shit" moment when he realized that he could turn his passion into a business.

Shaun remembers, "One woman came by and gave me a twenty-dollar bill. I asked her why she was giving it to me. She shared that she wanted to be part of our success by contributing a small sum of money when nobody else knew about us. When we got onto television, she had a small hand in helping us get there. I wasn't actively thinking about being rich and famous, but it was cool that someone else envisioned that for me."

Shaun's trip to South Africa, where the idea for the guitar came from, had been prompted by his growing disillusionment with pursuing a career in psychology. His family was from South Africa, and his aunt and uncle owned a well-known chain of clothing stores. As a kid, Shaun had accompanied his aunt on store visits, inventory reviews, and financial audits. This time, as an adult, Shaun wanted to clear his head.

He took his younger cousins out for a stroll to the local market to look for cool and unusual gifts to bring back to friends, and by chance, he happened upon a street artist who was playing with a guitar made from a vintage oil can attached to a broomstick. Shaun couldn't stop staring as he liked the look of guitars more than he actually enjoyed playing them. The music had a great vibe and his curiosity was piqued. He wanted to make one. Before he could even approach the street musician, his younger cousins got antsy and whisked him away, but the memory of that visual stuck with him until he could create his own replica.

Back in the US, Shaun continued to sell the guitars at local art fairs around the Atlanta metropolitan area. It was a barebones operation. There were no signs. Shaun felt the guitars sold themselves, so he just laid them on a table. This minimalist presentation was an invitation to stop, approach, and ask. A quizzical look accompanied the most typical question: "Do these really work?"

Shaun didn't have to do much work. His response was to try it for themselves. When they did try, it created this moment of excitement mixed with astonishment. How could a guitar made up of a vintage oil can create music on par with a normal model?

After ten art and craft shows, Shaun felt he was on to something. His plan was to continue down this path. He was making a living by doing what he loved the most. His brother Adam saw a greater market opportunity for Shaun's product. Adam saw the passion in his brother, but more important, he saw that same passion in whoever purchased a guitar from him. Word about the product traveled quickly as the guitar was so visually compelling and unusual. People had to tell their friends about what they had discovered.

As a kid, Adam, who was three years older, had always looked out for Shaun. Adam asked Shaun to submit his papers to him in high school and even throughout college. He wanted to make sure Shaun got the best grades. He truly took on the role of big brother. Starting a business was no different. Adam wanted his brother to succeed, and he wanted to play a role in that success by joining as an advisor at first and then as his cofounder later.

First, they had to come up with a name for the brand. The brothers thought the guitars looked very bohemian, so they settled on Bohemian Guitars. They then decided to launch a Kickstarter campaign where they could test if there was a market for their guitars. The Kickstarter campaign was a success, surpassing its goal of $25,000. It also gave Adam the validation he needed to quit his job as a project manager at a travel company and joined forces with his brother. Their parents thought they were crazy—one had dropped out of grad school and the other had quit a high-paying job to start a company around vintage oil-can guitars. But the brothers could not be dissuaded; they knew they were on to something much bigger.

Originally, Shaun assumed the role of president since he had conceived of the product, but he soon ceded this title to his older brother. Shaun was more interested in designing and creating the product. Shaun got to do what he loved and his brother, whom he fully trusted, handled the business side. It was a prescient decision as Adam could continue to look out for his brother and steer the company in a direction that put it on a path for growth.

Despite a successful Kickstarter campaign and a successful enrollment at 500 Startups, a prestigious accelerator program, building the brand was not an easy path from the outset. Their first big manufacturing run of 1,000 guitars was a disaster. The money committed for the initial production had disappeared with the rep who negotiated the initial production run. Nobody could find him. Even the Hong Kong police failed to track him down. The factory didn't want to start production without payment.

The Lee brothers were in a bind. They had trusted this manufacturing rep who came to them through a close, personal reference. They had a pre-order of 400 guitars and a major purchase order from Urban Outfitters. They flew to China to meet with the factory. It was in an old communist building. The building was decrepit. Chickens and stray dogs wandered around aimlessly. It was such a stark contrast to the manufacturing line, which used top of the line technology and hummed with efficiency, producing thousands of goods at the press of a button.

The Lee brothers sat at the table with the factory owners. It was tense. The factory owners were angry because they had invested the upfront capital to purchase the parts. They blamed the Lee brothers for failing to deliver payment. The only way to change this perception was to shift the blame to the manufacturing rep who had disappeared. Adam hounded the rep with phone calls. He tried again at the meeting. Miraculously, the rep picked up. He admitted to taking the money. The Lee brothers were absolved from guilt as they had intended to pay the factory on time. Both parties could now work together constructively knowing that they were in this situation together. They found a credit-based solution that allowed the first production run to take place.

As Adam predicted, Bohemian Guitars is now tapping into a market of consumers who want to learn guitar on a guitar customized to their style. Kids, for example, love the Hello Kitty version that the brothers have made. These customers are learning to love music because they love their instrument. Bohemian Guitars is not just a brand, but a community of guitar enthusiasts who are expressing their personality through their music and their instruments.

The company has also has caught the eyes of major artists like Hozier, who wrote the hit single "Take Me to Church." Shaun contacted his management team when Hozier was performing at State Bank Amphitheatre at Chastain Park, the largest amphitheater in Atlanta. They were interested and asked Shaun to bring five guitars for Hozier to try out before the show. There was nobody else on stage except Hozier and Shaun.

Shaun remembers, "I brought him five guitars. Hozier was plugging them in. He was talking to his sound guy, and he found the one that he liked. That night, I called all of my friends to come down as I had ten front row seats. It was insane. He played 'Someone New' on one of our guitars. We had a killer video of him playing with our guitar. It was more satisfying than making money. Seeing it on stage, it was a better feeling. If I failed tomorrow, I would have at least known that I had done something."

Bohemian Guitars is a product of Shaun's desire to build products that he loves. The product wasn't intended to disrupt the guitar industry; it just turned out that way. Shaun enlisted his brother to help him because he realized he couldn't do it alone. That move was never about ego. It was about making a decision that could scale the company and expose millions of people to music. What started out for Shaun as a hobby and a way to find himself turned into a business that has allowed others to explore their passion in music.

"Kids and adults learning guitar want something that is unique to them," comments Shaun. "We are able to give them that customization that allows them to enjoy the learning process. That is really cool about our company. We are more than just a product and more than just a brand. We are a community. We want to cultivate a community of guitar players who love to play music and enjoy the lifestyle that we promote through our brand."

CHAPTER 17

THE SERENDIPITOUS FOUNDER

THE CREATIVE ENTERPRISE

Entrepreneur: Mickey Meyer
Age: 33
Hometown: Clinton, New York
Company: JASH, a comedy collective featuring original content from partners Michael Cera, Tim & Eric, Sarah Silverstein, and Reggie Watts (acquired by Group Nine Media in November 2017)

The set was pulled together on a shoestring budget. There were two pieces of IKEA furniture, a tattered green-screen cloth, and a small, grey boom box for music playback. Mickey Meyer usually worked for large-scale production companies on well-established television shows. He was used to big sets, significant budgets, call sheets, and set parking. Every set had some level of chaos, but it was organized chaos with substantial resources at his disposal. In the case of this shoot, it was truly chaos. Nobody knew how to act on a real set, but it didn't matter. The crew believed in the video concept and wanted to share it with the world. This was the making of the first ever video of *Epic Rap Battles of History*.

At the time, Mickey was staffed on a commercial for *The Biggest Loser*. "There were two to three months' worth of work around this commercial. It was just boring," Mickey says. "I could get all of my work done in an hour. I was doing the most minuscule things to keep myself busy." Mickey needed a creative outlet. When his friend Dave McCary invited him to the *Epic Rap Battles of History* set, Mickey jumped at the opportunity. They had worked together previously when Mickey helped Dave direct videos for his sketch comedy group, Good Neighbor.

On set, Mickey became an integral part of the creative process and worked directly with the talent, Pete and Lloyd. For example, they worked together to capture the prickliness of their mustaches to heighten the parody of the insane rap battle between John Lennon and Bill O'Reilly. It wasn't perfect. But it didn't have to be. The imperfections made it raw but pure, which is the essence of what Pete and Lloyd wanted Dave and Mickey to capture.

The epic rap battle between John Lennon and Bill O'Reilly was posted on YouTube. There was an instant response that went from 10,000 views to 100,000 views to 1 million views. The numbers kept climbing. Comments poured in. Mickey watched in astonishment. Normally he had to wait months for the commercials he shot to air. "I had a creative itch that wasn't being satisfied in my current job," Mickey explains, "I had a camera and loved to shoot things. It was the most fun that I had done in the longest time."

Mickey always knew that he wanted to be a video producer. As a kid, he went into the local video store and rented *Rad* and *Robin Hood* at least 100 times. He went to USC to study film and theatre.

After graduating, he started at the bottom at a production company. He understood the different steps he needed to take to become a full producer on different jobs, but he was miserable.

"I was doing someone else's work. It wasn't creative that I cared about. It wasn't jobs that I cared about. It was something that allowed me to eat and have a place to stay. It rarely fulfilled me in any other way."

During his downtime, Mickey would shoot video on his camera. That was how he met Dave McCary, now a director on *Saturday Night Live*. Mickey produced several videos for Dave who was the director and editor of a comedy group called Good Neighbor. Dave had also connected Mickey to Danny Zappin, the business visionary behind Maker Studios, a new form of studio.

In the initial meeting, Mickey shares, "Danny twirled the back corner of his hair, which he still does today when he is plotting and scheming, and I wondered to myself who was the guy? He really cared about this thing. He saw something that I didn't yet. I wanted to know what he saw that allowed him to have this much fun and allowed them to make what they wanted to make. That was my first real encounter with successful entrepreneurship."

Mickey could continue to make something unique and have an impact like he did with *Epic Rap Battles of History*. Mickey shares, "I said fuck it, I would give it a month's worth of time, and see what it does. I wasn't going to skip a step in terms of what I was making then, which was about $2,000 per week. I asked Danny about the pay, he said 2,000. I thought, 'Great, let's do this.' When I found out it was actually $2,000 a month, I said, 'Screw it. I'm already in, let's do it.'" Mickey became addicted to the rush of shooting video in a much more raw, organic fashion.

He stayed at Maker Studios for three years and saw it go from a crazy, fun place where anything was possible to a company focused only on scaling. Investors had made a big bet on the company's growth and were itching for a big liquidity event. Mickey saw and felt this transition firsthand. The company lost its original fuel to experiment. The creativity in the content was being influenced less by ideas and more by what content was projected to generate increased audience numbers. Mickey became restless. He was no longer being challenged creatively. He wanted to leave, but he had acquired a significant financial stake in the company. It wasn't until Daniel Kellison, the producer of *The David Letterman Show* and creator of *Jimmy Kimmel Live*, called to pitch him on a startup idea around a comedy platform on YouTube that Mickey seriously considered leaving.

Mickey was in an enviable position as head of production for Maker Studios. Lots of people called him to ask for funding for their video ideas as well as to offer him jobs. Daniel had a TV pedigree, but he wanted to create a comedy channel leveraging the existing talent relationships he had. He wanted to work with Mickey because of his expertise in digital distribution and offered him a cofounder role in a new company called JASH. Mickey hesitated. Millions of dollars were at stake as Maker was poised for acquisition. But in the end, he decided to leave stability behind and make the jump to cofounder at a company where he could set the vision.

"At Maker, I had health insurance. I had a child. I had

stability. I had friends. I was making great pay, and I had a fair amount of equity. BUT, it was the most miserable that I felt in a long time. All of a sudden, I just was sitting underneath fluorescence lamps, and I was dreaming of ways to make money off of other people without them really seeing the benefit. I had financial stability but was unhappy."

JASH had financial runway for an entire year. YouTube was investing in content to boost the overall quality of its platform. Mickey churned out several videos. Nothing caught fire. The company was run with a production mindset: create a show; finish the show; move on to the next show. This was in contrast to running the company with a corporate mindset: build a product; monetize; sustain; diversify the product line. Soon enough, Mickey saw the writing on the wall. The company's initial round of funding from YouTube was almost gone. In a matter of months, JASH was going to shut down.

Mickey, the creative, became Mickey, the businessman. Just as he became engrossed in the creative formation of the shows, he drilled down into the economics of the online video business. He built budgets that had specific margin targets and staffed each show according to actual need, not according to anticipated, constant need. These were basic changes, but necessary ones to shift the mindset of the company to a media company that was a business, not a production house that lived project to project. It was a shift for Mickey too, one that he surprisingly enjoyed because he was able to build a business system that still protected the creative integrity of JASH.

Under Mickey's leadership, JASH became a company that generated sustainable and predictable cash flow. As Mickey explains, "I wanted this to work so badly. Why were we going to close our doors? We have people sitting around and doing nothing because we didn't budget correctly. We didn't have a long-term business model. That became the focus, which was to build a system and organizational processes where we were all coordinated on our portfolio of projects as a company versus scrambling one project at a time. We didn't do anything in a vacuum anymore."

Business has become a creative pursuit for Mickey. He still loves being creative on set where he can capture the spontaneity of a scene. But what surprised him is that he also enjoys the process of building a system to transform creative ideas into intellectual property that can be monetized repeatedly.

"I enjoy a lot from business that I never thought I would. I like building a process that validates my system," Mickey says, "We make a show, and we build a system around it that gives that show an opportunity to succeed creatively and monetarily. While each project is different, we take a very disciplined approach to give it the right funding, the right partners, and the right distribution to find an audience who would value that kind of content."

Mickey became an entrepreneur because his urge to create was greater than his urge to settle. That's why he moved on to found JASH. He left millions of dollars on the table when Maker Studios was acquired by Disney, but he became an entrepreneur because he stayed true to his creative integrity.

"Entrepreneurship. I do now associate myself with that term," Mickey concludes. "I didn't for a while. I felt uncomfortable when people referred to me as one. At Maker, I wasn't the one with the vision. I didn't feel like I had everything to lose. Now, I feel that I have earned it. I have gone a year without pay and fought and gone through every permutation in my head to be successful. I was always trying to find inspiration and evolve to stay that clip ahead. It is a drug. I understand why people are in this for life."

SHOWING UP, JUST BECAUSE

Entrepreneur: TJ Parker
Age: 31
Hometown: New Hampshire

Company: PillPack, a full-service pharmacy that delivers a better, simpler experience for people managing multiple medications

The first step to success is just showing up. That's what TJ Parker did when he decided to attend a planning meeting for the MIT $100K Entrepreneurship Competition. He wasn't a student at MIT. He didn't have a startup idea. He just had a hunch that something good would come out of being in this environment. His ideal outcome was landing an internship at a startup. Never did he dream that he would end up transforming how people receive and take their prescription meds.

At the time, TJ was enrolled in pharmacy school. His father was also a pharmacist, and a pharmacy degree seemed a way to ensure a secure financial future. On the other hand, TJ had a lot of interests outside of his pharmacy degree program. He bought and sold rare sneakers. He was a real estate agent. He did photo shoots for open houses. He worked at the pharmacy at Target. He took fashion and design classes by cross-registering at Massachusetts College of Art and Design. There was no consistent thread in any of these ventures except his curiosity.

"In retrospect, it was obvious how the pieces all worked together. I was learning about business, design thinking, customer experience, and the service industry—which would all be critical for PillPack's success. But in the moment, it was frustrating. I was exploring a lot of stuff. I didn't know what I wanted to do. I didn't know what I was good at. When I was twenty-one, I just wanted to understand who I was in the world."

What prompted him to join the planning committee for the MIT $100K Entrepreneurship Competition in the first place was reading *The Innovator's Dilemma* by Clayton Christensen, a professor at Harvard Business School. TJ had seen firsthand how the old model of healthcare worked, and Christensen's book gave him new ideas on how to use entrepreneurship to change that model. So he set out to find people who thought about the world from an entrepreneurial mindset, and that's what led him to the MIT $100K Entrepreneurship Competition.

He attended the organizing meetings for eighteen months. As he exposed himself to different startups and investment concepts, his confidence grew. He kept meeting people through networking events. While these conversations were productive, none of them led to a partnership or the formation of a startup. He started to question whether this time investment was leading to an outcome or just spinning his wheels.

"I'm in school. I'm also a real estate agent. I'm also driving to MIT twice a week to meet and do stuff for the $100K, and I often thought, 'Was this really worth it?' It felt like it was going to eventually be useful, and the people that I met would hopefully be helpful at some point in my life. But there was no clear payout nor was there even a clear benefit."

Over time, though, some relationships and connections started to stick. For example, when he met Elliot Cohen, his eventual cofounder, at a startup bootcamp weekend. Elliot had just moved to Boston and wanted to do something in the healthcare space. While there was no immediate flash of lightning, the two saw each other as smart, motivated, and skilled technically, so they made sure to keep in touch after the bootcamp.

In between TJ's last two semesters of school, he landed an internship at a startup in San Francisco—his goal all along. But neither the Bay Area nor the company were the right fit. Despite all the hype and press around the startup scene and digital health, it felt like too many ideas and not enough impact. He finished the internship and went back to school for his last semester.

After graduation, he took a pharmacist role at his dad's pharmacy back in New Hampshire. It was better than working at CVS or Walgreens. But he still thought to himself, "Shit, it came to this, right?" He wasn't happy there and, on nights and weekends, he drove from New Hampshire back down to Boston so that he could continue to immerse himself in the startup scene there.

Around this time, he started to formulate the idea for PillPack. For a long time, he had observed how difficult it could be for patients to stick with their medication regimen. For someone taking a handful or more meds every day, it was hard to stay on top of refills, follow instructions, and keep everything organized.

For example, one patient he had delivered medications to had really poor eyesight; she asked him to take a sharpie and mark her different medications with big bold letters so that she could see what she was taking. Another patient asked him to color code her medication bottles so that she knew when to take each of them.

TJ felt like he could simplify the system, making life easier for tens of millions of people. But he also knew that to achieve impact at scale would require rewriting all the backend software that power a pharmacy. He needed a technical cofounder. This is when he keyed in on Elliot as a potential partner. Two years had passed since they first met and Elliot, a passionate entrepreneur, already has a number of ideas for his next venture. TJ had to persuade Elliot to give up all these other ideas and give TJ's pharmacy concept a shot. Luckily, Elliot and TJ were both involved in an effort from MIT called Hacking Medicine, a group dedicated to bringing together different kinds of people to test new ideas in healthcare over the course of a very intense weekend. The two friends decided to try their own medicine and work on the pharmacy idea over a startup weekend at Massachusetts General Hospital. At the end of the hackathon, they would pitch the idea to investors.

"There was a lot of buildup for this event. It was at Mass General Hospital and had a number of well-known global and public health professionals attending. We worked on it for the weekend, and by the end of it, we had a box that represented what PillPack might be, along with a deck that outlined the market opportunity and how we were going to execute. It was enough to make it tangible. Then we pitched at the end of the hackathon to fifty or sixty people—doctors, engineers, and designers. I never went to Harvard, MIT or Princeton, but the crowd was made of this impressive group of people. For me to pitch in front of them, it was overwhelming."

TJ and Elliot won the competition. It gave them enough fuel to continue working on the idea for another three months. Elliot was still not convinced there was a strong market for their product. But on a trip back home to San Francisco, Elliot was chatting with his father when he accidentally knocked his pillbox over. His father started to freak out and the value of PillPack hit home for Elliot in that moment. His father shared his own personal horror stories of getting his medication from pharmacies. Elliot texted TJ at 2 a.m. and told him he was ready to commit to the business full time. That's when they set off to create the pharmacy of the future.

For TJ, it was easy to point to the milestones that now showcase their success. Admittance into the Techstars accelerator program. Venture funding totaling over $115 million. Six facilities that house more than 700 employees, including his father who came to work for the company as a regulatory expert. From an outsider's point of view, the path toward growth looks linear.

The path to starting, however, was serendipitous. It took time for TJ to figure out who he was in this world. He experimented with a lot of ideas before he settled on one that made sense to him. Even when he settled on that one idea, he had to spend almost a year convincing Elliot to join him. TJ could have given up on the idea, but something kept pushing him to explore. That intuition led him to trust his gut and drive him toward a place where he was in position to start a business that could not just transform an industry, but his own life and the lives around him as well.

IDEAS, IDEAS, IDEAS

Entrepreneur: Umang Dua
Age: 31
Hometown: Delhi, India
Company: Handy, the leading platform for connecting individuals looking for household services with top-quality, pre-screened, independent service professionals

Umang Dua settled into his chair. Across from him was a famous Bollywood movie director. Umang had pulled a few strings through his family network to get a meeting with him. He purchased a plane ticket to Mumbai from Delhi, booked a hotel room, and organized his entire schedule around this conversation. He hoped the director could offer him nuggets of wisdom for starting his career in film directing and went into the conversation with an open mind, hoping to glean some useful insights.

At that time, Umang had just graduated from Amherst College. He knew he wanted to start something but didn't know what. He often had ideas for products that he shared with friends. For instance, one idea he had was opening a sports bars in India. His country was crazy about cricket and the market lacked a proper venue for watching sports on big screen televisions. He soon backtracked on the idea when he realized the capital required to start such a venture.

Why not look at the film industry? He always had an interest in filmmaking and had a few connections in the industry. But he left that meeting with the director feeling disappointed because he had given him advice that was exactly the same as what he told other young students who came through his door. Start at the bottom. Work at it. It might be three years, five years, or even ten years before you achieve moderate success.

"When I heard this, part of my brain thought that this was too long of a slog," Umang says. "I was disappointed not with what he said because I agreed with what he said. I was disappointed because I had to rule out another field. I was feeling restless."

Finally, Umang settled on an idea that he liked and cofounded a company called College Connect, which helped students from India apply to colleges in the States. It became real when his first customer brought him an envelope of cash to pay for counseling. "We had this makeshift ledger, and we didn't have any entries yet. We put in the information, and we had cash. This was when it became real for us. It was a sign that we could deliver a service to our customers. There was trust."

But a year and a half into the business, Umang wanted to leave. On one hand, he didn't think the business was scaling fast enough. He had grander ambitions than a service-based business with a slow growth trajectory. On the other hand, he was afraid that he might miss out on an opportunity for a real job. He had applied to McKinsey & Company, a strategy consulting firm, and had received an offer. He went on to work for McKinsey for a year until he left for Harvard Business School. His experience as a consultant was important because it also made him realize once again that it wasn't what he wanted to do. It just didn't feel right to him because he wanted to focus on his own business ideas, not someone else's.

He went to business school with the very clear goal of starting a company. He didn't know what kind of company, but he knew he was in the right place to continue to test his ideas. He was surrounded by people who could help him further those ideas. It turned out that the person who was best at helping him sort through ideas was his roommate, Oisin. They didn't know each other before business school but ended up rooming together in an apartment off campus when neither of them was able to secure on-campus housing.

Umang and Oisin developed a rhythm to their conversations. Sometimes it was at home. Sometimes it was out at a bar. They talked about an idea, and then they assigned each other items to explore around it. They came back together to discuss their individual findings, and they dropped an idea if it didn't continue to interest them.

Eventually, they landed on the idea that became Handy. "This idea, somehow we kept talking about it—the second week, the third week, the fourth week. We were just working harder. 'Let's not go out tonight, and instead, let's work on this. Instead of the school assignment, let's work on this instead.' That was pretty easy because we were pretty passionate about the things we were working on."

Summer came. Instead of accepting internships, they decided to work on their business idea—a decision that helped them cement their trust in each other. They agreed to work on the idea for three months. If it didn't work out, they could return to business school. They also prepared for the possibility they could focus on it full time. They wouldn't have to make a decision until the summer ended and they had more data points on the business. The business did, indeed, start to gain some market traction.

"Week on week, it got a little more serious, and I was emotionally preparing myself to drop out because we were able to raise money," Umang says. "And then by the end of the summer, we were at a place where we generally believed we had built something that could work."

As a result, Umang and Oisin decided to drop out of business school. It wasn't a dramatic decision for Umang. He had previous experience launching College Connect from scratch. He knew what that felt like, and it didn't scare him or bother him to start something so uncertain. He wasn't even too worried about not having a work visa. He just knew that it felt right to build this company now.

Since 2012, Handy has been on a growth tear. Two years later, in 2014, the company went from twenty people to 100 in a nine-month period, and it continues to scale today. But still, the business is a work in progress. "I am a pretty ambitious person. I don't think Handy is as big yet as it can be. I look at companies like Uber, Facebook, or Amazon that impacts millions of people every day as inspiration for where Handy can go. Sometimes it's physically and emotionally tiring, and over the past few years, I've gotten punched in the face a lot. Every day, I don't wake up and say to myself that this is really working yet. It's more like, 'Fuck, this is not working. This is wrong, that is wrong, and here's where we need to improve.' There's definitely a few moments, though, when you take a step back and say, 'Wow. We've come a long way, but this is nowhere close to being done.'"

Umang is determined to continue on this path. "By the time I was sixteen or seventeen, I knew I wanted to start something. It was intrinsically inside me. I just didn't know what or where. I didn't know the path I'd have to take to start a company. That just happened very organically for me. It was lots of small things—not one magical moment. It was a little bit of following my gut to double down where I could do something, make it happen, and then watch it grow. I persisted and found something that had market traction."

CONCLUSION

The journey to write this book was born out of a personal crisis: I wanted to pick the brains of millennial entrepreneurs so that I could better understand why the relationship with my wife-turned-entrepreneur fell apart; I also finally made the move to leave corporate America and hoped to gather insights to inspire my own entrepreneurial ambitions. Of course, what I discovered through the process of interviewing more than 300 entrepreneurs was way beyond what I could have imagined when I first started this project.

Hopefully, now that you've read the stories in this book, you too have absorbed the hard-won wisdom of these young entrepreneurs and gotten a taste of what it's really like to be an entrepreneur. A few key moments stood out for me and helped me grow as a person. Here are the six essential lessons I took away from founders that you can apply to your own life:

#1 YOUR COMMUNITY IS MORE POWERFUL THAN YOUR NETWORK

Jon Levy, the founder of The Influencers, completely changed my idea of networking and what it means to connect people. He built a series that brings amazing people together in a way that goes beyond typical professional connections. Instead, it's a diverse community of people who are all tremendously accomplished in their given industry or profession.

While I was in Los Angeles in November 2015, Jon invited me to one of The Influencers' salons at a house in West Hollywood one Saturday night. I didn't know what to expect. I had been to many late-night concerts in the music industry. There was always a typical arc to those nights, which culminated in a performance. In this case, there wasn't a musical act. It was just a small and intimate affair at someone's house and the purpose was simply to connect with other people in a meaningful way.

When I arrived, there was a small crowd gathered around one presenter who turned out to be a forensic scientist for the FBI and consulted for the TV industry. Next up was Josh Beckerman, the foodie magician, who did amazing magic tricks for the crowd. The final talk was given by a film producer. Jon had orchestrated the entire evening as a way of bringing amazing people together who could offer fascinating glimpses into their rarefied worlds and also open up new avenues for impacting other people's lives. Jon was at the center of this community, but he didn't control it. He let it build organically, simply providing the space for the people in his world to make new connections with each other.

"Networking is a very sterile experience, which is I've met this person, and this person now adds additional utility to my life. I think this is shortsighted," Jon explains. "When I started The Influencers, I was looking at it as a general concept with the fundamental belief that what defines the quality of our lives is the people who we surround ourselves with and the conversations we have with them. If they are extraordinary, I want them to become my friends. As my friends lives get better, my life gets better. What I did was create a community because when you create a community around a group of people and you instill it with values or an intention, you have the greatest impact on participants."

I met some incredible people that night who I might never have met otherwise. But what I came away most impressed with was the sense of community that Jon had built. He had invested years of time and money into building this community. He kept at it, even embarrassing himself by shamelessly promoting the series at other friends' dinner parties, to the point where his screw-ups were cringeworthy. It didn't matter, though, as what drove Jon was building a community of extraordinary people around him, which was a much different approach than I had taken in my corporate career.

#2 COMMITMENT MATTERS MORE THAN TALENT

When I interviewed Candice Simons, the CEO of Brooklyn Outdoor, an outdoor advertising company, I immediately gravitated to her story of growing up as a competitive dancer. "My mom would come with me to our competitions every weekend. If we didn't have competitions, we would go to dance conventions," Candice shares. "During the week, I was in class from 6 a.m. in the morning to 6 p.m. at night. This experience really shaped my sense of discipline and focus, which has made me the founder I am today. I stayed out of trouble because I had my own regimen and structure that put me on the path to success that I have achieved today."

Candice's story brought back memories for me of playing chess. My father taught me how to play at age six. Soon after I got the hang of the basic moves, I was beating him with ease, which prompted my parents to enroll me in a local chess club. My winning ways continued. My parents saw my potential and took me to local tournaments, then state tournaments, and finally to national tournaments because I kept on winning. By age eight, I was the number one chess player in the nation in my age group.

I could sit at a chess board for hours and review different

combinations that would put me in the best position to win. I was so focused and disciplined. Nothing distracted me. Chess set the foundation for how I saw the world as a kid and later on as an adult. Because I achieved such a high level of success at such a young age, I thought I was invincible and infallible. My national chess ranking became my trump card, for example, to get into the best colleges because my application was so different than other students who didn't have this background.

My natural gift, though, was a curse in disguise. I didn't have to practice to win in my age category. My talent trumped everyone else around me. Over time, I faced stiffer competition who were not fooled by my normal bag of tricks. But I refused to practice or evolve my game. It wasn't because I didn't want to get better. I just didn't know how to practice in a way that would yield results on the board.

#3 WORK HARD, PLAY HARD, BUT DON'T FORGET TO REST

Matt Williams is relentless—that was my first impression when I met the founder of LavCup. Matt approached me after I spoke on an innovation panel about how big companies were integrating startups into their organizations. Matt's company invented a beverage platform, which incorporates built-in advertising. The LavCup is installed above toilets and sinks of bathrooms within sports and entertainment venues. The business model: provide venues with a much-needed amenity, while selling fun, fan-centric advertising on the platform. I was intrigued and wanted to learn more about his business as well as him.

What I loved about Matt was his sheer intensity. He had a story to tell but it wasn't forced. Matt shares, "I spent $3,000 to attend this conference where all of the new presidents of sports teams attended. It was a lot of money, but if I closed one deal, it was worth it. I rolled the dice and hustled like crazy at this conference. The president of the Seattle Seahawks just came offstage, and I sniped him out. Everyone else bombarded him, but I waited until he was exiting. I approached him, and he told me that he didn't have an internship to offer. But I pulled out my iPad and showed him my product. Before I could launch into my pitch, he cut me off because right away, he understood the benefit of LavCup, exclaiming how brilliant the idea was. He connected me to the right people, and ten weeks later, my product was in stadiums right as the Seahawks were making their Super Bowl run in 2014."

Matt was like many other entrepreneurs who were always hustling to find their next customer, their next investor, their next employee. His hustle was non-stop. Hustle was not work. Hustle was not a job. Hustle was simply the lifestyle. Hanging out with Matt made me realize why he and other entrepreneurs took the time to engage with me—because they needed an emotional break from the startup grind. They needed time to decompress and pause to enjoy their journey, not just motor through the next hurdle.

That might mean a night out with a random stranger. It might mean playing video games all night like Alex White from Next Big Sound did with his cofounders after a long day of coding. It might mean spending time with other entrepreneurs during a quarterly dinner to connect and console each other on the struggles of building a startup as Spencer Frye from Podia did. It might mean doing an intense workout like Adam and Ryan Goldston from Athletic Propulsion Labs to help balance their commitment to building their business.

As I traveled from city to city, I became obsessed with trying to interview as many people as I could while in a given location. I would meet with an entrepreneur anywhere, anytime. Scheduling time with Ben Lerer, the cofounder of *Thrillist*, took me to a chateau in Cannes, France, where he had a break in his schedule to meet. I was relentless in my pursuit to meet these founders so that I could discover their personal journey to becoming an entrepreneur.

That relentless pursuit was balanced by the need to

recharge elsewhere, whether that meant staying at my sister's house in San Francisco or catching up with a group of business school friends in Seattle. Finding emotional outlets in between my intense interview schedule, just as the entrepreneurs I interviewed did with their work, kept things balanced so that the obsessive commitment to an idea didn't result in a physical or emotional breakdown.

#4 LOOK TO YOUR FAMILY FOR INSPIRATION

When I spoke with Peter SerVaas, cofounder of Double-Map, a digital mapping service for transportation options, he shared the impact his grandfather, a successful serial entrepreneur in Indianapolis, had on him. Peter and his grandfather were very close. They met for a half day every month. Peter's grandfather didn't dispense advice during that time. Instead, he was absorbing what was going on in Peter's life. Asking lots of questions helped him get a feel for who Peter was as a person and who he was growing up to be. Peter's grandfather knew that he could have a greater impact on Peter if he could tailor his advice to what was currently going on in his life.

"My grandfather wanted me to be successful," Peter remembers. "When I was running for student body president, he asked me what he thought we needed to do to win. He didn't tell me what to do. He planned my campaign with me. When I moved back to Indianapolis to start a business, he took the exact same approach. He wanted me to find my own path to success, and he provided the support and passion for me to drive toward a business that I thought I could scale."

Before I met Peter in Indianapolis, I had been in St. Louis interviewing Jimmy Sansone, founder of The Normal Brand, a Midwestern lifestyle apparel brand. Jimmy shared how his grandparents had started a successful real estate business, which Jimmy's father works at with his brothers and continues to grow. None of Jimmy's siblings or cousins were allowed to join the real estate firm. "Statistically, only about 4 percent of third generation businesses succeed," Jimmy says. "My grandfather made the decision to close off the business to the third-generation family members because there were so many of us. This prevented all of the infighting that naturally occurs and allowed them to focus on running and building the business."

Growing up, Jimmy never saw the nine-to-five lifestyle like many of his friends whose parents had regular jobs. Jimmy was able to see the exhilarating highs and the debilitating lows when his father presented real estate development plans at city hall. He wanted a taste of that entrepreneurial life himself. After college, Jimmy labored through his prestigious investment banking job, but this lucrative path didn't appeal to him.

The entrepreneurial itch was something Jimmy had to scratch. He didn't want to follow the safe path. He wanted to start his own business with his brothers, and he started selling hats that he had designed. The first run sold out in two days. That was the first sign that there was something to his vision of selling a Midwestern lifestyle brand.

Jimmy shares how his father encouraged him to pursue his dream: "My father told me I was going to make it. He was very sincere and confident. He told me to believe in myself and don't focus on the short-term stuff, think long term. That was an amazing high for me and kept me going when I didn't believe in myself."

Peter and Jimmy's story helped me reflect on the legacy of my own grandfather who opened two Chinese restaurants in New York in the 1930s, one in Chinatown and the other in Midtown East. In fact, an old *New York Post* article claimed that the restaurateur Lum Fong was the first to bring the egg roll and wonton soup to America. I never met him as he died before I was born, but his legacy lives on in a collection of photos that my family still maintains. He was always happy, always checking in on his guests. He was the consummate host dressed impeccably in a suit. Our family shut the restaurant down in the mid-70s because they didn't want the responsibility of running it anymore.

I never lived in the shadows of my grandfather, and I didn't grow up relying on the restaurant to generate income for our family. But I knew about my grandfather and our history. I have always felt a deep connection to him because he came from nothing and created something incredibly meaningful for his family while also making an impact on Chinese cuisine in America.

My grandfather worked hard for his success. I feel a sense of obligation to honor what he built from nothing and create something of cultural significance. His entrepreneurial spirit runs through my veins and has directed me on a path that is uniquely my own.

#5 LIGHT YOUR OWN FIRE

At Columbia Records, I saw firsthand how scrappy musicians with humble beginnings became revered pop stars. During my last year at Columbia Records, I met Rachel Platten, an artist we had just signed to a recording contract. Prior to that signing, she had spent years playing music in small venues and house parties to keep her dream alive. She was just so appreciative and gracious because she knew getting signed to Columbia Records was her shot at becoming a pop star. She knew she still had to work for it, but this was her chance to prove that her music was ready for mainstream audiences.

I immediately took a liking to Rachel and organized a

small event for her at Rose Bar, a trendy bar at the Gramercy Park Hotel. I invited executives who represented major brands such as Pepsi, Budweiser, and BMW. The evening was a chance for her to make an impression, and she was so personable, warm, and caring that everyone liked her as a person before they really even heard her music. She wasn't going to take any chances as any one of those executives could transform her music career if, for example, her music was in one of their commercials.

We promised everyone that her song was going to be a hit. We said that a lot about songs, but this one was special. "Fight Song" took on meaning for everyone who listened to it because it inspires people to fight through whatever difficult situation they're going through. For Rachel, "Fight Song" was her anthem to fight through the tough times in her music career. Instead of chasing sounds that were trending, she had to find her own voice that is authentic to who she is. She didn't let the naysayers weigh her down; she believed in herself and in her music to continue to pursue this career.

This fire is what I saw burning in the entrepreneurs I interviewed like Umang Dua, cofounder of Handy, who was obsessed with starting a business that had true, scalable impact like Amazon and Google. Or like Alex Gassiter, cofounder at Gather, an event-planning software company, who picked himself up off of the ground after four failed attempts at starting a business; he founded Gather on his fifth try. Or with Matt Williams, who endured his entire startup journey alone as a single founder but never once thought to quit, despite only having $7.21 in his bank account. There was a fire that burned within each of these entrepreneurs and propelled them past the darkest days of their journeys to find their paths to success.

#6 DEFINE WHAT TRULY MATTERS

After spending an entire year flying across the country to interview entrepreneurs, I decided to take some downtime to reflect on all the stories I had heard. Interviewing entrepreneurs didn't make me an entrepreneur, even though I thought the experience would enrich my understanding of what an entrepreneur is. The only way I could become an entrepreneur was to take the leap and start my own business, and I was still as far as away from that goal as when I started interviewing the first entrepreneur.

It was only when I slowed down long enough to reflect and spend time with my sister that I started to understand what this journey was all about.

Sitting at my sister's dining room table after her kids went to sleep, I confided in her that I felt so lost, lonely, and sad after my separation. My shoulders were slumped. My head was down. Tears were welling up in my eyes as I recounted what happened and how it made me feel. I was supposed to be the big brother offering her advice, but she was the one who helped comfort me. That vulnerability brought us a lot closer.

I'm four years older than my sister. We never attended the same schools, and we've never lived in the same city together as adults. Our lives led us in different directions. She married her college sweetheart, became a surgeon, and built a life on the West Coast. I pursued a business career and remained on the East Coast. We were the kind of siblings who checked in on each other, but didn't rely on each other.

Opening up to my sister allowed us to have a deep and rich emotional exchange that truly changed the dynamic of our relationship. I needed someone to listen to what I was going through. I had pushed my own feelings aside to absorb the stories of the entrepreneurs I met. I identified with their emotions so that I didn't have to listen to my own. I had so many pent-up feelings about my separation, and I was fortunate that my sister was willing to listen to me with arms open—the same way I had listened to hundreds of entrepreneurs tell their stories.

That night, we embraced for a few minutes. Previously, when we said goodbye, we would embrace and then pat each other on the back. One pat. Two pats. Three pats. This time we even counted out the pats as a way of acknowledging the emotional awkwardness of the moment. But I felt comfort in my sister's arms that night, knowing she loved me no matter what happened to me. It was a moment of true emotional connection because I was vulnerable with her in a way that I had never been before. I started to understand the things that truly matter to me in my quest to understand what happened in my marriage.

One particular entrepreneur I met, Zak, changed directions several time as an entrepreneur in order to focus on what truly matters to him. He found a calling beyond the singular focus of starting and scaling a business, one that encompasses more than just professional success.

I visited Zak in Maine one weekend in July 2017 and spent the evening with him and his wife Leah, as well as her sister and father who came over to their house. Leah and her sister and father all played violin and wrote their own music. As children, the sisters had performed together. Now that Zak and Leah had moved to Maine to be close to the rest of the family, they had the opportunity to rekindle their musical connection. They played, laughed, and goofed around on their violins.

In that moment, like the moment I had shared with my sister, I realized what I wanted was a family—people who I could rely on and would always be there to catch me when things got tough. I saw what Zak's brand of entrepreneurship afforded him: a lifestyle that prizes emotional intimacy with the people he loves, while also allowing him to pursue a path that is at the core of who he is. He had left the world of technology behind to run for public office, a decision that was not built on wild ambition to become popular, but simply a desire to change the world. His goals are rooted in the tremendous conviction and belief that he needs to help change today's political climate because he has the ability, resources, and vision to do so. Most important, he is able to do it together with someone he loves and is building a family with.

Initially, when I set out on the journey of writing this book, it was to understand what I could have done differently with my ex-wife who was an entrepreneur. I plowed myself into doing as many interviews as I could so that I could understand the story of our separation, why it happened, and what I could have done differently. What I didn't do was look inside myself and see what I truly wanted in life. I saw glimpses of other people's lives and now have the privilege of sharing their stories. But what I didn't do was ask myself the hard question: what do I want?

Entrepreneurship is full of ups and downs: the challenge of taking on impossible problems, the adrenaline rush of risking everything for an idea, and the thrill of reaping the rewards when you finally make it to the other side and taste sweet success. But entrepreneurship isn't everything.

I discovered that what I want, more than just being an entrepreneur, is to find ways to be closer to the people I love, like my sister and parents. That's what fulfills me. That idea crystallized when I looked at Zak and Leah, a loving couple who deeply care about family and about each other. That's the true gift of finding a purpose that is beyond just starting a business—building something meaningful together that stands the test of time.

I still have the desire to break out on my own as an entrepreneur one day. You likely do too, and thankfully, you now have a more intimate understanding of the challenges, hardships, and perils you may face on the journey to becoming one. My parting piece of advice to you is this: if you truly want to become an entrepreneur, find an idea you believe in, plunge yourself into it, and just do it. Do it armed with the entrepreneurial lessons and confessions you have read in this book and find a calling you can truly commit to.

ACKNOWLEDGMENTS

Thank you to my family and friends for supporting me through this endeavor. This has been an emotional journey that allowed me to learn a lot about myself and how I can become a better person, both on a personal and professional level.

ABOUT THE AUTHOR

ELLIOT LUM is the Senior Vice President of Talent Strategy and Program Development for the Educational Foundation of the Association of National Advertisers, leading the organization's efforts to recruit exceptional students into the marketing and advertising industry. He previously worked at Columbia Records, where he forged marketing partnerships for some of the world's most popular recording artists, including Beyoncé, Tony Bennett, T.I., and One Direction. Elliot received his MBA from MIT Sloan and earned a BA in art history from Columbia University. He lives in Brooklyn, New York.